ENGLISH LANGUAGE NOTES

Addictions

REBECCA LEMON, Special Issue Editor

Of Note

Reframing Addiction
Devotion, Commerce, Community

....

REBECCA LEMON

L ike so many accounts of addiction, this special issue begins with a solitary figure: Picasso's *The Absinthe Drinker: Portrait of Angel Fernández de Soto* (1903)
captures a moment in time, a wobbly drinker with a drained glass (fig. 1). The image
in blue and gray might stand as an emblem of the hope and challenge of conceptu-
alizing addiction. For even as the painting showcases a single figure, holding a pipe
with a glass of absinthe at his table, de Soto is not alone. The absinthe bar serves a
community, one that is implied yet invisible. There is bar staff providing the drinks
to customers. There is Picasso himself, who captures de Soto, a friend and fellow
painter, on canvas. This preoccupied drinker is lost in thought, yet he is surrounded
by those who supply and chronicle his addiction.

 This opening paragraph telegraphs a shift in the field of addiction studies
itself: turning away from a broken brain model of addiction, addiction studies is
experiencing what we might call a "humanist turn." This special issue of *English
Language Notes* contributes to such a turn: devoted to the topic of addiction and the
humanities, "Addictions" draws attention to the range of fields—from history, literature, and critical race studies to theology, philosophy, and creative writing—that
wrestle with this phenomenon, shaping the portraits and stories around it. In the
same spirit of considering the people around Picasso's de Soto, this special issue is
born of a desire to investigate around and behind familiar portraits of addiction,
reframing the conversation in several key areas: addiction and history, addiction
and bias, and addiction and the author. This introduction takes up each of these concerns in turn, laying the groundwork for the essays that follow.

 First, this issue approaches addiction not as the story of an isolated individual
but instead as a study in relationships. An addict exists, most obviously, in relation
to a substance or behavior, figured in Picasso's framing of the man and his glass.
And there has been much to say about this singular addict, with a body driven by a
set of compulsions or desires: the field of addiction research routinely approaches
its subject by considering biology,[1] personal history, or what has been called the
damaged will.[2] But, as the absent presence in Picasso's barroom reveals, the phenomenon of addiction relies on a human community. This community might include
others who share the addiction, or the structures and people that supply the addictive

ENGLISH LANGUAGE NOTES

60:1, April 2022 DOI 10.1215/00138282-9560188

Figure 1. Picasso, *The Absinthe Drinker: Portrait of Angel Fernández de Soto* (1903). Oil on canvas, 70.3 × 55.3 cm (27.67 × 21.75 in). Private collection.

substance or provide the occasion for addictive behavior. The community includes the figures who support, exploit, condemn, or sit with the addict. This group might be chosen or assigned, a group of believers or of those profiled by policies, a set of friends or those figures structurally positioned together. This issue brings greater visibility to that addict community, reaching out beyond the singular figure to locate addiction in a group, culture, or nation.

The issue's second major intervention is the link of addiction to historical epistemes and capitalist systems, which is again implied yet invisible in Picasso's portrait. The figure of de Soto, a friend and studio mate of Picasso's who later dies in the Spanish Civil War, speaks to a time and place: he is a young man, as Picasso himself describes him, an "amusing wastrel" who is part of a community of artists and drinkers.[3] Does de Soto see himself as a wastrel, imbricated in this specific time and place and conscripted to tell a particular story of addiction for an audience? De Soto does not, at least here, seem to be telling his own story. He instead stands in for an interwar community of artists, and his image becomes a highly commercialized one.[4] The necessity of studying addiction in terms of historical and political epistemes—and in connection to capital, from the sale of the drink to the sale of the painting itself—has come into sharp relief in the last decade. How is addiction linked to economic systems and interests, including the commercializing of the addict's cravings?[5] How do race and gender, in particular, figure in such systems surrounding addiction?[6] This last question fuels some of the most pressing current research on addiction, as scholars in this issue and beyond wrestle with the kinds of prejudice and social injustice that surround the label *addict*.

Finally, in depicting de Soto, Picasso represents a fellow artist and painter, another preoccupation of this special edition. The connection between addiction and artists and writers is long-standing, extending from Socrates's symposium to the present day.[7] Addiction has been deemed a source of inspiration, as the spirit that breathes creative expression into the artist, yet it has also been called a force of destruction, unraveling art and lives.[8] This special issue takes up this link of addiction and artistry, posing the kinds of questions that might arise in looking at the portrait: Is Picasso participating in this scene he paints, chronicling de Soto's consumption of absinthe as he drains his own glass? Is he, to pose a question familiar from Bronislaw Malinowski forward, a witness or participant?[9] Likely, of course, the answer is both, and ultimately, Picasso's portrait challenges perspective and perception, representing a wobbly figure who seems a physical representation of a phenomenon: drunkenness.

In different ways, then, each of the essays here moves behind the singular image of the addict to view instead a history of relationships, communities, faith, and capital that is at times surprising, and at other points all too familiar. The conversations that unfold in this issue, across history, literature, philosophy, creative writing, and medicine, testify powerfully to the range of innovative research on and thinking about addiction. Working within distinct disciplines, geographies, and cultural contexts, the authors in this edition contribute to and effect the "humanist turn" in addiction studies.

Definitions

This introduction opened by laying out three ways in which the issue pushes on current studies of addiction by reframing the field: addiction and history, addiction and bias, and addiction and the author. I return to this framework in introducing the essays in the issue itself. But first it is worth noting those definitional essays that bookend the collection: beginning with Phil Withington's exploration of the term *drunkard* and its longitudinal uses, the collection ends with the careful study of *addiction* by Steve Sussman and Erika Wright. Taken together, these essays offer anatomies of key terms associated with the phenomenon of addiction. They also reveal the continuing challenges of defining a concept that so many readers and writers imagine they already know. As Sussman and Wright illuminate in detail, the *Diagnostic and Statistical Manual of Mental Disorders* (*DSM*), which helps physicians diagnose and categorize illnesses, continues to debate what to call this phenomenon of addiction. While earlier editions of the *DSM* included alcoholism and compulsive disorders under the mantle of addiction, the most recent issue forgoes the notion of substance dependency and the category of addiction.[10] Instead, as Sussman and Wright discuss, it classifies substance use in connection with a range of other disorders. As a result, the *DSM* no longer classifies addiction as a singular phenomenon. It exists on a continuum of disorders, attaching itself to particular substances, to behaviors, or to perceptions.

Does this mean that addiction no longer exists? No. But it does mean that the cordoning off of addiction and the addict as a singular problem—an individual affliction that is discrete and different from other medicalized diseases—seems no longer helpful or accurate. Rather, addiction might be seen as one mechanism among a range of others for coping with human life and its attendant pains. Addiction might be a phenomenon common to all of us, an insight offered in this issue with both Jose Cree's study of early modern addiction as theory of mind and Anthony Cunningham's investigation into addiction as a way of being in the world. Everyone has more or less successful ways of meeting and of psychologically reacting to the challenges of human life. Redefining addiction away from a model of the substance-dependent addict begins the process of rethinking judgmental constructs between one group and another, between addicts and nonaddicts, the ill and the healthy. "It is questionable," as one study puts it, "whether 'normal' performance should be a norm."[11]

Addiction: History and Community

Reframing the study of addiction away from the singular individual's struggles with substances or behaviors, this issue's first section, "Early Addictions," offers three essays that challenge the modern historical boundaries of addiction. Doing so illuminates addiction in relation to faith and nation, decentering the individual addict to concentrate instead on collective practices. This longer history of addiction, which is only beginning to be told, revises its conventional medical history, which dates the concept to the turn of the nineteenth century.[12] This is when physicians in both Britain and America diagnosed alcoholism as a nervous disorder. First, around 1800 the British navy physician Thomas Trotter, who has been called "the first scientific investigator of drunkenness," argued that habitual drunkenness is itself a disease.[13] Nearly simultaneously, Benjamin Rush in America (one of the original signatories of the Declaration of Independence and a man deemed the father of American psychiatry) also defined drunkenness as a disease.[14]

The work of Trotter and Rush ushered in a "new paradigm," medical historians tell us. This new paradigm "constituted a radical break with traditional ideas about the problems involved in drinking and alcohol."[15] Specifically, opinion shifted on habitual drunkenness (and in turn on opium use and other addictive behaviors) from moral condemnation to a disease model, the key feature of modern definitions of addiction. As the historian of science Roy M. MacLeod notes: "Not until the last half of the 19th century did the scientific appreciation of alcoholism become general. It was too easy to view alcoholism simply as immoral excess, its cure, simple moral restraint, and its expense, a personal responsibility."[16]

In understanding the shift in viewpoint on excessive drinking, scholars not only stress the moralizing of earlier periods, but they also point to earlier conceptions of drinking as a matter of choice. Harry Levine, for example, discusses how "during the 17th century, and for the most part of the 18th, the assumption was that people drank and got drunk because they wanted to, and not because they 'had' to." By contrast, "in the modern definition of alcoholism, the problem is not that alcoholics love to get drunk, but that they cannot help it—they cannot control themselves."[17]

If 1800 has been deemed a watershed moment in the "discovery" of addiction, the essays in "Early Addictions" by Withington, Jeffrey Wilson, and Cree instead reveal the rich variety of discourses on addiction before this point. The term *drunkard* emerged, we learn, as the result of religious and social pressures that pushed this term to the fore, replacing other labels for the drinker. State and religious figures deployed this derogatory term as fodder in the rise of a Puritan chorus, a process Withington chronicles in his essay. Wilson also investigates drinking in relation to social groups: his reading of *Hamlet* excavates the culture of alcoholism in relation to institutions, drawing attention to a privileged, upper-class expression of addiction as it relates to a royal, male community. Doing so highlights the connections between early modern drinking culture and modern fraternity life, underscoring the long history of addictive practices institutionally as well as personally, as seen in Wilson's skillful weaving of autotheory into his essay.

Jose Cree's study of addiction contrastingly studies addiction as a routine output of a properly functioning human body: addiction is formed within the self through a process of mind related to passion, the will, and habit. Yet, she argues, this addictive process differs between men and women, with women more likely to become addicted yet less likely to sustain an addiction, a contradiction that she explores in its prejudicial attitudes toward female subjects (a prejudice also taken up in Ellen Lansky's essay on the drinking woman). In all three essays in "Early Addictions," then, not only is addiction viewed as a premodern phenomenon but it is also one entangled with expressions of self and state sovereignty as they intersect with religion, nationality, and gender. Addiction is not, it turns out, a recent discovery or phenomenon—nor is it a solitary one.[18]

If addiction has a longer timeline than conventional scholarship acknowledges, it also has a more capacious and positive definition than modern audiences might expect. This issue pushes against modern conceptions of addiction by linking it to devotional practices globally. Three of the issue's essays weave through positive forms of addiction: Ben Breen links addiction to study in the figure of Psalmanazar, whose opium addiction comes to signal his devotion to intellectual life; Utathya Chattopadhyaya's essay reveals the devotional addiction at stake in consumption of bhang (cannabis) by rebels in India as they rise against British colonial rule; and Tony Cunningham's reading of Mr. Stevens in Kazuo Ishiguro's *The Remains of the Day* illuminates the challenges facing a devotional figure who relinquishes his own will, and indeed himself, in the service of a fading empire.

In their attention to devotional addiction, these essays take up an invitation delivered with the first uses of the term *addict* in English, when the word appeared in connection with religious communities. *Addict* experienced its first sustained use in printed texts from the 1530s, in the work of theologians who were translating the Bible and introducing the Reformed faith of Luther and Calvin to England.[19] George Joye, who produced the first printed translation of several books of the Old Testament, offers one of the earliest usages of the term. Joye warns of mortal men "addict to this world" and against the ungodly who are "addict unto wickedness," and "addict and all given to wickedness."[20] He also praises the faithful follower of God as an addict, asking God to "make fast thy promises to thy servant which is addict unto thy worship."[21]

This range of the term *addict* suggests its broad association with different forms of attachment, including those linked to religion. Specifically, Reformed writings overtly celebrate addiction as an intense mode of devotion and commitment, and they express concern for misguided addictions to the improper faith. Following the etymology of "addiction" as *ad + dīcere* (to speak, to declare), these writings trumpet a model of addictive living. Positive invocations of addiction fill guidebooks on pious living. Barnabe Googe suggests that the addict dedicate himself specifically to prayer, and the collection *A posie of gilloflowers* (1580) inspires its readers to "addict all their doings towards the attainment of life everlasting."[22]

Addiction, in these early guides to pious living, is encouraged. At the same time, writers admit that addiction is difficult. Not just anyone can achieve it. The popular text *Of the Imitation of Christ* (1580) concedes the challenge, writing how "few there be which addict themselves to the study of celestial things, because few can withdraw themselves, wholly from the love of this world."[23] Addiction requires a natural disposition and ability; it is not purely a matter of hard work or instruction. As John Huarte writes in 1594 that if a "child have not the disposition and ability, which is requisite for that science whereunto he will addict himself, it is a superfluous labor to be instructed therein by good schoolmasters."[24] Addiction is an inclination that the individual both does and does not control. Lancelot Andrewes states how only by "being so visited, redeemed and saved, we might wholly addict, and give over ourselves, to the Service of Him who was Author of them all."[25] The ability to addict is both a gift and an effort.

For most of the sixteenth century, addiction, in its link to God and service, was not a problem; it was an achievement. To be an addict required commitment, vulnerability, hard work, and courage. To be an addict meant devoting oneself entirely to a calling —to scripture, to scholarship more generally, or to Christ. This notion of addiction as devotion, while largely unfamiliar to modern audiences, has not disappeared, as the essays by Breen, Chattopadhyaya, and Cunningham illuminate: such sixteenth-century links of addiction and devotion persist, in different time periods and geographies.

Addiction's Biases

If this issue's second section, "Addiction and Empire," gently weaves through a sense of devotional addiction, it also offers a trenchant investigation of addiction's more sinister uses for colonial and imperial rule. This section's essays approach addiction in relation to organized systems of capital or, as Susan Zieger's reframing reveals, logistics. Viewed through a colonial lens, addiction appears increasingly as disease or pathology, as with the preconceptions of Europeans toward Chinese opium users in Breen's analysis, the English racialization of cannabis use in India in Chattopadhyaya's piece, or the logistical nightmares of colonial trade and capital in Zieger's essay.

The colonial context of addiction comes into sharp focus in Breen's reading of impersonator George Psalmanazar who, playing to European ignorance, fashioned a fictive identity that drew on multiple addictions, including to idolatry, opium, God, and study. Breen illuminates opium's Enlightenment-era associations with exotic foreignness from the European vantage point looking east, while also opening up the range of addictions indexed by a figure like Psalmanazar: he was able to transform his drug use from "vanity" or "extravagance" to a devotional aid in the study of God as part of an historical shift on views of opium within the British empire more broadly.

Chattopadhyaya's analysis of cannabis, or bhang, also exposes the shifting and oppositional attitudes toward addiction, this time between rebels in India and the British colonial authorities who attempted to condemn and dismiss such political resistance. The colonial characterization of bhang operated as part of the broader English racialization of Indians as violent, irrational, and rebellious. Such discourses portrayed insurgency as lunacy, thereby robbing it of any rationality. Against this prejudicial view of bhang, Chattopadhyaya draws out the longer use of the substance in devotional and daily practice in India, as well as the European reliance on bhang as an object of colonial revenue. As in the case of Withington's essay on the shifting representations of the drunkard, Chattopadhyaya reveals a lack of consistency in the descriptions of the effects of cannabis due to ideological and political motivations under colonial rule.

Addiction's connection to sociopolitical systems, evident in the framing of the Indian rebels through imperialist logic, is a phenomenon explored directly in Zieger's essay for this issue. She draws particular attention to the role of systems in understanding addiction: the structural organization of the state, and the compromised agency of subjects hampered within logistical systems. Zieger's essay speaks to precisely how this "humanist turn" in addiction studies exposes the histories and political economies at stake in addiction. Addiction, she writes, "is never solely about individuals; it is the outcome of relations between broader systems," which in the case of her essay concern labor, empire, and opium.

The capitalizing, commercializing, and racialization of drug use addressed in this section's three essays by Breen, Chattopadhyaya and Zieger anticipates more recent events, namely the specter of addiction as it spans from the war on drugs to the opioid crisis. Recent US history telescopes the historical connection of discourses of addiction to prejudice—be it gendered, religious, nationalistic, or class prejudice. From President Ronald Reagan's war on drugs to the opioid crisis, drug policies and addiction treatment fall along stark and particularly racialized lines. The war on drugs is one of the most prominent examples of a state-sanctioned discriminatory practice, one that led to the disproportionate incarceration of people of color.[26] Even as Reagan claimed to address a pressing social problem when he announced this new war, only a tiny fraction of the American public considered the issue of drugs to be significant.[27] "This fact was no deterrent to Reagan," Michelle Alexander writes, "for the drug war from the outset had little to do with public concern about drugs and much to do with public concern about race. By waging a war on drug users and dealers, Reagan made good on his promise to crack down on the racially defined 'others'—the undeserving."[28]

The link of racialized bias to drug policy continues in the opioid crisis of the twenty-first century. Indeed, as Donna Murch puts it, "race made the opioid crisis."[29] She writes how "the success of OxyContin hinged on racially bifurcated understandings of addiction. The fundamental division between 'dope' and medicine, after all, has always been the race and class of users."[30] White drug users are sanctioned as "licit health seekers," while Black users are condemned as "illicit pleasure seekers." "Our ideas of drug use—which kinds are legal, and which are not—are steeped in the metalanguage of race," Murch writes.[31]

The use of drug policy to criminalize communities of color stands in stark contrast to the linking of drugs to pain management in white communities. In their research on the opioid epidemic—what Helena B. Hansen and Julie Netherland call the "white drug war"—white drug use is treated as a clinical problem, a medical disease that remains decriminalized.[32] Indeed, the opioid crisis is labeled a public health issue while, as Anjali Om writes, "crack addition was only ever considered a criminal justice issue that prompted decades of mass (and hugely disparate) incarceration."[33]

Further, access to both pain medications and treatment for addiction falls along class and racial lines as the pain of middle- and upper-class white patients is taken more seriously than that of patients of color or poorer patients in general.[34] "Physicians prescribed to people who persuasively represented their suffering as medical," David Herzberg writes. And this task proves "easiest for the white-collar men and especially women portrayed in medical literature (and pharmaceutical advertising) as prone to nerves, anxiety, obesity, lack of 'pep,' and so forth."[35] Both policy and treatment options preserve middle- and upper-class white privilege: white patients are granted access to legal pain medications and then, as addicts, offered treatment options in recovery programs.[36] By contrast, Black and Latinx patients suffering from drug addiction are more frequently arrested and incarcerated rather than treated, in part because of drug policy itself.[37] This distinction between prescription opioid medication and illicit drugs bifurcates white addiction as a product of neurochemical addiction associated with medication and racialized addiction as associated with crime.[38] Indeed, the more lenient laws and sentencing for users of opioids causes one writer to "wonder if this new policy [on opioids] is motivated by a desire to provide much needed health support for predominately white victims of opioid addiction while increasing harsh sentences for black dealers."[39]

Beyond policy and treatment, media reporting on addiction further reinforces racialized bias. The corruption of pharmaceutical companies has become a mainstream media topic, and the white users addicted to opioids frequently appear in such media accounts as the victims of corporate greed. Accounts of "suburban" drug use frequently feature an element of surprise and a detailed etiology of an individual, framed through the lens of tragedy.[40] Emphasis lies on the role of big pharma and the medical establishment, from doctors to pharmaceutical suppliers, in pushing a product associated, early on, with problems.[41] By contrast, when reporting on people of color arrested for using or selling drugs—often framed as arrests in "urban" communities—media reports chronicle criminal charges, without any etiology to build empathy and without recognition of the biased policies or uneven enforcement that led to such arrests in the first place. Drugs, when linked to communities of color, come with threats of violence and criminal activity; drugs, when reported in white communities, evoke specters of tragedy and wasted potential.

This oppositional dynamic in addiction policy and reporting—between treatment for white users and incarceration or disenfranchisement for people of color—is not new. The specific link of drugs to racialized attacks extends back to the first uses of drugs in America. For even as soldiers wounded during the Civil War received opium and laudanum (a pain killer derived from opium), claims of opium use among Chinese immigrants offered fodder in the Chinese exclusion debates of the 1880s and 1890s. "In the United States, opium and opioid derivatives distributed to sick and wounded soldiers during the Civil War made opium the first mass-consumption narcotic in US history," Max Mishler writes. Yet "the negative connotations of opium use, however, were reserved for Chinese immigrants rather than veterans or middle-class white women addicted to morphine."[42] Just as Reagan's war on drugs effectively disenfranchised millions of prisoners, largely Black and Brown men, from voting life, the nineteenth-century division between white and Chinese opium users disenfranchised and excised communities of color from the political realm.[43]

This survey of addiction and racial discrimination chronicles an acute policy problem. But it also reveals the importance of history. It uncovers a clear through line, from the attack on Chinese immigrant communities in the nineteenth century, to the arrest of Black and Brown individuals under Reagan's war on drugs, to the current attitudes toward white opioid users. And this through line extends even further backward. It connects to the prejudicial attitudes evident from the first introduction of the word *addict* in English, as suggested above in relation to gender, religion, class, and nation. *Addict* is a term affiliated with allegedly weak women, as Cree reveals, and drinking women come under attack more broadly.[44] The charge of *addict* also underpinned religious tensions between the godly Protestants and their Catholic or high-Protestant foes.[45] Or, in another articulation of addiction and prejudice, the nationalist accusations against the sosspot Dutch, the swaggering Germans, or the drunken Danish filled early English drinking literature, upholding a sense of English superiority against their European counterparts, as Wilson's essay reveals.[46] By the eighteenth century, Hogarth's gin lane, like the gin acts regulating distribution and consumption, chronicled anxiety about working-class drinking, as cheap distilled liquor became available to masses of people beyond aristocratic tipplers.[47] Such English practices of control at home were intimately linked to British imperial efforts in Taiwan (Formosa) and India, as the essays by Breen, Chattopadhyaya, and Zieger illuminate.

Addiction and the Author

Women, religious dissidents, foreigners, colonial subjects, people of color, and the working classes: all come under attack as addicts. This is the longer history of fear surrounding addiction, excessive consumption, and social control. And, as suggested above, such derision of one group by another punctuates narratives on addiction going forward in ways that morph and change with context and geography. Such preoccupations about addicts and the structures that contain them drive the essays in the issue's penultimate section, "Addiction and the Author." The two essays by Lansky and Cunningham wrestle with figures emmeshed in structural forces beyond their control, as gendered and national identities constrain the individual addict. Lansky's essay for this issue, offered as both analysis and autotheory, takes up the issue of the drinking woman through a reading of Hemingway. "Hills Like White Elephants" centers on a drinking woman in conversation with her male partner, a sharp contrast to a history that excises or condemns the voices of female drinkers. Highlighting the female drinking buddy, Lansky teases out this portrait's long but, she suggests, often overlooked history. Yet the apparent freedom of Hemingway's unnamed female character is undercut by the story's atmosphere of stifling constriction. Lansky investigates this conflict around addiction, drinking, and gender in the context of the relationship between the reader and the author, offering a creative and moving account of addiction in the process. Her essay resonates with Cree's reading of the addicted woman, Wilson's shared use of autotheory in his study of male drinking culture, and Breen's analysis of gender play in Psalmanazar. In each of these essays, gender emerges as a crucial concern in weighing up the different kinds of addictive cultures and their impacts on individual bodies.

Tony Cunningham offers a complementary account of the addict in fiction, also exploring how a singular figure, in this case Ishiguro's famous butler in *The Remains of the Day*, might be caught in a historical moment. If earlier essays such as Cree's illuminate "addiction" in relation to the "will" as a repeated form of choice, Cunningham teases out how this notion of choice might be historically compromised. Using a philosophical lens to ask what constitutes notions of the good life, Cunningham illuminates how addiction is a paradoxical challenge: devotional pursuits give life a sense of meaning, yet these pursuits may come to define us and limit our choices. The devotional form of addiction to one's vocation, exercised by Ishiguro's protagonist Mr. Stevens, toggles between admirable and necessary service, or misguided and enabling myopia. In all cases Stevens remains inhibited in his ability to act freely. In analyzing the structural constraints so deftly drawn in Ishiguro, Cunningham's essay builds on the devotional addiction emphasized in this issue and addressed explicitly by Breen and Chattopadhyaya as well.

The issue ends as it began, with a definition of a key term. Sussman and Wright excavate the long history of the term *addiction* and expose the significant variety in understandings and expressions of this phenomenon. From the distinction between addictive substances and behaviors to the range of definitions offered in the *DSM*, the attempt to understand the phenomenon of addiction is, they reveal, ongoing and multilayered. This special issue represents a significant step forward in this process of understanding. Here, in *English Language Notes*, scholar-researchers enjoy the rare luxury of engaging in a truly cross-disciplinary conversation, meditating on a topic with contributors from a range of fields. Addiction, here, is a phenomenon that is communal, political, historical, and variable. By insisting on addiction's multiple communities and perspectives, this issue seeks to participate in, and encourage, the humanist turn in addiction studies.

REBECCA LEMON is professor of English at the University of Southern California. Her award-winning writing on Shakespeare, law, political philosophy, and the history of medicine has been supported by numerous fellowships. She is author of *Treason by Words: Literature, Law, and Rebellion in Early Modern England* (2006), *Shakespeare's King Richard III: Language and Writing* (2018), and *Addiction and Devotion in Early Modern England* (2018). Her work in *Addiction and Devotion*, which challenges conventional theories of addiction by tracking its longer history from the sixteenth century, has been featured in a range of venues, including popular radio broadcasts, political blogs, podcasts, and scholarly reviews. See www.rebeccalemon.org.

Acknowledgments

I owe a deep debt of gratitude to my research assistant and copyeditor for this issue, Reavant Singh. His research for this issue was painstaking; furthermore, he was an ideal and brilliant interlocutor through this process, and I will miss our conversations about the long history of scholarship on addiction. He will see my debt to his work throughout this issue. I am also grateful to Nan Goodman for her encouragement, as well as for her insights and feedback on this introduction, and to Kaela Walker for shepherding the issue through, from start to finish.

Notes

1   For studies on addiction and the brain, see National Institute of Drug Abuse, "Drugs, Brains, and Behavior"; Leshner, "Addiction Is a Brain Disease"; Satel and Lilienfeld, "Addiction and the Brain-Disease Fallacy"; Satel and Lilienfeld, "If Addiction Is Not Best Conceptualized a Brain Disease"; and Wiers and Verschure, "Curing the Broken Brain Model of Addiction." For studies on history and habit, see Courtwright, *Forces of Habit*; and Goodman, Lovejoy, and Sherratt, *Consuming Habits*.

2   For studies of choice and will, see Radoilska, *Addiction and Weakness of Will*; Valverde, *Diseases of the Will*; Poland and Graham, "Introduction"; and Moore, "Addiction, Responsibility, and Neuroscience."

3   *artdaily*, "Christie's to Offer."

4   The painting became the subject of a legal dispute when Andrew Lloyd Webber, who had bought it from Christie's for $29.1 million in 1995, was informed by the heirs of the original owner that it had been sold under pressure by the Nazis. Webber settled with the heirs and so, four years after he had originally planned to sell the painting, offered it for auction through Christie's. See Crow, "Christie's Sells Picasso for $51.2 Million."

5   Alexander, *Globalisation of Addiction*; Dumit, *Drugs for Life*; Happe, Johnson, and Levina, *Biocitizenship*; Macy, *Dopesick*; Van Zee, "Promotion and Marketing of OxyContin"; Ryan, Girion, and Glover, "'You Want a Description of Hell?'"; Bogdanich and Forsythe, "McKinsey Proposed Paying Pharmacy Companies."

6   Murch, *Racist Logic*; Netherland and Hansen, "White Opioids"; Mendoza, Hatcher, and Hansen, "Race, Stigma, and Addiction"; Herzberg, "Entitled to Addiction?"; Ruppert, Kattari, and Sussman, "Prevalence of Addictions"; Tuchman, "Women and Addiction."

7   Roth, "Socrates Undrunk"; Cook, *Alcohol, Addiction, and Christian Ethics*.

8   Biello, "Is There a Link between Creativity and Addiction?"; Knafo, "The Senses Grow Skilled in Their Craving."

9   Reed-Danahay, "Participating, Observing, Witnessing."

10 See Sussman and Wright in this issue. See also Flanagan, "Addiction Doesn't Exist."

11 Wiers and Verschure, "Curing the Broken Brain Model of Addiction."

12   Premodern categories of addiction include witchcraft, study, and religious devotion, overlooked as "addictions" by modern researchers. See Willis, "*Doctor Faustus* and the Early Modern Language of Addiction"; Cree, "Protestant Evangelicals"; Lemon, "Scholarly Addiction"; and Lemon, *Addiction and Devotion*. This section on "addiction's history" is adapted from my introduction in that book.

13   Trotter, *Essay, Medical, Philosophical, and Chemical*, 18.

14   Rush, *Inquiry into the Effects of Ardent Spirits*, 8. See also Rush, *Medical Inquiries and Observations*, 264.

15   Levine, "Discovery of Addiction," 144.

16   MacLeod, "Edge of Hope," 223.

17   Levine, "Discovery of Addiction," 144, 148.

18   Recent scholarship has challenged the notion of addiction as a modern discovery. See Lemon, *Addiction and Devotion*; Porter, "Drinking Man's Disease," 385; Warner, "'Resolv'd to Drink No More'"; Warner, "'Before There Was Alcoholism'"; Warner, *Craze*; White, "'Slow but Sure Poyson,'" 37; and Herring et al., "Starting the Conversation," 3–4.

19   On the definition of the term *addict*, see Lemon, *Addiction and Devotion*; Cree, "Protestant Evangelicals"; and Rosenthal and Faris, "Etymology and Early History of 'Addiction.'"

20   Joye, *Psalter of Dauid in Englyshe*, n.p.

21   Joye, "Fyfth Octonary," in *Psalter of Dauid in Englyshe*, n.p.

22   Googe, "Capricornus, the Tenth Booke," in *Zodiake of Life*, NNiiir; Gifford, *Posie of Gilloflowers*, 64–65.

23   Rogers, *Of the Imitation of Christ*, 70, 191.

24   Huarte, *Examination of Mens Wits*, B1r.

25   Andrewes, *Sermon*, 2.

26   Alexander, *New Jim Crow*; Mendoza, Hatcher, and Hansen, "Race, Stigma, and Addiction."

27   "At the time he declared this new war, less than 2 percent of the American public viewed drugs as the most important issue facing the nation" (Alexander, *New Jim Crow*, 62).

28   Alexander, *New Jim Crow*, 62–63.

29   Murch, "How Race Made the Opioid Crisis."

30   Murch, "How Race Made the Opioid Crisis," 2.

31   Murch, "How Race Made the Opioid Crisis," 3.

32   Hansen and Netherland, "Is the Prescription Opioid Epidemic a White Problem?"

33   Om, "Opioid Crisis in Black and White," 615.

34   "A 2012 study by a University of Pennsylvania researcher found that black patients were thirty-four per cent less likely than white patients to be prescribed opioids for such chronic conditions as back pain and

migraines, and fourteen per cent less likely to receive such prescriptions after surgery or traumatic injury" (Talbot, "Addicts Next Door").

35   Herzberg, "Entitled to Addiction?" On the issue of racial bias in medical understandings of pain, see Sabin, "How We Fail Black Patients in Pain"; and Hoffman et al., "Racial Bias."

36   On the challenge of admission to hospitals and to rehab programs for poorer addicts, see Talbot, "Addicts Next Door."

37   Mendoza, Hatcher, and Hansen, "Race, Stigma, and Addiction"; Volkow, "Addiction Should Be Treated, Not Penalized"; Forati, Ghose, and Mantsch, "Examining Opioid Overdose Deaths."

38   Netherland and Hansen. "White Opioids."

39   Om, "Opioid Crisis in Black and White."

40   Netherland and Hansen, "The War on Drugs That Wasn't."

41   Ryan, Girion, and Glover, "'You Want a Description of Hell?'"; Bogdanich and Forsythe, "McKinsey Proposed Paying Pharmacy Companies."

42   Mishler, "Race and the First Opium Crisis," 25; Courtwright, *Forces of Habit*.

43   Mishler summarizes the cycles in this way: "Racist depictions of Chinese opium use underscored the Chinese threat to US society and bolstered racist political campaigns for Chinese exclusion during the 1880s and 1890s. Meanwhile, black resistance to racial terror was interpreted through the lens of 'Negro cocaine madness.' By the 1930s, in response to Mexican immigration and Latinx urbanization, white observers worried about 'reefer madness'" (Mishler, "Race and the First Opium Crisis," 25).

44   Skelton, *The Tunning of Elynour Rumming*. See Herman, "Leaky Ladies and Droopy Dames." On women and gendered drinking perceptions and practices, see Britland, "Circe's Cup"; Bennett, *Ale, Beer, and Brewsters in England*; Capp, "Gender and the Culture of the English Alehouse"; and Martin, *Alcohol, Sex, and Gender*.

45   See Wrightson, "Puritan Reformation of Manners"; Wrightson, "Postscript"; Ingram, "Reformation of Manners in Early Modern England"; and McIntosh, *Controlling Misbehavior in England*.

46   On nationalist drinking, see Lemon, "Compulsory Conviviality"; Ludington, *Politics of Wine in Britain*; Brown, "Sons of Beer and Sons of Ben"; and Wrightson, "Alehouses, Order, and Reformation in Rural England."

47   See Warner, *Craze*; and White, "'Slow but Sure Poyson.'"

Works Cited

Alexander, Bruce. *The Globalisation of Addiction: A Study in Poverty of the Spirit*. Oxford: Oxford University Press, 2008.

Alexander, Michelle. *The New Jim Crow: Mass Incarceration in the Age of Colorblindness*. New York: New Press, 2010.

Andrewes, Lancelot. *A Sermon Preached before His Majestie at Whitehall the Fifth of November Last, 1617*. London, 1618.

artdaily. "Christie's to Offer Andrew Lloyd Webber's Picasso Masterpiece from His Blue Period." March 18, 2010. artdaily.cc/news/36901/Christie-s-to-Offer-Andrew-Lloyd-Webber-s-Picasso-Masterpiece-from-His-Blue-Period.

Bennett, Judith M. *Ale, Beer, and Brewsters in England: Women's Work in a Changing World, 1300–1600*. Oxford: Oxford University Press, 1999.

Biello, David. "Is There a Link between Creativity and Addiction?" *Scientific American*, July 26, 2011. www-scientificamerican-com.libproxy1.usc.edu/article/is-there-a-link-between-creativity-and-addiction.

Bogdanich, Walt, and Michael Forsythe. "McKinsey Proposed Paying Pharmacy Companies Rebates for OxyContin Overdoses." *New York Times*, November 27, 2020; updated December 17, 2020.

Britland, Karen. "Circe's Cup: Wine and Women in Early Modern Drama." In *A Pleasing Sinne: Drink and Conviviality in Seventeenth-Century England*, edited by Adam Smyth, 109–26. London: Brewer, 2004.

Brown, Cedric C. "Sons of Beer and Sons of Ben: Drink as a Social Marker in Seventeenth-Century England." In *A Pleasing Sinne: Drink and Conviviality in Seventeenth-Century England*, edited by Adam Smyth, 3–20. London: Brewer, 2004.

Capp, Bernard. "Gender and the Culture of the English Alehouse in Late Stuart England." In *The Trouble with Ribs: Women, Men, and Gender in Early Modern Europe*, edited by Anu Korhonen and Kate Lowe, 103–27. Helsinki: Helsinki Collegium for Advance Studies, 2007.

Cook, Christopher C. H. *Alcohol, Addiction, and Christian Ethics*. Cambridge: Cambridge University Press, 2006.

Courtwright, David. *Forces of Habit: Drugs and the Making of the Modern World*. Cambridge, MA: Harvard University Press, 2001.

Cree, Jose Murgatroyd. "Protestant Evangelicals and Addiction in Early Modern English." *Renaissance Studies* 32, no. 2 (2018): 446–62.

Crow, Kelly. "Christie's Sells Picasso for $51.2 Million." *Wall Street Journal*, June 23, 2010.

Dumit, Joseph. *Drugs for Life: How Pharmaceutical Companies Define Our Health*. Durham, NC: Duke University Press, 2012.

Flanagan, Owen. "Addiction Doesn't Exist, but It Is Bad for You." *Neuroethics* 10, no. 1 (2017): 1–8.

Forati, Amir M., Rina Ghose, and John R. Mantsch. "Examining Opioid Overdose Deaths across Communities Defined by Racial Composition: A Multiscale Geographically Weighted Regression Approach." *Journal of Urban Health: Bulletin of the New York Academy of Medicine* 98, no. 4 (2021): 551–62.

Gifford, Humphrey. *A Posie of Gilloflowers*. London, 1580.

Goodman, Jordan, Paul E. Lovejoy, and Andrew Sherratt, eds. *Consuming Habits: Global and Historical Perspectives on How Cultures Define Drugs*. London: Routledge, 1995.

Googe, Barnabe. *The Zodiake of Life Written by the Godly and Zealous Poet Marcellus Pallingenius Stellatus*. London, 1565.

Hansen, Helena B., and Julie Netherland. "Is the Prescription Opioid Epidemic a White Problem?" *American Journal of Public Health* 106, no. 12 (2016): 2127–29.

Happe, Kelly E., Jenell Johnson, and Marina Levina, eds. *Biocitizenship: The Politics of Bodies, Governance, and Power*. New York: New York University Press, 2018.

Herman, Peter C. "Leaky Ladies and Droopy Dames: The Grotesque Realism of Skelton's *The Tunnynge of Elynour Rummynge*." In *Rethinking the Henrician Era: Essays on Early Tudor Texts and Contexts*, edited by Peter C. Herman, 145–67. Champaign: University of Illinois Press, 1993.

Herring, Jonathan, Ciaran Regan, Darin Weinberg, and Phil Withington. "Starting the Conversation." In *Intoxication and Society: Problematic Pleasures of Drugs and Alcohol*, edited by Jonathan Herring, Ciaran Regan, Darin Weinberg, and Phil Withington, 1–32. Basingstoke: Palgrave Macmillan, 2013.

Herzberg, David. "Entitled to Addiction? Pharmaceuticals, Race, and America's First Drug War." *Bulletin of the History of Medicine* 91, no. 3 (2017): 586–623.

Hoffman, Kelly M., Sophie Trawalter, Jordan R. Axt, and M. Norman Oliver. "Racial Bias in Pain Assessment and Treatment Recommendations, and False Beliefs about Biological Differences between Blacks and Whites." *Proceedings of the National Academy of Sciences of the United States of America* 113, no. 16 (2016): 4296–4301.

Huarte, John. *The Examination of Mens Wits*. London, 1594.

Ingram, Martin. "Reformation of Manners in Early Modern England." In *The Experience of Authority in Early Modern England*, edited by Paul Griffiths, Adam Fox, and Steve Hindle, 47–88. London: Macmillan, 1996.

Joye, George. *The Psalter of Dauid in Englyshe*. London, 1534.

Knafo, Danielle. "The Senses Grow Skilled in Their Craving: Thoughts on Creativity and Addiction." *Psychoanalytic Review* 95, no. 4 (2008): 571–95.

Lemon, Rebecca. *Addiction and Devotion in Early Modern England*. Philadelphia: University of Pennsylvania Press, 2018.

Lemon, Rebecca. "Compulsory Conviviality in Early Modern England." *English Literary Renaissance* 43, no. 3 (2013): 381–414.

Lemon, Rebecca. "Scholarly Addiction: *Doctor Faustus* and the Drama of Devotion." *Renaissance Quarterly* 69, no. 3 (2016): 865–98.

Leshner, Alan I. "Addiction Is a Brain Disease, and It Matters." *Science*, no. 5335 (1997): 45–47.

Levine, Harry G. "The Discovery of Addiction: Changing Concepts of Habitual Drunkenness in America." *Journal of Studies on Alcohol* 39, no. 1 (1978): 143–74.

Ludington, Charles. *The Politics of Wine in Britain: A New Cultural History*. Basingstoke: Palgrave Macmillan, 2013.

MacLeod, Roy M. "The Edge of Hope: Social Policy and Chronic Alcoholism, 1870–1900." *Journal of the History of Medicine and Allied Sciences* 22, no. 3 (1967): 215–45.

Macy, Beth. *Dopesick: Dealers, Doctors, and the Drug Company That Addicted America*. New York: Little, Brown, 2018.

Martin, A. Lynn. *Alcohol, Sex, and Gender in Late Medieval and Early Modern Europe*. London: Palgrave Macmillan, 2001.

McIntosh, Marjorie Keniston. *Controlling Misbehavior in England, 1370–1600*. Cambridge: Cambridge University Press, 1998.

Mendoza, Sonia, Alexandrea E. Hatcher, and Helena Hansen. "Race, Stigma, and Addiction." In *The Stigma of Addiction: An Essential Guide*, edited by Jonathan D. Avery and Joseph J. Avery Jr., 131–52. Cham: Springer, 2019.

Mishler, Max. "Race and the First Opium Crisis." In Murch, *Racist Logic*, 22–26.

Moore, Michael S. "Addiction, Responsibility, and Neuroscience." *Illinois Law Review* 2020, no. 2: 375–470.

Murch, Donna. "How Race Made the Opioid Crisis." In Murch, *Racist Logic*, 7–21.

Murch, Donna, ed. *Racist Logic: Markets, Drugs, and Sex*. Cambridge, MA: MIT Press, 2019.

National Institute of Drug Abuse, National Institute of Health, Department of Health and Human Services. "Drugs, Brains, and Behavior: The Science of Addiction." April 2007. www.drugabuse.gov/scienceofaddiction /sciofaddiction.pdf.

Netherland, Julie, and Helena B. Hansen. "The War on Drugs That Wasn't: Wasted Whiteness, 'Dirty Doctors,' and Race in Media Coverage of Prescription Opioid Misuse." *Culture, Medicine, and Psychiatry* 40, no. 4 (2016): 664–86.

Netherland, Julie, and Helena B. Hansen. "White Opioids: Pharmaceutical Race and the War on Drugs That Wasn't." *BioSocieties* 12, no. 2 (2017): 217–38.

Om, Anjali. "The Opioid Crisis in Black and White: The Role of Race in Our Nation's Recent Drug Epidemic." *Journal of Public Health* 40, no. 4 (2018): 614–15.

Poland, Jeffrey, and George Graham. "Introduction: The Makings of a Responsible Addict." In *Addiction and Responsibility*, edited by Jeffrey Poland and George Graham, 1–20. Cambridge, MA: MIT Press, 2011.

Porter, Roy. "The Drinking Man's Disease: The 'Pre-history' of Alcoholism in Georgian Britain." *British Journal of Addiction* 80, no. 4 (1985): 385–96.

Radoilska, Lubomira. *Addiction and Weakness of Will*. Oxford: Oxford University Press, 2013.

Reed-Danahay, Deborah. "Participating, Observing, Witnessing." In *The Routledge Companion to Contemporary Anthropology*, edited by Simon Coleman, Susan B. Hyatt, and Ann Kingsolver, 57–71. London: Routledge, 2016.

Rogers, Thomas. *Of the Imitation of Christ*. London, 1580.

Rosenthal, Richard J., and Suzanne B. Faris. "The Etymology and Early History of 'Addiction.'" *Addiction Research and Theory* 27, no. 5 (2019): 437–49.

Roth, Marty. "Socrates Undrunk: Literature Writing Philosophy in Plato's *Symposium*." In *Drunk the Night Before: An Anatomy of Intoxication*, 47–58. Minneapolis: University of Minnesota Press, 2005.

Ruppert, Ryan, Shanna K. Kattari, and Steve Sussman. "Prevalence of Addictions among Transgender and Gender Diverse Subgroups." *International Journal of Environmental Research and Public Health* 18, no. 16 (2021): 8843.

Rush, Benjamin. *An Inquiry into the Effects of Ardent Spirits upon the Human Body and Mind*. 8th ed. Boston, 1823.

Rush, Benjamin. *Medical Inquiries and Observations upon the Diseases of the Mind.* 5th ed. Philadelphia, 1835.

Ryan, Harriet, Lisa Girion, and Scott Glover. "'You Want a Description of Hell?': Oxycontin's Twelve-Hour Problem." *Los Angeles Times,* May 5, 2016.

Sabin, Janice A. "How We Fail Black Patients in Pain." Association of American Medical Colleges, January 6, 2020. www.aamc.org /news-insights/how-we-fail-black-patients -pain.

Satel, Sally, and Scott O. Lilienfeld. "Addiction and the Brain-Disease Fallacy." *Frontiers in Psychiatry,* March 3, 2014. doi.org/10.3389/ fpsyt.2013.00141.

Satel, Sally, and Scott O. Lilienfeld. "If Addiction Is Not Best Conceptualized a Brain Disease, Then What Kind of Disease Is It?" *Neuroethics* 10, no. 1 (2017): 19–24.

Skelton, John. *The Tunning of Elynour Rumming.* London, 1521.

Talbot, Margaret. "The Addicts Next Door." *New Yorker,* June 5–12, 2017. www.newyorker.com /magazine/2017/06/05/the-addicts-next-door.

Trotter, Thomas. *An Essay, Medical, Philosophical, and Chemical, on Drunkenness, and Its Effects on the Human Body.* 4th ed. London, 1810.

Tuchman, Ellen. "Women and Addiction: The Importance of Gender Issues in Substance Abuse Research." *Journal of Addictive Diseases* 29, no. 2 (2010): 127–38.

Valverde, Mariana. *Diseases of the Will: Alcohol and the Dilemmas of Freedom.* Cambridge: Cambridge University Press, 1998.

Van Zee, Art. "The Promotion and Marketing of OxyContin: Commercial Triumph, Public Health Tragedy." *American Journal of Public Health* 99, no. 2 (2009): 221–27.

Volkow, Nora D. "Addiction Should Be Treated, Not Penalized." *Neuropsychopharmacology* 46 (2021): 2048–50.

Warner, Jessica. "'Before There Was Alcoholism': Lessons from the Medieval Experience with Alcohol." *Contemporary Drug Problems* 19, no. 3 (1992): 409–29.

Warner, Jessica. *Craze: Gin and Debauchery in an Age of Reason.* London: Profile, 2003.

Warner, Jessica. "'Resolv'd to Drink No More': Addiction as a Preindustrial Concept." *Journal of Studies on Alcohol* 55, no. 6 (1994): 685–91.

White, Jonathan. "The 'Slow but Sure Poyson': The Representation of Gin and Its Drinkers, 1736– 1751." *Journal of British Studies* 42, no. 1 (2003): 35–64.

Wiers, Reinout W., and Paul Verschure. "Curing the Broken Brain Model of Addiction: Neurorehabilitation from a Systems Perspective." *Addictive Behaviors* 112 (2021): 1–10.

Willis, Deborah. "*Doctor Faustus* and the Early Modern Language of Addiction." In *Placing the Plays of Christopher Marlowe,* edited by Sara Munson Deats and Robert A. Logan, 136–48. Farnham: Ashgate, 2008.

Wrightson, Keith Edwin. "Alehouses, Order, and Reformation in Rural England, 1590–1660." In *Popular Culture and Class Conflict, 1590– 1914: Explorations in the History of Labour and Leisure,* edited by Eileen Yeo and Stephen Yeo, 1–27. Hassocks: Harvester, 1981.

Wrightson, Keith Edwin. "Postscript: Terling Revisited." In *Poverty and Piety in an English Village: Terling, 1525–1700,* edited by Keith Edwin Wrightson and David Levine, 186–220. 2nd ed. Oxford: Oxford University Press, 1995.

Wrightson, Keith Edwin. "The Puritan Reformation of Manners, with Special Reference to the Counties of Lancashire and Essex, 1640– 1660." PhD diss., Cambridge University, 1973.

Remaking the Drunkard in Early Stuart England

PHIL WITHINGTON

Abstract   This article traces the changing semantics of *drunkard* in English during the first half of the seventeenth century. Combining methods of "distant reading" (made possible by the Early English Books Online–Text Creation Partnership) and the "close reading" of didactic printed materials, it shows how this venerable Middle English word became unusually prevalent and ideologically charged in the six decades after the ascension of James VI and I to the English throne. Key to these developments was the new monarch's *Counterblaste to Tobacco* (1604), in which James I at once delineated a capacious concept of *drunkard* as someone who simply liked drinking, rather than became demonstrably drunk, and confirmed the consumption of tobacco and alcohol as an appropriate subject for the burgeoning printed "public sphere." The article suggests that the separation of *drunkard* from *drunkenness* proved very useful for ministers and moralists concerned with the moral and economic consequences of unnecessary and "superfluous" consumption for individuals, households, and communities. Resorting to populist and didactic genres like pamphlets, sermons, dialogues, and treatises, writers ranging from the Calvinist John Downame to the regicide John Cook deployed the category of the drunkard to critique not only English drinking habits but also social and economic practices more generally. In pushing the concept so hard, however, reformers inevitably rubbed against more conventional notions of "civil society" and the sociable practices constituting it.
Keywords   drunkard, seventeenth century, England

When John Downame decided to publicly discuss "drunkenness, and what it is" in 1609, he began by defining his subject.[1] On the one hand, the influential Calvinist minister observed that men engaged in drunkenness "when by immoderate swilling and tippling they are deprived of the use of their reason, understanding, and memory; so as for the time, they become like unto beasts." On the other hand, he argued that drunkenness involved habitual "excess, when as they addict themselves to much drinking, and make it their usual practise to sit at the wine or strong drink." Downame immediately followed this identification of singular and repetitive "excess" with an important gloss: that "neither are they alone to be esteemed as drunkards who deprive themselves of the use of reason, and become brutish; but those who take their chief pleasure in drinking and carousing, though their brain will bear it without any great alteration."[2] For Downame, that is, it was not simply intoxication that marked a man as a drunkard, be it occasional or habitual. Rather, a drunkard was someone who derived pleasure from the consumption of alcohol whatever its physiological and cognitive affects.

The same year Robert Elton, a husbandman from Blackburn in Lancashire, also struggled with the definition of *drunkard*. However, the circumstances were somewhat different. Elton had been called as witness to a case of defamation in the church courts between his master's wife, Beatrice Bolton, and a local man called Adam Clayton. Bolton accused Clayton of calling her "his whore" and declaring to her husband and anyone who would listen that "he had had his pleasure of her in every corner of that house where they dwelled and at every apple and plum tree in the orchard."[3] When on June 15, 1609, Elton testified to the court that he had heard Clayton defame Bolton in these terms, he was also asked about the reliability of another witness for Bolton, John Salisbury, who had been with Elton when Clayton made his boasts. Clayton had queried Salisbury's trustworthiness as a witness by characterizing him as "a common haunter and frequenter of alehouses and a common drunkard a quarreller a brawler and a fighter [who] used to be so drunk or overcome in drink that he cannot go stand or speak."[4] Elton now responded, "That Salisbury is taken for an honest man but saith that he will be merry amongst the gent and good fellows but cannot discern of a drunkard."[5] It seems that for Elton, contra Downame, simply taking pleasure from drinking rituals and sociability—from making merry and enjoying good fellowship—did not make someone a "common drunkard," with the implication that becoming senseless through drinking still did.

This article is about the label *drunkard*—a venerable Middle English word that, it argues, became unusually prevalent and ideologically charged in the first half of the seventeenth century. What follows outlines a spike in discursive noise about drunkards after the ascension of James VI and I to the English throne and looks at the role of learned and godly discussions of the term in populist and didactic genres—such as pamphlets, sermons, and dialogues—in amplifying the sound. Downame was an early and influential contributor to this literature, helping make drunkards a minor obsession of the early Stuart printed "public sphere." Following the example of his monarch, he and other reformers developed a new and capacious conception of the drunkard that could be deployed as a critical tool not only of English drinking habits but also of society, culture, and economy more generally. The "discernment" of Elton indicates, in turn, the difficulties and potential resistance facing reformers—a reluctance to recognize a more extensive and intrusive sense of *drunkard* that perhaps helps explain the relative dissipation of the concept after 1660. This article examines the intellectual influences and analytic techniques that went into the Jacobean remaking of *drunkard* and shows, semantically speaking, how new wine could be served in old wineskins.

From a historiographical perspective, the public interest in drunkards in Jacobean England should not be especially surprising. Social historians have long identified the first half of the seventeenth century as a moment in which magisterial concerns with drunkenness, articulated through parliamentary legislation and governmental orders, were extensively implemented across English communities.[6] Not only did Jacobean legislators add the final details to the premodern system of licensing alehouses—the most popular institution for the public retail of alcohol—but certain sorts of householder increasingly embraced licensing to regulate the public retail and consumption of alcohol in their neighborhoods.[7] In the meantime, however, this was also a period when the commercialization of the drinks trade (especially beers and wines) gathered pace and tobacco was first popularized as an accompaniment and possible incitement to drinking.[8] And it was when different kinds of drink-fueled sociability were valorized across the social spectrum—not least forms of merriment and fellowship alluded to by Elton.[9] The prominent role of religious writers in framing these antithetical developments has likewise been noted. While for Keith Wrightson it was ministers who provided the ideological urgency to regulate alehouses, with drunkenness a prominent and often controversial target of the more widespread "reformation of manners," for Jessica Warner it was Downame and other Jacobean preachers who first elucidated the insights and principles on which a "disease"-based concept of alcohol addiction would subsequently be founded.[10] As Rebecca Lemon notes, it was precisely this generation of "Puritans" who were instrumental in transforming drunkenness from one of the familiar "deadly sins" of medieval culture into a source of "disease and reprobation."[11]

Examining how *drunkard* was redefined in print provides an opportunity to explore in more detail these cultural and social developments and, more particularly, how didactic writers pulled together a range of moral, economic, medical, and social ideas to outline a new concept of the drunkard. So doing helps delineate a key moment in both the longer history of the reformation of manners and the modern conceptualization and regulation of intoxicants.[12] The first section accordingly uses digitized "distant reading" to trace the diachronic history of the term during the sixteenth and seventeenth centuries.[13] The second and third sections then focus on the moment when reformers and moralists distinguished the character of the drunkard from singular or repetitive acts of drunkenness and, in creating this conceptual space, remade a familiar stereotype into a tool of social, economic, and cultural critique. The article shows that these reformers were quite as concerned with the economic ramifications of superfluous drinking as with the spiritual or physiological damage it might cause. And it argues that, by imposing an increasingly capacious concept of the drunkard, they risked jeopardizing the habits and customs on which civil society depended.

The Rise and Fall of *Drunkard*

It is possible to trace diachronically the use of *drunkard* in vernacular print using the "Early English Books Online–Text Creation Partnership" (EEBO-TCP), which has so far made around 45 percent of texts cataloged on *EEBO* fully searchable between 1473 and 1700. This large sample of text can be supplemented with a full search of *all* the title pages of texts cataloged on *EEBO* and the *English Short Title Catalogue* (*ESTC*) (see table 1).[14]

Trends evident from the printed data can in turn be compared with appearances of *drunkard* in depositional evidence from the ecclesiastical courts over a sim-

Table 1. Total number of English titles and text cataloged on *ESTC* and EEBO-TCP, 1490s–1690s

Decadal	All texts in the ESTC	All texts in EEBO	No. of EEBO-TCP texts	% EEBO texts in TCP
1490s	142	118	52	44
1500s	248	430	74	17
1510s	268	208	70	34
1520s	382	336	103	31
1530s	807	807	274	34
1540s	1,178	1,235	422	34
1550s	1,343	1,280	444	35
1560s	1,303	1,297	533	41
1570s	1,702	1,730	699	40
1580s	2,194	2,140	951	44
1590s	2,587	2,562	1,177	46
1600s	3,562	3,894	1,682	43
1610s	4,295	4,169	1,794	43
1620s	5,220	5,105	2,147	42
1630s	5,706	5,585	1,946	35
1640s	19,135	26,471	10,629	40
1650s	12,794	15,408	6,532	42
1660s	11,503	11,413	5,492	48
1670s	12,471	10,936	5,227	48
1680s	19,898	18,360	9,322	51
1690s	19,240	15,407	7,925	51
Total	125,978	128,891	57,495	45

Sources: *ESTC* (estc.bl.uk/F/?func=file&file_name=login-bl-estc) and *EEBO* (search-proquest-com.sheffield.idm.oclc.org/eebo/advanced). Figures collated in June 2020.

ilar period—that is, from the kind of archive recording Robert Elton's understanding of *drunkard* in 1609. The ecclesiastical courts were a distinct jurisdiction in early modern England, hearing cases of a moral nature either brought by parishioners against each other or by the court itself against ecclesiastical officeholders, and the evidence of deponents offers unusual insight into quotidian language and attitudes.[15] Series of depositions can be examined systematically using the database of the "Intoxicants and Early Modernity" project (IEM), which enables keyword searches of all legal cases with a drinking dimension heard in the ecclesiastical or consistory courts in Norwich and Chester between the 1570s and 1740s, with a gap in the records during the 1640s and 1650s, when the courts were discontinued.[16] Although there is unfortunately no space here to unpack the depositional evidence in any detail, the extent to which deponents used the word *drunkard* over time is nevertheless a useful way to gauge whether printed discourse coincided with legal and everyday conversation.

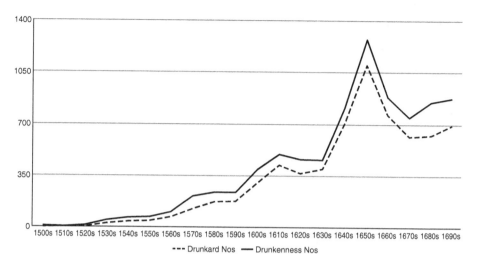

Figure 1. *Drunkard* and *drunkenness* in EEBO-TCP texts, 1500–1700 (numbers of texts per decade).

Figure 1 shows the number of EEBO-TCP texts in which *drunkard* or *drunkenness* (with variant spellings) were used between 1500 and 1700. It reveals two trends (fig. 1). First, *drunkard* by and large shadowed the more commonplace *drunkenness* across the period. Second, both terms enjoyed successive changes in usage: a gradual rise in the last four decades of the sixteenth century; a steep rise between the 1600s and 1620s; a climactic spike in the 1640s and 1650s; and a significant dip and plateau at the Restoration. As table 1 suggests, these trends reflect in part that more texts were produced (and survived) during the period, especially during the 1640s. Figure 2 shows that if we outline the *percentage* of EEBO-TCP texts in which *drunkard* or *drunkenness* were used, then a slightly modified picture emerges. First, the gap in usage between *drunkenness* and *drunkard* becomes clearer (with

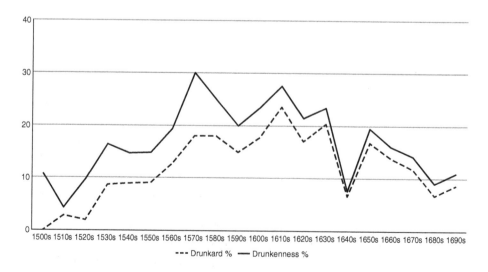

Figure 2. *Drunkard* and *drunkenness* in EEBO-TCP texts, 1500–1700 (percentage of all TCP texts).

Table 2. Subject classifications of printed texts with *drunkenness* or *drunkard* on the title page, 1490s–1690s

Group 1	"Liberal Arts"	Travel (A), History (B), Biography (C), Classics (E)
Group 2	"Religion"	Religious instruction (D), Religious controversy (M), Sermons (N)
Group 3	"Society"	Social description (F), Occupational instruction (X), Education (AA)
Group 4	"Pragmatics"	Substance specific (DD), Medical (G), Household economy (I), Astrology (Y), Witchcraft (BB), Recipes (CC)
Group 5	"Literary"	Poetry (J), Language (K), Miscellanies (L), Folk lore (H), Stage-plays (O), Prose fiction (P), Music (R), Ballads (W), Visual culture (GG)
Group 6	"Public"	Public debate (II), Military (S), Political economy (T), Legal (U), Political/moral theory (Z), Politicking (EE), News (V)
Group 7	"Spatial"	Spatial designation (HH), Material culture (JJ)

drunkard less commonplace in the sixteenth century). Second, both terms dip significantly in the 1640s and 1650s amid the anomalous slew of texts produced during the civil war and commonwealth era. Third, the climactic spike for *drunkard* is, in fact, the first four decades of the seventeenth century rather than the civil war era. This peak is preceded by a steady increase in use over the previous hundred or so years and is followed by a relative decline in the use of both *drunkenness* and *drunkard*—to about pre-Reformation levels—after 1660.

These patterns of use within EEBO-TCP texts can be supplemented by the total number of vernacular texts in the *ESTC* and *EEBO* to have *drunkenness* and/ or *drunkard* on their title page. This describes the number of texts advertised by the term *drunkard*; the smaller number of texts involved means, in addition, that it is also possible to categorize them according to subject and genre, as outlined in table 2. Figure 3 shows a significant increase in the number of vernacular printed texts explicitly about drunkenness or drunkards from the 1600s, with spikes of just below or above twenty titles in the 1620s, 1640s, and 1670s. It also shows how until the 1620s it was "religious" texts (Group 2)—which includes texts of religious instruction, treatises, and sermons—that were the most likely to use this language, and to a much lesser extent literary works (Group 5), including works of popular literature like ballads and plays. Thereafter, however, the subject matter and genre became more diverse, with works of political and household economy also represented from the middle of the seventeenth century. Of course, throughout the period the number of title pages inscribed with *drunkenness* or *drunkards* was a small

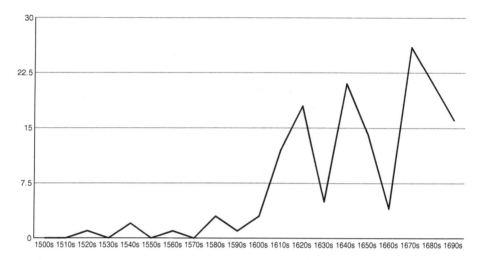

Figure 3. *Drunkard* and *drunkenness* on printed title pages, 1500–1700.

proportion of all published works: figure 4 shows that, when presented as a percentage of all EEBO-TCP texts, there was only one spike of note. This was in the 1610s and 1620s, when between 13 and 18 title pages amounted to around 0.7–0.8 percent of all EEBO-TCP texts (the peak in the 1520s is caused by 1 title page out of 104 cataloged texts).

Viewed quantitatively, then, the first three decades of the seventeenth century were clearly significant for printed discourse about drunkenness and, in particular, drunkards. Not only did they see a marked jump in texts and title pages using the terms, but the language was proportionally more prominent. But as striking is how this intensification of Jacobean printed discourse correlated with trends in the ecclesiastical courts in Norwich and Chester. Figure 5 breaks down the number of cases

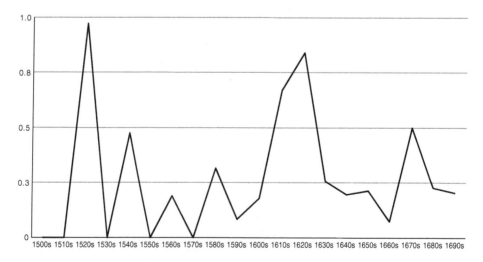

Figure 4. Percentage of EEBO-TCP texts with *drunkard* or *drunkenness* on the title page, 1500–1700.

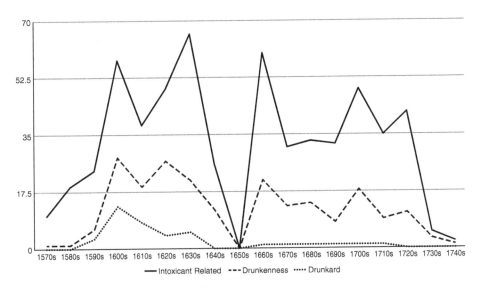

Figure 5. Norwich and Chester Consistory Court cases involving any mention of intoxicants, drunkenness, and *drunkard*, 1570s–1740s.

heard in these courts in three ways. First, the figures show the entire number of cases with any kind of reference to intoxicants recorded between the 1570s and 1740s (these might range from innkeepers allegedly receiving stolen goods to violent arguments breaking out in an alehouse). Second, they show the number of cases involving references to alleged drunken behavior (either as the main point of the case or an incidental feature). Third, they show the number of cases in which deponents or examinees explicitly used the term *drunkard* to describe another person.

Figure 5 demonstrates that aside from the 1640s and 1650s, when court business was disrupted by political events, the ecclesiastical courts at Chester and Norwich recorded more than thirty cases per decade involving some reference to intoxicants, with that figure significantly higher in the first four decades of the seventeenth century (peaking in the 1630s), the 1660s, and the 1700s. It shows that within that trend, allegations of drunkenness were at a rate of between twenty and thirty cases per decade in the forty years before the civil war and between ten and twenty cases per decade in the sixty years after 1660. And it shows that *drunkard* began to be mentioned in the depositional record in the 1590s; peaked in the 1600s; continued to appear—albeit less frequently—in legal and everyday conversations until the 1640s; but then all but disappeared at the Restoration (getting mentioned in one case per decade until the 1720s, when the term disappears entirely). Thus, while the printed data indicates the dissipation of *drunkard* after 1660, the depositional material suggests an even more marked degree of absence.

Making the Jacobean Drunkard

The rise of *drunkard* in print can be understood as one example of a more general, public concern among vernacular religious preachers and writers for the moral and spiritual condition of the populace following the break with Rome in the middle of the sixteenth century. As is well known, this "reformation of manners" was an English variant of a European-wide phenomenon whereby reformers in both Protestant and Catholic territories looked to establish institutional authority over the different aspects of Christian worship while exerting tangible influence over the behavior and attitudes of their congregations. As part of this process, the "deadly sins" of pre-Reformation culture received renewed and energetic treatment, with the relatively new technology of print providing a convenient and powerful medium through which to reach wider audiences.[17]

As a variant of gluttony with complicated ramifications for both the self and society, drunkenness was an ideal sin to receive such reformatory treatment. As the influential preacher and writer Henry Smith explained in the early 1590s, "there is no sin but hath some shew of virtue, only the sin of drunkenness is like nothing but sin."[18] This was because whereas most sins were at least explicable in the sense that they resulted in worldly and material gain for the sinner (however misconceived), drunkenness was "so unthankful that it makes no recompense: so noisome, that it consumes the body." Smith accordingly wondered that "any man should be drunk that hath seen a drunkard before, swelling, and puffing, and foaming, and spewing, and grovelling like a beast for who would be like a beast, for all the world?"[19] Drunkards did not merely risk their soul and relinquish their humanity for no obvious return. Like pride, drunkenness was an "impudent sin, because she decries herself in the eye, in the speech, in the gesture, in the look, in the gait." Smith explained: "Many that know him not, shall point at him with their fingers in the streets, & say, there goes a proud fellow: which they pronounce of no [other] vice, but the drunkard, because these two betray themselves."[20] He accordingly beseeched his listeners to "look upon the drunkard when his eyes stare; his mouth drivels, his tongue faulters, his face flames, his hands tremble, his feet reel" and consider "how ugly, how monstrous, how loathsome doth he seem to thee, so loathsome dost thou seem to others when thou art in like taking? And how loathsome then dost thou seem to God."[21]

This intensification of public discourse about drunkards was driven in part by the increasing numbers of highly educated clerics coming through the universities. Trained in humanistic skills like rhetoric and philology, and conscious of the power of print as a means to patronage as well as propaganda, they treated drunkenness, like other sins, in increasingly sophisticated and persuasive terms. Educated in Cambridge in the 1570s, Smith, for example, was recognized as one of the most skillful and effective communicators of the late Elizabethan era.[22] Thomas Nashe nicknamed him "silver-tongued" on account of his successful vernacularization of classical literary techniques and eulogized that "I never saw abundant reading better mixt with delight, or sentences which no man can challenge of prophane affectation, sounding more melodious to the ear or piercing more deep to the heart."[23] Arthur Dent, a contemporary of Smith's at Cambridge, was another preaching and print sensation whose *The Plaine Mans Path-way to Heauen*, published in 1601, reached its twenty-fifth edition by 1640. Like Smith, he drew on "some of the ancient writers, and some of the wise Heathen also" in order "to bear witness of the ugliness of some vices, which we in this age make light of."[24] Choosing the classical dialogic form to maximize his populist appeal, Dent nevertheless eschewed the relative light and shade discernible in Smith's analysis for something more absolute. He proclaimed drunkenness "so brutish and beastly a sin . . . that all reasonable men should even abhor it, & quake to think of it." He lamented "yet almost nothing will make men leave it: for it is a most rife and over common vice." And he thundered that "all drunkards are notorious Reprobates, and hell-hounds, branded of Satan, and devoted to perpetual destruction and damnation."[25]

Dent's representation of drunkenness as the diametric opposite to godliness was consistent with an emergent vernacular Calvinism that, in its framing by polarities, vindicated more general tendencies within public life toward political conflict, religious "apartheid," and cultural "disassociation."[26] Over the next three decades a new generation of university graduates accordingly contributed to a corpus of work explicitly dedicated to the problem of drunkenness—and the drunkard—conceived broadly in these terms. They included Downame, with whom this article started, as well as other university-educated and eminent preachers like Robert Bolton, Robert Harris, and Samuel Ward.[27] So marked was this surge in vernacular moral critique that the young lawyer William Prynne could approvingly reference it as a distinctly "modern" tradition in his own polemic against drinking healths in 1628; and the likes of lawyer and regicide John Cook and reformer Richard Younge continued in the same vein into the 1640s and 1650s.[28]

There was, nevertheless, more to this characterization of the drunkard than the ungodly and senseless reprobate against whom the godly and the elect could define themselves. First, early Stuart commentators inherited the humanistic training of previous generations and continued to look both to the primitive church and Greco-Roman writers to understand and reform their world. While this reinforced the Protestant emphasis on temperance and moderation, it also provided other intellectual tools to explain excessive and possibly compulsive consumption. Second, these commentators were responding to a world that was changing rapidly both in terms of the availability and consumption of alcohols—and their accompaniments, like tobacco—and the social, economic, material, and legal contexts shaping consumption. In developing their critiques, they deployed modes of socioeconomic and cultural analyses that supplemented core shibboleths about sin and damnation and extended the concept of the drunkard in significant ways.

Influential in each of these respects was James VI and I. This was most obvious in his role as legislator. James agreed the definitive version of the *Constitutions and Canons Ecclesiastical of the Church of England* in 1603, reaffirming drunkenness as a crime to be presented to the ecclesiastical courts along with adultery, whoredom, and incest, and for perpetrators to be excluded from Holy Communion until they reformed.[29] A year later James's first parliament passed an act outlining "several penalties of alehouse-keepers, for their several offences." This confirmed the assumption of the statute of 1552 that it was the responsibility of licensed proprietors and local officeholders, in particular constables, to ensure that only "necessary" or "urgent" drinking occurred in alehouses and inns. But the subsequent act of 1606, titled "The Penalty of the Drunkard, and of him that continues drinking in an Alehouse," made individuals culpable for "offences of Drunkenness and of excess and unmeasurable Drinking."[30] Two years later, Downame noted that "our days this vice more reigns then ever it did in former ages; as may appear in that our wise Statesmen thought it necessary in Parliament, to enact a law for the suppress-ing of this sin."[31] Now was an opportunity for "Magistrates and Ministers to join together, and not only labour by the sword of the word, but also by the sword of Justice, to suppress this vice."

Historians have noted how this legislation came to reshape relationships in local communities.[32] Less recognized is that, when it came to drunkards, James was an influence on the sword of the word as well as the sword of justice. When he ascended the English throne in 1603 the Scottish king was already a distinguished contributor to the printed public sphere, with learned and humanistic treatises on kingship, biblical exegesis, civil conduct, and witchcraft as well as books of poetry to his name.[33] These were now republished, along with a new short treatise that deployed cultural analysis and medical theory to argue against the pleasurable and excessive consumption of the American-Spanish intoxicant—an expensive luxury and "novelty" that had become deeply fashionable among the English ruling classes.[34]

Counterblaste to Tobacco was an important intervention for the concept of the drunkard for at least four reasons. First, James noted the similarities between tobacco and alcohol in terms of their effects on mind and body, recognizing the abuse of tobacco as "a branch of the sin of drunkenness, which is the root of all sins."[35] Just as "the only delight that drunkards take in Wine is in the strength of the taste, & the force of the fume thereof that mounts up to the brain," so are "those (I meane the strong heat and the fume) the only qualities that make Tobacco so delectable to all the lovers of it."[36] More important, he suggested a process of acculturation by which people came to depend on the intoxicants. If "no man likes strong heady drink the first day . . . but by custom is piece and piece allured . . . ," then "is not this the very case of all the great takers of Tobacco? which therefore they themselves do attribute to a bewitching quality in it."[37] Second, England's new king repurposed a classical conception of "custom" to explain more precisely this "bewitching quality."[38] Asking why "many in this kingdom have had such a continual use of taking this unsa-voury smoke, as now they are not able to forbear the same, no more than an old drunkard can abide to be long sober, without falling into an incurable weakness and evil constitution," he answered "that for their continual custom hath made to them, *habitum, alterā naturam*": that is, the force of habit eventually became second nature, "so to those that from their birth have been continually nourished upon poi-son and things venomous, wholesome meats are only poisoned."[39] Third, *Counter-blaste* reiterated that personal consumption did not simply carry cultural and social significations—nor merely compromise the individual's relationship to God—but was also an issue of political authority and economy. James asked his subjects whether it was "not the greatest sin of all, that you the people of all sorts of this King-dom, who are created and ordained by God to bestow both your persons and goods for the maintenance both of the honour and safety of your King and Common-wealth, should disable yourselves in both?"[40] Fourth, the drunkenness described by James was not the preserve of an impoverished and desperate people seeking consolation and respite through intoxication. Rather, it was symptomatic of the "Peace and wealth [that] hath brought forth a general sluggishness, which makes us wallow in all sorts of idle delights, and soft delicacies."[41] Indeed, the drunkard was indicative of how "our Clergy are become negligent and lazy, our Nobility and Gentry prodigal, and sold to their private delights, Our Lawyers covetous, our Common-people prodigal and curious; and generally all sorts of people more careful for their private ends, then for their mother the Common-wealth."[42]

As well as sinful and inhumane, therefore, drunkards were the product of custom—by which social practices engendered powerful habits and biological dependencies—and subjects of political economy, exemplifying how the opportunities of affluence, excess, and private consumption rubbed against the demands of citizenship, commonwealth, and public virtue. These were not original insights: Elizabethan satirists like Thomas Lupton were aware of the economic and public problems posed by the "rich drunkard" who not only devotes himself to "drinking, bibbing and belly-cheer" but also "brags" about it when sober.[43] But articulated and authorized by a new monarch, these insights provided wide scope for addressing the problem of drunkenness with renewed and didactic intent.

Downame was especially concerned, for example, with how customs became "second nature" and why ostensibly rational men invented rituals and practices that led them into "slavery" and madness."[44] He reported in shocked tones how modern drinkers "use . . . glasses without feet, that so they may go about in a continual motion [because they cannot be put down]; they carouse by the bell, by the dye, the dozen, the yard, and so by measure, drink out of measure." The practices of drunkards were intended to manipulate not only behavior but also the physiology or nature of the person. Downame explained that because "nature is content with a little, and soon cloyed and oppressed with excess, they use all their art and skill to strengthen it for these wicked exploits." Tricks included "salt meats to whet their appetite [. . . and . . .] tobacco, that by drunkenness they may expel drunkenness, and being glutted with wine, they drink smoke, that by this variety it may not grow tedious."[45] This sociological analysis was supplemented by Samuel Ward, who replaced the usual rhetorical technique of listing the fate of infamous classical and biblical drunkards—men like Noah, Lot, and Alexander the Great—with contemporary instances of God's judgment. In what was an early exercise in social surveying, Ward collated cases like the "two servants of a Brewer in Ipswich, drinking for a rump of a Turkey, struggling in their drink for it, fell into a scalding Caldron backwards: whereof the one dyed presently, the other lingeringly, and painfully since my coming to Ipswich."[46] And like any good social scientist, he was even careful to keep "The names of the parties thus punished" anonymous "for the kindred's sake yet living."[47]

Across this burgeoning reformatory discourse, it is possible to discern at least three analytic and methodological threads spinning across the didactic literature. These included concern with the social practices and customs that created the drunkard; the language determining how drunkards and their opponents were defined, condemned, or valorized; and the relationship between drunkards and socioeconomic structures over time. Each was meant to explain why contemporaries engaged in such calamitous behavior and why, as pressingly, drunkards seemed more prevalent now than in the past. But by interrogating customs, language, and political economy so critically, reformers also ratcheted up the like-lihood of conflict over the concept of the drunkard itself. Rather than some-one simply overtaken by drunkenness—whether occasionally or recurringly—the drunkard morphed into anyone who drank for any reason other than necessity, with necessity defined in increasingly restricted terms.

Robert Harris's *The Drunkard's Cup* was a case in point. Harris prefaced his sermon, which he dedicated to Justices of the Peace in Oxfordshire, with various economic and political reasons for why "there is an Art of Drinking now, and in the world it has become a great profession."[48] One factor was the breakdown of the manorial system and the commercialization of the drinks trade: just as "the want of Hospitality" in manor and parsonage required the establishment of paying ale-houses, so "want of upholding tilling and husbandry" led to evictions, urban migra-tion, and the reemployment of landless husbandmen as badgers, maltsters, and the alemen.[49] Other causes included the bad example set by gentry households ("were I to seek a Tobacconist, I would as soon look him in a Gentleman's house, as in any man's") and the reluctance of governors to enforce the law against drunkards.[50] Having contextualized the problem, Harris elaborated on the concept of the drunk-ard that encompassed pleasurable as well as disordered drinking. Asking "who is a drunkard?," he invoked the ghost of Solomon to explain that drink "is not only abused when it turns up a man's heels, and makes the house run round (as one speaks) but when it steals away the affections": "If a man drink too much for his purse, too much for his calling and occasions, too much for his health and quiet of body and mind, Solomon calls him a drunkard."[51] Put simply, men need not have "lost their legs, tongues, senses" or "lie tumbling in their own vomit" to qual-ify. Like Ward, Harris did not rely on ancient or biblical exemplar to make the point. In a passage almost ethnographic in its details, Harris argued that

> It's your mannerly, sober Methodical drunkard, that drinks by the hour, and can tell the clock, that drinks by measure, and by rule, first so much Ale, then such a quantity of Beer, then of Sack, then to Rhenish . . . who knows his proportions, for wine, for sugar, for spring-water, Rose-water . . . [who] have his tools about him, Nutmegs, Rosemary, Tobacco . . . just so much as will make him hearty, cheerful, witty, healthful, and no more: this is the man that Solomon speaks of, a man of measures, and mixtures.[52]

Audiences were left in no doubt that these customs of "regular drinking" were as much "abusive drinking"—the drinking of the drunkard—as the descent into "senselessness."[53]

The Drunkard and Socioeconomic Critique

These analytic strands were pulled together most systematically by William Prynne in 1628 to explain "why Drunkenness doth so much increase and superabound among us."[54] Aside from the innate depravity of man and the demonstrable influ-ence of the devil, for Prynne the cause of the current crisis of "excess, and Drunk-ards" in England was a particular convergence of custom, language, and social emulation. Prynne accordingly observed that while the "common ceremonies" involved in the "Art of Drinking" were described in "popular, goodly, flattering, and insinuating titles; so Temperance and Sobriety are deformed, vilified, derided, sentenced, condemned, and scoffed at, under . . . opprobrious and disdainful names."[55] The result was that "Drunkards are likewise magnified, and extolled, under the amiable, reverenced, and applauded terms of good-fellows, wits; Poets; courteous, sociable, merry, jovial, and boon-companions." In the meantime, those "who make a conscience of excess" were reviled as "Puritans, Praecisians, Stoics; unsociable, clownish, rustic, perverse, peevish, humorous, singular, discourteous niggardly, pragmatical, proud, unmannerly, degenerous, base, scrupulous, melancholic, sad or discontented persons."[56] So significant was this semantic politics that "great men, Gentlemen, Clergymen, and others . . . instead of being patterns of temperance and sobriety unto inferior and meaner persons, are oft times made their presidents & plot-forms of Drunkenness and excess."[57] This was a deadly scenario given that "inferiors . . . commonly adore [their] Superiors' chief and greatest vices, as so many glorious and resplendent virtues." It was even more so because of "the negligence and coldness of Justices, Magistrates, and inferior Officers, in the due and faithful execution of those laudable and pious Lawes and Statutes, enacted by our King, and State."[58] Prynne opined that if England's rulers were "as diligent to suppress and pulldown Drunkenness and Alehouses, as they are industrious and forwards to Patronize and set them up, [then] the wings of Drunkenness would soon be clipped."[59]

As well as triangulating the Jacobean concern with custom, semantics, and emulation, Prynne conveyed the urgent social and economic critique informing the discussions of his predecessors. Following the initial example of James himself, this critique aimed at the affluent and powerful in the first instance. All commentators were conscious that poor drunkards could only make their families and neighborhoods poorer and that drunkenness, like idleness, was antithetical to industriousness.[60] But in print those who could afford to be bewitched by tobacco in 1604 or 1609 and who, in the words of Harris, were guilty of the "unsufferable abuse of their wealth and plenty, partly in the getting, and partly in the spending," attracted the most ire.[61] This coupling of "the getting"—as "Covetousness and Ambition"—with "the spending"—as "riotous . . . and abusive drinking"—was a powerful fixture in the evaluative and critical lexicon that developed around the Jacobean conception of the drunkard.[62] Not only did it make the inequitable accumulation of wealth and its consumption two sides of the same economic and moral problem, but it also reinforced another assumption among reformers: drunkards were the result of recent historical processes.[63] For Harris, as we have seen, their root cause was agrarian capitalism and the breakdown of manorialism: while "heretofore it was a strange sight to see a drunken man, now it is no news; heretofore it was the sin of Tinkers, Ostlers, Beggars, etc, now of Farmers, Esquires, Knights etc."[64] Another explanation was the Germanic dynamic within Protestantism, John Cook making the "sad observation that Drunkards came not into this Kingdome till the Reformation of Religion, and a sadder observation which I have found true, that Protestants generally are greater Drinkers then Papists, who are far more libidinous and unchaste."[65] For Prynne, the more specific problem of oathing and healthing lay not so much with the Germans—although he acknowledged the ancient and "modern Germans" were great drunkards, he also made a specific point of explaining that rumors of Luther's dissoluteness were Catholic lies—as with the educated elites' obsession with classical culture and their adaptation of heathenish practices.[66]

Prynne, however, went a few steps further with this critique than his Jacobean predecessors. He implicated the monarchy in the problem of drunkenness by asserting that it was healths of love and loyalty to the king that were especially used to vindicate drunkenness; and he dedicated his analysis to the new king, James's son Charles, as a kind of challenge to do something about it.[67] Repeating the same trick a few years later over the related problem of stage plays, he was tried for sedition and physically mutilated.[68] If this was one way to mark the end of the "Jacobethan consensus"—such as it was—then twenty years later John Cook could nevertheless adopt the insights of Harris to make the drunkard the pivot of his reformatory political economy.[69] As a lawyer and future regicide, Cook published *Unum Necessarium: or, The Poore Mans Case* from the albeit bedraggled center of parliamentary power. After six years of civil war, Charles by 1648 was the prisoner of a regime struggling to deal with dearth and famine and a politically and religiously divided nation. It was these dire circumstances that prompted Cook to observe that the "English follow extremes too much." On the one hand, "one man is too prodigal, his mouth like a Sepulchre, his throat like a hot Oven, that consumes all; the Drunkard and intemperate person."[70] But "another is so extremely penurious, that he will not afford himself food, and raiment, according to his quality"—the sort of men Cook also labeled "cruel misers" and "covetous persons."[71] In times of scarcity and hardship—such as now—it was "between these two Millstones [that] the poor labouring man is squeezed to death": just as "covetous misers" looked to profit from grain shortages and inflated prices, so drunkards wasted scarce barley on unnecessary drinking.[72] Cook hazarded that "were it not for the hardness of some men's hearts; and the riotous excess and Intemperance of others, we need not much fear a Dearth."[73] Indeed, "would Christians were so merciful, to part with their superfluities, without question, that which is excessively spent in apparel and Diet would comfortably relieve all the poor in the Kingdom."[74]

In making these arguments Cook explicitly combined the humanism of Thomas More and Michel de Montaigne with Jacobean sermonizing on drunkenness.[75] Not only did he elaborate on Harris's economic model of "getting" and "spending" as the key to understanding the sociopathology of the drunkard, but he also rejected popular conceptions of the drunkard as simply one who "staggers," "reels," or "does not understand himself" for the more capacious sense of one "who hath taken more than his body requires for health or strength inordinately."[76] Cook had in mind, that is, "no drunkard like the old Drunkard that can sit all day from morning to night, & by the help of that witch Tobacco (against the moderate or unlustful use whereof I except not,) as K. James calls it, which will make a drunken man sober, & a sober man drunk, will be as fresh at night as at the first cup."[77] But whereas his predecessors had mainly sought to deal with drunkards by the proper enforcement of laws against alehouses, the encouragement of godliness and stoicism on the part of householders, and the wholesale withdrawal of the godly and honest from "bad company," Cook preferred an altogether more draconian remedy.[78] This involved an escalation from short imprisonment for the first offense, to a fine for the second offense, to a pardon for the third offense, and "for the fourth offence to sustain the pain of death, as unworthy to live in a well-governed Kingdome, a Drunkard being the greatest robber of poor people which are ready to famish for want of bread, a rebel against divine and humane authority, and a sworn enemy to all humanity."[79]

Conclusion

Cook's treatise of 1648 coincided with widespread popular demand for governmental action against alehouses and middlemen that was driven by both "godly zeal" and fear of dearth.[80] The intersection of rhetoric and policy was not unprecedented. As John Walter and Wrightson long ago demonstrated, over the previous forty years the reformatory tradition informing Cook's arguments had led to "concrete action" in times of economic hardship and was "certainly attractive to those of the 'middling sort' of town and country who stood in an intermediate position between the poor and the local representatives of church and state."[81] The campaigns against drunkenness are accordingly presented as religious and moral crusades, centering primarily on the alehouse, that were most likely to engender popular assent when linked to the pressures of economic necessity.[82] Focusing on how early Stuart moralists constructed the character of the drunkard points, however, to a multiple rather than singularly religious identity. Not simply moral agents defined in terms of sin and damnation, early Stuart drunkards were also perceived by moralists as economic beings—what contemporaries were learning to describe as "consumptioners" and "consumers"—whose excessive and superfluous consumption had obvious economic consequences in much the same way that the behavior of "covetous misers" broke salient codes of equity and religion.[83] Indeed, just as contemporary economic theorists were far from shy in importing moral assumptions and prerequisites into their discussions, so reformers and moralists eagerly engaged in political—moral—economy.[84] In this sense, the rise and fall of the drunkard is as much a part of economic history as the history of drinking and manners.

It is also the story of much more besides. The remaking of the drunkard involved classical as well as biblical learning; it built on Elizabethan fears about drunkenness and encouraged a range of contemporary socioeconomic and cultural analyses. The result was a powerful tool of criticism and didacticism that was not only economic and moral in nature but also social, medical, and political. This character of the drunkard proscribed not only the loss of reason and humanity but also the pursuit of pleasure and recreation. It warned against mannerly, regular, and sober drinking as well as intoxication of the instant. It drew a sharp distinction between superfluous and necessary consumption of not simply alcohols but also other intoxicants—most notably tobacco. It held all social groups—but especially social and political elites—to serious public account. And from the mid-1620s it was conflated with partisan and anti-Puritan identities, with conflict about intoxicants personalized in the character of the drunkard in the same way that it was spatialized in the alehouse. Given the force of this reformatory discourse, it is hardly surprising that churchwardens in Northamptonshire should declare in 1619 that "we cannot define a . . . drunkard and therefore crave advice (how to present such) until the next court."[85] Martin Ingram argues this was a canny way to resist the intensification of regulatory tendencies that can be traced back well into the medieval era.[86] But it also indicates more immediate and unprecedented attempts to redefine the drunkard and the social confusion this caused.

Telling this story has meant focusing on the rise of *drunkard* rather than its decline. It has also left no time to consider concurrent and alternative discourses that valorized drinking, nor the history of the label in the kind of depositional material from which Robert Elton's more "discerning" definition was recorded. While these issues must be treated in more detail elsewhere, it is worth concluding with a couple of speculative points. The first concerns the popular purchase of reformist ideas about drunkards, about which this discussion has raised more questions than answers. One is whether the critique of social elites explicit to the tag *drunkard* also resonated with the "middling sort": did their activism work upward, as the rhetoric against drunkards encouraged, or was it mostly directed toward the poor, as regulation of alehouses seemed to encourage?[87] Another is whether the attendant and more complicated notions of *drunkard* propagated by reformers found purchase with parishioners: not least ideas about custom, habituation, and second nature. Did they take seriously, for example, Richard Younge's warning in 1658 that "if physick be taken too oft, it will not like physick: but nature entertains it as a friend, not as a Physician: yea poison by a familiar use becomes natural food. As Aristotle (in an example of a Maid, who used to pick spiders off the walls and eat them) makes plain"?[88] Younge suspected not: "it is sad to consider, how many Drunkards will hear this Charge, for one that will apply it to himself. For confident I am that fifteen of twenty, all this City over, are Drunkards."[89] He explained that "perhaps by the Laws of the Land, a man is not taken for drunk, except his eyes stare, his tongue stutter, and his legs stagger," but "he that drinks more for lust, or pride, or covetousness, or fear, or good fellowship, or to drive away time, or to still conscience, then for thirst, is a Drunkard in Solomon's esteem."[90]

But here, perhaps, was the crux of the reformist problem. Although rooted in concerns about inequity, addiction, and waste—as well as sin—the centrality of alcohol to most aspects of early modern life meant that an expansive concept of the drunkard risked criminalizing the customs by which civil and commercial society functioned. Reformers in the 1600s had been sensitive to the tension, Dent arguing that it was "pot-companionship" rather than "brotherly fellowship" that "the plain man" should avoid and even Downame reassuring readers that it was not only lawful to drink "for necessity, but also for honest delight, and that not only in Christian and religious feasting, when for some public benefit we offer unto God public thanks and praise, but also in love feasts and civil meetings, for the maintenance and increase of amity and friendship amongst neighbours."[91] By the midcentury these sensitivities, at least for some, had hardened. For Younge, "in cases of this nature, things are rather measured by the intention and affection of the doer, than of the issue, and event." On this basis, the archetypal drunkard "constantly clubs it, first for his mornings draught, secondly at Exchange time, thirdly at night when shops are shut in; as is the common, but base custom of most Tradesmen; and the Devil so blinds them, that they will plead a necessity of it; and that it is for their profit."[92] This was not so much an assault on superfluity and waste as on the very practices of everyday life.[93]

The imperialism of this concept of the drunkard—together with the relentlessness of its didacticism and increasing politicization from the mid-1620s—perhaps explains why it could not survive in its evolved semantic state at the Restoration. Like other terms that underwent discursive enclosure after 1660—"commonwealth" comes to mind—the language of *drunkard* was too compromised by the revolutionary era to be current thereafter.[94] It did not disappear in print in the way it slipped from the depositional record, however; indeed, its revival in the 1670s (as described in figures 3 and 4) was driven by reeditions of early Stuart texts and new popular genres that worked their didacticism through balladry and fiction. But John Wilkin's influential *Essay towards a Real Character, and a Philosophical Language* relegated *drunkard* to a subset of *sot* and collocated it with *fool, dull,* and *dotage* rather than confirm the more capacious concept.[95] Medical writers began to take an altogether more benign interest in the relationship between intoxicants and second nature.[96] And Enlightenment definitions of *drunkard* accordingly retreated to denote "one given to excessive use of strong liquor, one addicted to habitual ebriety."[97] In the meantime, powerful counterdiscourses proclaiming the public benefits of private consumption, pleasure, and happiness began to pose serious questions of the civic asceticism promulgated earlier in the century.[98] As importantly, the economic conditions that had made the pre–civil war era so challenging—and the emphases of *drunkard* so plausible—relented: real wages rose, inflation abated, and demographic pressures eased.[99]

That is not to say that the insights and methodologies of early Stuart reformists were lost. Increase Mather transported the reformist concept of the drunkard to New England in 1673, berating those colonists who "love to drink Wine to excess, though he should seldom be overcome thereby" and additionally lamenting how "Some amongst us (who they are the Lord knows) out of Covetousness have sold Liquors and strong drinks to these poor *Indians*, whose lands we possess, and have made them drunk therewith."[100] Aside from critiquing the political and economic purposing of liquor by his fellow colonists, Mather delineated the "traditional" and "Puritan" definition of *drunkard* that, according to Harry Levine, preceded the coining of a modern "disease" concept of addiction a hundred years later.[101] But it is now clear that this "traditional" concept not only was itself a relatively recent construction but came out of the insistent corralling of ideas and observation by reformers that "modern" and medicalized conceptions of temperance and addiction—including "disease" conceptions—emerged.[102] More ironic, perhaps, is that as the primary describers of drunkards in early Stuart print, reformers did most both to promulgate the "lurid" customs they ostensibly abhorred and to establish the importance of representing them in print.[103] Their conception of the drunkard may have been contested, but the construction of a prurient public sphere was more perennial.

PHIL WITHINGTON is professor of social and cultural history at the University of Sheffield. He has worked extensively on intoxicants and intoxication, publishing numerous articles and chapters on the subject (most recently in the *Economic History Review* and the *Journal of Modern History*) and coediting the *Past and Present* special supplement "Cultures of Intoxication" (2014) and the *Historical Journal* special issue "Intoxicants and Early Modern European Globalisation" (2021). He is leading the project "Intoxicating Spaces" (www.intoxicatingspaces.org), funded by the Humanities in the European Research Area, and is writing a monograph provisionally called *The Holy Herb and Other Stories*.

Acknowledgments

Thanks to Cathy Shrank and Keith Wrightson for reading earlier drafts of this article. The research was generously funded by the Humanities in the European Research Area project "Intoxicating Spaces" (www.intoxicatingspaces.org).

Notes

1   Downame, *Foure Treatises Tending to Disswade*, 83.

2   Downame, *Foure Treatises Tending to Disswade*, 83.

3   EDC 5/1609/17 (unfol.) [i.e., n.p.] Bolton c [i.e., v.] Clayton, available on the Intoxicants and Early Modernity database at www .intoxicantsproject.org/publications/database.

4   EDC 5/1609/17 (unfol.) Bolton c Clayton, deposition of Adam Clayton.

5   EDC 5/1609/17 (unfol.) Bolton c Clayton, deposition of Robert Elton.

6   Walter and Wrightson, "Dearth and the Social Order"; Wrightson, *English Society*, chap. 6.

7   Brown, "Alehouse Licensing and State Formation"; Wrightson, "Alehouses, Order, and Reformation in Rural England."

8   Stephens, "English Wine Imports"; Taylor, "Tobacco Retail and State Formation"; Unger, *Beer in the Middle Ages and Renaissance*, chap. 6; Withington, "Intoxicants and the Early Modern City"; Withington, "Intoxicants and the Invention of Consumption."

9   Hailwood, *Alehouses and Good Fellowship*, esp. sec. 2; Hailwood, "Sociability, Work, and Labouring Identity"; McShane, "Material Culture and 'Political Drinking'"; McShane, "Drink, Song, and Politics"; Withington, "Intoxicants and Society." See also Smyth, *Pleasing Sinne*.

10   Wrightson, "Alehouses, Order, and Reformation in Rural England," 11, 17–18; Warner, "'Resolv'd to Drink No More.'"

11   Lemon, *Addiction and Devotion*, 13.

12   Ingram, "Reformation of Manners"; Nicholls, *Politics of Alcohol*, 1–2.

13   For a smart use of "distant reading" to facilitate targeted semantic analysis, see Cree, "Protestant Evangelicals and Addiction in Early Modern English," 447–52.

14   Withington, *Society in Early Modern England*.

15   For an introduction to the courts and their historical potential, see Gowing, *Domestic Dangers*, esp. chap. 2.

16   See Intoxicants and Early Modernity.

17   Wrightson, *English Society*, chap. 6; Ingram, "Reformation of Manners"; Ingram, *Carnal Knowledge*, 8–29.

18   Smith, "Looking Glass for Drunkards," 590.

19   Smith, "Looking Glass for Drunkards," 590; Shrank, "Beastly Metamorphoses."

20   Smith, "Dissuasion from Pride," 441.

21   Smith, "Looking Glass for Drunkards," 590.

22   Gary W. Jenkins notes how Smith's London parishioners petitioned the church authorities in 1589 that he "had done more good among them than any other that had gone before or, which they doubted, could follow after" ("Smith, Henry").

23   Nashe, *Pierce Penilesse*, D3r.

24   Dent, *Plaine Mans Path-way to Heauen*, A3r.

25   Dent, *Plaine Mans Path-way to Heauen*, 162.

26   Lake, "Anti-popery," 73–74; Collinson, "Cohabitation of the Faithful with the Unfaithful," 63, 65; Walsham, "Ordeals of Conscience," 47–48; Wrightson, *English Society*, 232–36.

27   Bolton, *Two Sermons Preached at Northampton*; Bolton, *Some Generall Directions for a Comfortable Walking with God*; Harris, *Drunkards Cup*; Ward, *Woe to Drunkards*.

28   Prynne, *Healthes: Sicknesse*, 35–36; Cook, *Unum Necessarium*; Younge, *Drunkard's Character*; Younge, *Blemish of Government*.

29   *Constitutions and Canons Ecclesiastical of the Church of England*, cix.

30 W.B., *Collection of Certain Statutes*, 10–12, 14–17.

31 Downame, *Foure Treatises Tending to Disswade*, 79–80.

32 Wrightson, "Alehouses, Order, and Reformation in Rural England," 11–12; Clark, *English Alehouse*, 172–76; Nicholls, *Politics of Alcohol*, 13–15.

33 James VI and I, *His Maiesties Lepanto*; James VI and I, *Fruitefull Meditation*; James VI and I, *Dæmonologie in Forme of a Dialogue*; James VI and I, *Basilikon dōron*; James VI and I, *True Lawe of Free Monarchies*.

34 James VI and I, *Counterblaste to Tobacco*.

35 James VI and I, *Counterblaste to Tobacco*.

36 James VI and I, *Counterblaste to Tobacco*.

37 James VI and I, *Counterblaste to Tobacco*.

38 Shapin, "Why Was 'Custom a Second Nature'?," 4.

39 James VI and I, *Counterblaste to Tobacco*, C3r.

40 James VI and I, *Counterblaste to Tobacco*, C4.

41 James VI and I, *Counterblaste to Tobacco*, A3r.

42 James VI and I, *Counterblaste to Tobacco*, A3r.

43 Lupton, *Sivquila*, 56.

44 Lemon, *Addiction and Devotion*, 84–85.

45 Downame, *Foure Treatises Tending to Disswade*, 80.

46 Ward, *Woe to Drunkards*, 20.

47 Ward, *Woe to Drunkards*, 29.

48 Harris, *Drunkards Cup*, A2r.

49 Harris, *Drunkards Cup*, A3r.

50 Harris, *Drunkards Cup*, A4.

51 Harris, *Drunkards Cup*, 11.

52 Harris, *Drunkards Cup*, 12.

53 Harris, *Drunkards Cup*, 16, 15; Bolton, *Some Generall Directions for a Comfortable Walking with God*, 204.

54 Prynne, *Healthes: Sicknesse*, B2.

55 Prynne, *Healthes: Sicknesse*, A3–A3r.

56 Prynne, *Healthes: Sicknesse*, A3r.

57 Prynne, *Healthes: Sicknesse*, B1.

58 Prynne, *Healthes: Sicknesse*, B1.

59 Prynne, *Healthes: Sicknesse*, B1.

60 Dent, *Plaine Mans Path-way to Heauen*, 166; Wrightson, *English Society*, 175; Clark, *English Alehouse*, 167.

61 Harris, *Drunkards Cup*, 2.

62 Harris, *Drunkards Cup*, 2.

63 McShane, "Material Culture and 'Political Drinking,'" 257–61.

64 McShane, "Material Culture and 'Political Drinking,'" 22.

65 Cook, *Unum Necessarium*, 9; Downame, *Foure Treatises Tending to Disswade*, 80.

66 Prynne, *Healthes: Sicknesse*, 33, 19, 24.

67 Prynne, *Healthes: Sicknesse*, "The Epistle Dedicatory."

68 Lamont, *Marginal Prynne*, 28–48; Kishlansky, "'Whipper Whipped.'"

69 Hunt, "A Jacobean Consensus?"

70 Cook, *Unum Necessarium*, 70.

71 Cook, *Unum Necessarium*, preface, 13, 16, 41, 43, 73, 70, 74.

72 Cook, *Unum Necessarium*, 70, 74.

73 Cook, *Unum Necessarium*, 29.

74 Cook, *Unum Necessarium*, 45.

75 Cook, *Unum Necessarium*, 36, 52, 54.

76 Cook, *Unum Necessarium*, 22.

77 Cook, *Unum Necessarium*, 22.

78 Dent, *Plaine Mans Path-way to Heauen*, 166; Downame, *Foure Treatises Tending to Disswade*, 85, 95, 105, 114.

79 Cook, *Unum Necessarium*, 19.

80 Walter and Wrightson, "Dearth and the Social Order," 37–39.

81 Walter and Wrightson, "Dearth and the Social Order," 29.

82 Walter and Wrightson, "Dearth and the Social Order," 38.

83 Withington, "Intoxicants and the Invention of Consumption," 390–93.

84 Withington, "Intoxicants and the Invention of Consumption," 394–98; Waddell, "Economic Immorality," 165–67, 176–77.

85 Cited in Ingram, "Reformation of Manners," 76.

86 Ingram, "Reformation of Manners," 68–69, 80–81.

87 Wrightson, "Alehouses, Order, and Reformation in Rural England," 16–17; Clark, *English Alehouse*, 166–68.

88 Younge, *Blemish of Government*, 2.

89 Younge, *Blemish of Government*, 10.

90 Younge, *Blemish of Government*, 10.

91 Dent, *Plaine Mans Path-way to Heauen*, 166; Downame, *Foure Treatises Tending to Disswade*, 82.

92 Younge, *Blemish of Government*, 10.

93 Wrightson, "Alehouses, Order, and Reformation in Rural England," 6.

94 Withington, *Society in Early Modern England*, chap. 5.

95 Wilkins, *Essay*, s.v. "sot."

96 Withington, "Addiction, Intoxicants, and the Humoral Body."

97 Johnson, *Dictionary of the English language*, s.v. "drunkard."

98 Slack, "Politics of Consumption," 611–16.

99 Wrightson, *Earthly Necessities*, sec. 3.

100 Mather, *Wo [sic] to Drunkards*, 21.

101 Levine, "Discovery of Addiction," 45.

102 Porter, "Drinking Man's Disease," 393; Warner, "'Resolv'd to Drink No More,'" 689–90; Lemon, *Addiction and Devotion*, 84; Withington, "Addiction, Intoxicants, and the Humoral Body."

103 Wrightson, "Alehouses, Order, and Reformation in Rural England," 6.

Works Cited

Bolton, Robert. *Some Generall Directions for a Comfortable Walking with God Deliuered in the Lecture at Kettering in Northhamptonshire, with Enlargement.* London, 1626.

Bolton, Robert. *Two Sermons Preached at Northampton at Two Severall Assises There[.] The One in the Time of the Shrevalty of Sir Erasmus Dryden Baronet[,] Anno Domini, 1621. The Other in the Time of the Shrevalty of Sir Henry Robinson Knight, Anno Domini, 1629.* London, 1635.

Brown, James. "Alehouse Licensing and State Formation in Early Modern England." In *Intoxication and Society: Problematic Pleasures of Drugs and Alcohol,* edited by Jonathan Herring, Ciaran Regan, Darin Weinberg, and Phil Withington, 110–32. Basingstoke: Palgrave Macmillan, 2013.

Clark, Peter. *The English Alehouse: A Social History, 1200–1830.* London: Longman, 1983.

Collinson, Patrick. "The Cohabitation of the Faithful with the Unfaithful." In *From Persecution to Toleration: The Glorious Revolution and Religion in England,* edited by Ole Peter Grell, Jonathan I. Israel, and Nicholas Tyacke, 51–76. Oxford: Oxford University Press, 1991.

Constitutions and Canons Ecclesiastical of the Church of England (1603). www.anglican.net/doctrines /1604-canon-law/#p1-1 (accessed January 7, 2021).

Cook, John. *Unum Necessarium: or, The Poore Mans Case: Being an Expedient to Make Provision of All Poore People in the Kingdome.* London, 1648.

Cree, Jose. "Protestant Evangelicals and Addiction in Early Modern English." *Renaissance Studies* 32, no. 3 (2017): 446–62.

Dent, Arthur. *The Plaine Mans Path-way to Heauen. Wherein Euery Man May Clearly See, Whether He Shall be Saued or Damned. Set Forth Dialogue Wise, or the Better Understanding of the Simple.* London, 1601.

Downame, John. *Foure Treatises Tending to Disswade All Christians from Foure No Lesse Hainous Then Common Sinnes; Namely, the Abuses of Swearing, Drunkennesse, Whoredome, and Briberie.* London, 1609.

Gowing, Laura. *Domestic Dangers: Women, Words, and Sex in Early Modern London.* Oxford: Oxford University Press, 1996.

Hailwood, Mark. *Alehouses and Good Fellowship in Early Modern England.* Woodbridge: Boydell, 2014.

Hailwood, Mark. "Sociability, Work, and Labouring Identity in Seventeenth Century England." *Cultural and Social History* 8, no. 1 (2011): 9–29.

Harris, Robert. *The Drunkards Cup.* London, 1619.

Hunt, Arnold. "A Jacobean Consensus? The Religious Policy of James VI and I." *Seventeenth Century* 17, no. 1 (2002): 131–40.

Ingram, Martin. *Carnal Knowledge: Regulating Sex in England, 1470–1600.* Cambridge: Cambridge University Press, 2017.

Ingram, Martin. "Reformation of Manners in Early Modern England." In *The Experience of Authority in Early Modern England,* edited by Adam Fox, Paul Griffiths, and Steve Hindle, 47–88. Basingstoke: Palgrave Macmillan, 1996.

Intoxicants and Early Modernity: English, 1580–1740. Database. www.intoxicantsproject.org /publications/database (accessed January 7, 2021).

James VI and I. *Basilikon dōron. Or His Maiesties Instructions to His Dearest Sonne, Henry the Prince.* Edinburgh, 1603.

James VI and I. *A Counterblaste to Tobacco.* London, 1604.

James VI and I. *Dæmonologie in Forme of a Dialogue, Diuided into Three Books.* Edinburgh, 1603.

James VI and I. *A Fruitefull Meditation Containing. A Plaine and Easie Exposition, or Laying Open of the 7. 8. 9. and 10. Verses of the 20. Chap. of the Reuelation, in Forme and Maner of a Sermon.* London, 1588; repr. 1603.

James VI and I. *His Maiesties Lepanto, or Heroicall Song Being Part of His Poeticall Exercises at Vacant Hours.* London, 1603.

James VI and I. *The True Lawe of Free Monarchies, or, The Reciprock and Mutuall Dutie betwixt a Free King, and His Naturall Subiects.* London, 1603.

Jenkins, Gary W. "Smith, Henry (c. 1560–1591)." In *Oxford Dictionary of National Biography,* September 23, 2004. www.oxforddnb.com /view/10.1093/ref:odnb/9780198614128.001 .0001/odnb-9780198614128-e-25811.

Johnson, Samuel. *A Dictionary of the English Language.* Vol. 1. London, 1770.

Kishlansky, Mark. "'The Whipper Whipped': The Sedition of William Prynne." *Historical Journal* 56, no. 3 (2003): 603–27.

Lake, Peter. "Anti-popery: The Structure of a Prejudice." In *Conflict in Early Stuart England: Studies in Religion and Politics, 1603–1642,* edited by Richard Cust and Ann Hughes, 72–106. London: Routledge, 1989.

Lamont, William. *Marginal Prynne, 1600–1669.* London: Routledge, 1963.

Lemon, Rebecca. *Addiction and Devotion in Early Modern England.* Philadelphia: University of Pennsylvania Press, 2018.

Levine, Harry Gene. "The Discovery of Addiction: Changing Conceptions of Habitual Drunkenness in America." *Journal of Substance Abuse Treatment* 2, no. 1 (1985): 43–57.

Lupton, Thomas. *Sivquila Too Good, to Be True.* London, 1580.

Mather, Increase. *Wo [sic] to Drunkards: Two Sermons Testifying against the Sin of Drunkenness, Wherein the Wofulness of That Evil, and the Misery of All That Are Addicted to It, Is Discovered from the Word of God.* Boston, 1673.

McShane, Angela. "Drink, Song, and Politics in Early Modern England." *Popular Music* 35, no. 2 (2016): 166–90.

McShane, Angela. "Material Culture and 'Political Drinking' in Seventeenth-Century England." *Past and Present*, no. 222, suppl. no. 9 (2014): 247–76.

Nashe, Thomas. *Pierce Penilesse HIS SUPPLICATION to the Divell.* London, 1592.

Nicholls, James. *The Politics of Alcohol: A History of the Drink Question in England.* Manchester: Manchester University Press, 2009.

Porter, Roy. "The Drinking Man's Disease: The 'Pre-History' of Alcoholism in Georgian Britain." *British Journal of Addiction* 80, no. 4 (1985): 385–96.

Prynne, William. *Healthes: Sicknesse. Or a Compendious and Briefe Discourse; Prouing, the Drinking and Pledging of Healthes, to Be Sinfull, and Utterly Unlawfull unto Christians.* London, 1628.

Shapin, Steven. "Why Was 'Custom a Second Nature' in Early Modern Medicine?" *Bulletin of the History of Medicine* 93, no. 1 (2019): 1–26.

Shrank, Cathy. "Beastly Metamorphoses: Losing Control in Early Modern Literary Culture." In *Intoxication and Society: Problematic Pleasures of Drugs and Alcohol*, edited by Jonathan Herring, Ciaran Regan, Darin Weinberg, and Phil Withington, 193–209. Basingstoke: Palgrave Macmillan, 2013.

Slack, Paul. "The Politics of Consumption and England's Happiness in the Later Seventeenth Century." *English Historical Review*, no. 497 (2007): 609–63.

Smith, Henry. "A Dissuasion from Pride." In *The Sermons of Henrie Smith, Gathered in One Volume*, 427–49. London, 1593.

Smith, Henry. "A Looking Glass for Drunkards." In *The Sermons of Henrie Smith, Gathered in One Volume*, 575–96. London, 1593.

Smyth, Adam. *A Pleasing Sinne: Drink and Conviviality in Seventeenth-Century England.* Cambridge: Boydell, 2004.

Stephens, W. B. "English Wine Imports c. 1603–1640, with Special Reference to the Devon Ports." In *Tudor and Stuart Devon: The Common Estate and Government*, edited by Todd Gray, Margery Rowe, and Audrey Erskine, 141–72. Exeter: University of Exeter Press, 1992.

Taylor, Alexander. "Tobacco Retail and State Formation in Early Modern England and Wales." *Economic History Review* 72, no. 2 (2019): 433–58.

Unger, Richard. *Beer in the Middle Ages and Renaissance.* Philadelphia: University of Pennsylvania Press, 2004.

Waddell, Brodie. "Economic Immorality and Social Reformation in English Popular Preaching, 1585–1625." *Cultural and Social History* 5, no. 2 (2008): 165–82.

Walsham, Alexandra. "Ordeals of Conscience: Casuistry, Conformity, and Confessional Identity in Post-Reformation England." In *Contexts of Conscience in Early Modern Europe, 1500–1700*, edited by Harald E. Braun and Edward Vallance, 32–48. Basingstoke: Palgrave Macmillan, 2003.

Walter, John, and Keith Wrightson. "Dearth and the Social Order in Early Modern England." *Past and Present*, no. 71 (1976): 22–42.

Ward, Samuel. *Woe to Drunkards: A Sermon.* London, 1622.

Warner, Jessica. "'Resolv'd to Drink No More': Addiction as a Preindustrial Construct." *Journal of Studies of Alcohol* 55, no. 6 (1994): 685–91.

W.B. *A Collection of Certain Statutes in Force: with Full and Ready Notes in the Margent, Containing Their Effect in Briefe as Also the Ordinances for the Better Observation of the Lords Day, and the Fast Dayes.* London, 1644.

Wilkins, John. *An Essay towards a Real Character, and a Philosophical Language.* London, 1668.

Withington, Phil. "Addiction, Intoxicants, and the Humoral Body." *Historical Journal*, April 23, 2021. doi.org/10.1017/S0018246X21000194.

Withington, Phil. "Intoxicants and Society in Early Modern England." *Historical Journal* 54, no. 3 (2011): 631–57.

Withington, Phil. "Intoxicants and the Early Modern City." In *Remaking English Society: Social Relations and Social Change in Early Modern England*, edited by Steve Hindle, Alexandra Shepard, and John Walter, 135–64. Woodbridge: Boydell, 2013.

Withington, Phil. "Intoxicants and the Invention of Consumption." *Economic History Review* 73, no. 2 (2020): 384–408.

Withington, Phil. *Society in Early Modern England: The Vernacular Origins of Powerful Ideas.* Cambridge: Polity, 2010.

Wrightson, Keith. "Alehouses, Order, and Reformation in Rural England, 1590–1660." In *Popular Culture and Class Conflict, 1590–1914: Explorations in the History of Labour and Leisure*, edited by Eileen Yeo, 1–27. Brighton: Harvester, 1981.

Wrightson, Keith. *Earthly Necessities: Economic Lives in Early Modern Britain, 1470–1750*. London: Routledge, 2002.

Wrightson, Keith. *English Society, 1580–1680*. London: Routledge, 1982.

Younge, Richard. *The Blemish of Government, the Shame of Religion, the Disgrace of Mankind, or, A Charge Drawn Up against Drunkards and Presented to His Highness the Lord Protector*. London, 1658.

Younge, Richard. *The Drunkard's Character, or, A True Drunkard with Such Sinnes as Raigne in Him Viz. Pride. Ignorance. Enmity. Atheisme. Idlenesse. Adultery. Murther. with Aany the Like*. London, 1638.

Sigma Alpha Elsinore
The Culture of Drunkenness in Shakespeare's *Hamlet*

JEFFREY R. WILSON

Abstract   Claudius likes to party—a bit too much. He frequently binge drinks, is arguably an alcoholic, but is not an aberration. Hamlet says that Denmark is internationally known for heavy drinking. That's what Shakespeare would have heard in the sixteenth century. By the seventeenth, English writers feared that Denmark had taught their own nation its drinking habits. Synthesizing criticism on alcoholism as an individual problem in Shakespeare's texts and times with scholarship on national drinking habits in the early modern age, this essay asks what the tragedy of alcoholism looks like when located not on the level of the individual but on the level of a culture, as Shakespeare depicts in *Hamlet*. Our window into these early modern cultures of drunkenness is sociological studies of American college fraternities plus social-learning theories that explain how one person—one culture—teaches another its habits. For Claudius's alcoholism is both culturally learned and culturally significant. And, as in fraternities, alcoholism in *Hamlet* is bound up with ethnicity, wealth, masculinity, and tragedy. Thus alcohol imagistically reappears in key moments of *Hamlet*—the vial of "cursed hebona," Ophelia's liquid death, and the poisoned cup in the final scene—that stand out in recent performances and adaptations with alcoholic Claudiuses and Gertrudes.
Keywords   alcoholism, *Hamlet*, William Shakespeare

A pack of drunk assholes stumbles onstage—Danish royalty looking like American frat boys. The alpha, King Claudius, just married, slurs through the affairs of state. Upstage, resentful staff stock the bar, rolling their eyes at these rich-kid antics. Annoyed waiters circulate trays of cold meats. Like them, Prince Hamlet is disgusted. Gertrude can tell. Claudius tries to help but makes things worse. *A toast!* Claudius climbs atop the bar, loses his balance, steadies himself, chuckles about it with a nearby chump, hiccups, raises his glass, and through a burp says to Hamlet, "You are the most immediate to our throne" (1.2.109).[1] Hamlet concedes a smile and hurries to end the scene, but not before Claudius declares—to cheers—that tonight they will rage:

> No jocund health that Denmark drinks today
> But the great cannon to the clouds shall tell,

> And the King's rouse the heaven shall bruit again,
> Re-speaking earthly thunder. (1.2.125–28)[2]

They're going to get drunk and shoot off their guns. What could go wrong?

In Shakespeare's *Hamlet*, Denmark is a culture of drunkenness. I'm not talking about happy hours, your evening glass(es) of wine, or one too many on nights out with friends. In Elsinore, blackout drinking is the goal and the norm. Think American frat houses and high schools. As in those settings, Claudius's binge drinking is both culturally prompted and culturally consequential.

⋯

"The King's intemperance is very strongly impressed," Samuel Johnson wrote of Claudius's "rouse" in 1765. "Every thing that happens to him gives him occasion to drink."[3] Thomas Davies disagreed in 1784, emphasizing culture over individual: "I cannot think, with Dr. Johnson, that these lines particularly mark the King's fondness for drinking. Drunkenness was the national vice, as Hamlet himself afterwards confesses."[4] These readings are not opposed; they are inextricable. Both then and now, in literature and in life, binge drinking involves an interplay between individual and culture. Social customs contribute to alcohol abuse. Alcoholics affect the worlds they live in.

Shakespeare's Elizabethan audiences may have seen Claudius as a Tamburlaine. "Then wil we triumph, banquet and carouse," Marlowe's tragic hero announces after one conquest.[5] Shakespeare and Marlowe both associated binge drinking with cultural competition, upper-class self-congratulation, and the performance of masculinity. Similarly, American fraternities, to borrow Gina Bloom's description of upper-class early modern English drinking cultures, "rewrite unruly drunkenness as proper recreation for the gentleman."[6]

Danes of Shakespeare's day would have recognized Claudius as their King Christian IV.[7] During an English embassy to Denmark in 1603, "the king went aboard the English ship, and had a banket prepared for him upon the upper decks. . . . Every health reported sixe, eight, or ten shot of great Ordinance, so that during the kings abode, the ship discharged 160. shot."[8] Christian—whose older sister Anne married King James I—came to England in 1606 and, like a senior to a freshman pledge during rush, taught James to party:

> King James, Queene Anne, Prince Henry, with certaine other Brytaine princes
> and peeres, about ten a clocke in the fore noone, went a boord the King of
> Denmarkes greatest shippe . . . and as they sat at Banquet, greeting each other
> with kindness and pledges of continuing amity, and hearts desire of lasting
> health, the same was straightwayes knowne, by sound of Drumme, and
> Trumpet, and the Cannons lowdest voyce.[9]

For European royals and American college students alike, binge drinking is learned behavior. Early modern Danes, their English contemporaries, citizens of Shakespeare's Elsinore, audiences of *Hamlet*, and analysts of American colleges all confront the same questions: Why is binge drinking central to leading cultural institutions? How does a culture of binge drinking affect the lives and minds of its population? How are cultures of drunkenness passed from one society to another, from older generations to younger? Where does responsibility lie for tragedies that arise out of drunkenness—with the individual or with the culture?

In *Shakespeare and Alcohol* Buckner B. Trawick counts seventeen allusions in *Hamlet*, "an indication that the subject is of great significance to the play."[10] Yet alcohol only surfaces in hints and glimpses, obscured behind the ghosts, murders, and madnesses more readily visible in *Hamlet*. How does Denmark's drunkenness connect with the play's more prominent lines, scenes, and themes—crime, ambition, revenge, despair, and tragedy?

Imagine, for instance, in act 1, scene 2, as Claudius's party stumbles offstage like college kids parading to the pub, Hamlet alone with his wineglass, swirling it, raising it up, slowly pouring its contents to the floor, where it splatters down as he says, "Oh, that this too, too solid flesh would melt / Thaw, and resolve itself into a dew" (1.2.127–28 in folio).[11] The liquor of Claudius's "rouse" sloshes into the liquid imagery of Hamlet's first soliloquy, with all its "tears" (1.2.149, 154). That association of imagery creates questions about how Claudius's culture of binge drinking relates to Hamlet's depression, the rottenness he sees in Denmark, and the tragedy that awaits.

···

Hi, my name is Jeff, and I'm a Shakespeare scholar. The first step was admitting I had a problem. I spend a lot of time making amends. I'm also a recovering alcoholic, which is why I flinch at gimmicks like Shit-Faced Shakespeare, where actors see how far into their benders they can remember their lines.[12] Good fun, but Shakespeare thought alcohol was a major social problem. Many examples support this argument—Christopher Sly, Falstaff, Bardolph, Claudius, Cassio, the Porter in *Macbeth*, Barnadine, Lepidus, Trinculo, Stephano, and Caliban—and not many stand against it ("Dost thou think because thou art virtuous, there shall be no more cakes and ale?" [*Twelfth Night*, 2.3.106–7]).

Studies of Shakespeare and alcohol filter into two lines of thought. The first—older and more prominent—is about individuals and the morality of excessive consumption. Shakespeare presented moderate drinking as "a sign of hospitality or friendship," Trawick wrote, but "excessive drinking often leads to unhappiness, disaster, even death," and "alcohol is associated with murder in a significant number of instances."[13] Stephen Greenblatt worked up Shakespeare's frequently tragic scenes of alcohol into the observation that he "depicted heavy drinkers from close-up—he noted the unsteadiness of their legs, the broken veins in their nose and cheeks, their slurred speech," and then into the conjecture that Shakespeare's father, John, may have fallen from grace as an alcoholic.[14] Alcohol suggestively surfaced in Shakespeare's own life, at least in apocryphal recollections. One story from John Aubrey's *Brief Lives* (1669–96)—though disputed—gives an abstemious Shakespeare avoiding the party scene: he was not a "company keeper . . . wouldn't be debauched, and if invited to, writ: he was in pain."[15] Another story—also dubious—from the diary of

John Ward, vicar of Stratford from 1662 to 1681, offers the counterimage of Shakespeare drinking himself to death: "Shakespeare, Drayton, and Ben Jonson had a merry meeting, and it seems drank too hard, for Shakespeare died of a fever there contracted."[16] Scholars looking at Shakespeare's texts and times have shown that his antipathy to alcohol was consistent with and influenced by contemporary moral entrepreneurs, from religious homilies and prose satires to King James and contemporary dramatists.[17] Breakthroughs in this line of thought came in 2009 when David Houston Wood argued that Shakespeare represented excessive drinking as "a disabling disease that should properly be termed alcoholism," and in 2013 when Rebecca Lemon identified challenges to English law in Shakespeare's depiction of alcoholic criminals.[18] Since then, critics have emphasized the sympathetic, rather than judgmental, aspects of Shakespearean characters associated with alcohol, like Falstaff and Mistress Quickly.[19]

The second line of thought—newer and less developed—shifts attention from the individual to the cultural aspects of alcohol in Shakespeare's plays. Nations came to be associated with their alcohols and drinking habits. "The characterization of the Englishman as a beer-drinker reflects a growing sense of national identity and racial stereotyping," Charlotte McBride wrote in 2004.[20] Alcohol imported from foreign countries signified an emergent globalization, and the alcohol trade brought opportunities to exchange cultural traditions of alcoholism, as illustrated in the 2016 collection *Culinary Shakespeare*.[21] "Every time wine appears in Shakespeare's plays," Karen Raber argues, "it activates 'England' and 'Englishness' as concepts—at once newly revivified yet still fluid—that rely on a body/state analogy."[22]

Mixing these two lines yields a new question. What does the tragedy of alcoholism look like when identified not in an individual but in an entire culture? Shakespeare's emphasis on culture contrasts with the focus on an individual's thirsty adventures and psychological despair in the modern literature and film of alcoholism.[23] Yet our question is not only one Shakespeare asked in *Hamlet* but one sociologists ask about American teenagers.

···

Sociological studies of American fraternities can round out the picture of the culture of drunkenness that is suggested—but not fully developed—in *Hamlet*, providing depth and detail to a frequently overlooked aspect of this frequently studied text. While not exact, the analogy between Claudius's binge drinking and frat boys is tight enough that an analysis of the social structures of American fraternities helps us imagine life in Elsinore—not only the adolescence of Claudius, but also life behind the scenes of Shakespeare's play. This approach challenges some conventional readings of *Hamlet*, such as Claudius as a sinister villain, and Elsinore as a dark, dank, gloomy, enclosed, claustrophobic, haunted, mysterious—in a word, Gothic—place, whether that view comes from Hamlet himself ("How weary, stale, flat, and unprofitable" [1.2.133]), from the moody productions of Burbage, Garrick, Kean, Olivier, and Cumberbatch, or from recent scholarship with brooding titles like *Hamlet in Purgatory*, *Hamlet's Negativity*, and *Hamlet and the Vision of Darkness*.[24]

Recognizing Elsinore as party central adds feeling to Hamlet's isolation while creating new understandings of the origin, operation, and outcome of the catastrophe at the end of the play.

There are many forms of Greek life on American college campuses. Binge drinking is mostly associated with historically white fraternities on predominantly white campuses in the American Midwest and South.[25] They don't publish demographic data, but fraternities involve largely homogeneous populations of males in their late teens and early twenties, typically white, wealthy, straight, and Christian.[26] "Top-tier fraternities" are even less diverse. In America and Elsinore alike, binge drinking is bound up with race and ethnic—specifically white—customs.

Might these fraternities take us into Claudius's adolescence? Boys who join fraternities usually party hard and play sports. Their friends' fathers may be lawyers able to get them out of trouble when they run afoul of the law. Peers from high schools join the military or go straight to work; not them. These boys are young and insecure, just want to fit in, long for acceptance. Fraternities are a place to make friends, build networks for future careers, and open up pathways to leadership, success, and fortune, with traditions of money and power perpetuating these social systems, plus histories of racial discrimination. Imagine the privilege of growing up in Elsinore.

Students join fraternities while transitioning from their parents' households, where there was much oversight, to independent living. With the lack of adult supervision comes increased opportunities to drink. Many students, like adults, drink to relax, loosen up, and become more sociable.[27] Fraternity members drink more frequently and more heavily than nonfraternity college students.[28] Most binge drink— *party 'til you puke*. It's a performance of masculinity.[29] Excessive consumption is seen as a sign of virility. *I can drink more, party harder, go crazier than you.* The masculinity performed in binge drinking is not for women (who often find it repulsive) but for the other men in the fraternity. Since fraternity life is about male fellowship, binge drinking is one way to show you belong. These fraternities therefore invite Phil Whitington's analysis of early modern England: "For many educated and relatively affluent men, drinking and smoking were normative and stylized aspects of their social identity."[30] Fraternity life suggests, like the "cultures of intoxication" Withington describes, that "to be able to retain demonstrable levels of self-discipline and stamina in the midst of both immanent and purposeful intoxication distinguishes (usually male) elites from the incontinent and indiscriminate masses."[31] Imagine a young Claudius just trying to fit in, trying to prove himself, cup in hand.

Sociologists offer two additional theories about the centrality of binge drinking in fraternities. The first is the predisposition argument: because of their reputation for partying, fraternities attract heavy drinkers to join their ranks.[32] You partied hard in high school, and a fraternity is the best venue to continue. The second is the social-learning model: fraternities create binge drinkers.[33] They teach binge drinking to people who may have joined for fellowship and future career opportunities. Here binge drinking is learned behavior. Impressionable young members see how established elders drink and model their behavior on them—again, imagine Claudius coming of age.

Because alcohol is so central to fraternity life, social bonds are based around drinking. Binge drinkers flock together. They create a community and a culture of drunkenness.[34] It is not unhinged, random chaos. Themed party nights and pledge initiation rituals evoke Gina Bloom's reading of binge drinking as "disciplined play" in early modern England, "as an organized and measured activity, subject to rules."[35] The group's informal mechanisms of social control show a high tolerance for binge drinking. It is excused and justified. The fraternity offers members protection when drinking creates problems with the school or the police. Or the school looks the other way. Historian Alexandra Shepard could be describing today's colleges and universities when explaining excessive consumption by upper-class students at early modern English schools: "At times youthful misrule was tolerated and even implicitly condoned by those in authority over them."[36] Claudius's alcoholism implicates Elsinore's institutional neglect during his formative years. Positive reinforcement for binge drinking makes it normative.[37] Younger members feel pressure to conform to the binge drinking habits of the group, literalized in hazing rituals where group members force rushes to drink as part of their initiation. These American fraternities exhibit the "compulsory conviviality" that Rebecca Lemon identifies in early modern cultures of drunkenness: "At risk of 'abuse,' 'disgrace,' and indeed violence, the health drinker might stay in the ritual even against his own will and to the point of endangering his health."[38] The civilizing process of early modern England and American fraternities alike involves initiation to the culture of drunkenness.

There are consequences for individuals, the group, and society at large. Drinkers can experience the escalating consequences of blackouts, hangovers, fights, risky sex, alcohol poisoning, traffic accidents, and arrests, along with poor academic performance and problems at work. In the longer term, heavy drinkers can develop dependencies and depression, plus other diseases and mental illnesses.[39] Meanwhile friends, family, and bystanders are subjected to verbal abuse, sexual harassment, vandalism, violence, and sexual assault, along with the stress and frayed relationships that result from repeated experience with these outcomes. Consider how much more complex an adolescent Claudius now becomes. And then there are the tragic deaths we read about in the news—of the binge drinkers themselves, those around them, and complete strangers caught in their path. Alcohol brings the community both to life and to death—which is also true of the play *Hamlet*.[40]

Because Greek organizations often set the tone for campus life, their cultures of drunkenness become models for nonmembers. On a larger scale, the wealth, power, and prestige of fraternities make binge drinking normative in American society, normalizing in turn the concomitant features of this subculture: toxic masculinity, elitism, exclusion, sexual misconduct, academic dishonesty, aggression, violence, homophobia, glib racism, and variously covert, unconscious, and in-your-face white supremacy. We can imagine the same in the hallways of Elsinore. In America, college administrators fret but seem helpless to curb binge drinking on campus. They create intervention and education programs, while critics call for the abolition of fraternities.[41] That's the position of Prince Hamlet.

···

After his first soliloquy, Hamlet cynically welcomes Horatio to Denmark: "We'll teach you to drink deep ere you depart" (1.2.173 in folio). Three points. First, Denmark's national reputation for heavy drinking was well established in England by a string of writers including Barnabe Rich in 1578 ("Goe to the dronken contries of *Denmarke* and *Swethen*"),[42] Thomas Nashe in 1591 ("The Danes shall this yeere bee greatlye giuen to drincke"),[43] Ben Jonson in 1603 ("The Danes that drench / Their cares in wine"),[44] and Samuel Rowlands in 1604 ("The Dane, that would carowse out of his Boote").[45] Nashe also voiced this sentiment in *Pierce Penilesse* (1592), which would become a key source for Shakespeare's *Hamlet*: "The Danes are bursten-bellied sots, that are to bee confuted with nothing but Tankards or quart pots."[46]

Second, as E. H. Seymour wrote in 1805, "Hamlet would intimate that drunkenness was the only thing that could be learned at the usurper's court."[47] Hamlet's word *teach* evokes social learning theory. Adapting the sociologist Edwin Sutherland's first three statements on "differential association," we could say that (1) binge drinking in Denmark "is learned," (2) binge drinking in Denmark "is learned in interaction with other persons in a process of communication," and (3) "the principal part of the learning of [binge drinking in Denmark] occurs within intimate personal groups."[48] Just as American fraternity members learn more in college than what they study in their classes, early modern Englanders such as Thomas Young described drinking cultures as educational institutions: "There are in London drinking schooles: so that drunkennesse is professed with vs as a liberall Arte and Science."[49] As Withington argues, "The early seventeenth century was an especially significant moment in this learning process."[50] If "drink[ing] deep" is culturally learned in Shakespeare's Denmark, and is widespread, however, Hamlet stands against it.

Third, the binge drinking Hamlet fears Horatio will learn in Elsinore reflects the culture of drunkenness Elizabethans saw England learning from Denmark and the Low Countries. "We doo so much exceede al those that haue gone before vs," George Gascoigne wrote in *A Delicate Diet, for Daintiemouthde Droonkardes* (1576): "In this accusation, I doo not onely summon the Germaines (who of auncient tyme haue beene the continuall Wardens of the Droonkards fraternitye and corporation,) but I would also cyte to appeare our newfangled Englyshe men."[51] In 1592 Nashe's *Pierce Penilesse* said "superfluitie in drinke" was "a sinne, that euer since we haue mixt our selues with the Low-countries, is counted honourable: but before we knew their lingring warres, was held in that highest degree of hatred that might be."[52] The Germans were famous for their binge drinking, as B. Ann Tlusty illustrates, quoting Fynes Moryson, an Englishman who traveled in Germany between 1591 and 1597, anticipating something Prince Hamlet will say about Denmark a few years later: "All of the Germans haue one National vice of drunckenness in such excesse . . . as it staynes all theire nationalle vertues."[53] At the same time, as Bloom records, a German visitor to England in the 1590s could insist, "I have never seen more taverns and alehouses in my whole life than in London."[54] The culture of drunkenness was migrating.

In 1598 the Elizabethan philosopher Richard Barkley sounded like a modern sociologist, or maybe a college president:

> Vahappie are they and farre from felicitie, that think it a glorious thing to contend for the superioritie in carowsing: and to carrie away the victory in such a *Bacchanalian* combat: which pestiferous disease beginneth so to creepe into our Nation by the infection of our neighbours, that if it be not prevented by authoritie or lawes, it is to bee feared, lest it will grow to bee habituall, and take such roote, that it will bee impossible to bee removed, and so consequently that they which last received it will goe beyond them from whom they first had it. For, the imitation of evill alwayes exceedeth the example.[55]

That same year Barnabe Rich wrote of a fellow English soldier complaining of "Low country Captains, who vnder the pretence of the excellency of the weapons of fire, would bring in carowsing and drunkennesse"; his Continental interlocutor replies, "And for carowsing it was new christned in England from a carowse to a hearty draught, I thinke before the most of our Low country Captaines were borne."[56] Written around the turn of the seventeenth century, Shakespeare's *Hamlet* came at a turning point when drunkenness was shifting from the national trait of Denmark to that of England.

Shakespeare's play captures that trajectory, as does the movement in a 1609 line from Thomas Dekker, where the word *teach* again invokes a social learning model of cultural drunkenness: "Awake thou noblest drunkerd Bacchus, thou must likewise stand to me (if at least thou canst for réeling) teach me (you soueraigne Skinker) how to take the Germanies vpsy freeze; the Danish Rowsa, the Switzers stoap of Rhenish, the Italians Parmizant: the Englishmans healthes." Around that time, Beaumont and Fletcher called Englishmen "stubborn drinkers" who could "knocke a Dane downe."[57] This transmission of the culture of drunkenness informed a note on English merriment in William Camden's *Remaines* (1614): "This good cheare causeth the Germans to recharge vs with gluttony when we charge them with drunkenness which as we receiued from the Danes."[58] By the time of Henry Peacham's *The Complete Gentleman* (1622), the transfer of drinking from Denmark to England was fully formalized with reference to the Elizabethan soldier John Norris (ca. 1547–97) and his involvement in the Dutch war for independence from Spain (1566–1609):

> Within these fiftie or threescore yeares it was a rare thing with vs in *England*, to see a Drunken man, our Nation carrying the name of the most sober and temperate of any other in the world. But since we had to doe in the quarrell of the *Netherlands*, about the time of Sir *Iohn Norrice* his first being there, the custome of drinking and pledging healthes was brought ouer into *England*: wherein let the Dutch bee their owne Iudges, if we equall them not; yea I thinke rather excell them.[59]

On this war more generally, Camden wrote, "Our Englishmen who of all the Northerne Nations haue beene most commended for sobrietie, haue learned since these

Low-Country warres so well to fill their cups, and to wash themselues with Wine, that whilest they at this day drinke others healths, they little regard their owne."[60]

Then England's Charles I became a Christian IV, as courtier historian James Howell recorded in a letter from October 9, 1632: "The King feasted my Lord once, and it lasted from eleven of the clock, till towards the Evening, during which time, the King began thirty five healths; the first to the Emperour, the second to his Nephew of England, and so went over all the Kings and Queens of Christendom. . . . The King was taken away at last in his Chair."[61] As Rebecca Lemon has illustrated, "Whereas Elizabethan writers found national solidarity in satirizing healthing as a foreign and villainous practice, later Jacobean and Caroline poets instead frame health drinking as a means of establishing political allegiances."[62] Drunken English royalist revelry culminated in the restoration of Charles II, as in broadside ballads like *England's Royall Conquest* (1666): "The bells did ring and bone-fires shine, / and healths caroused in beer and wine."[63] In a ballad called *England's Triumph*, "Our drinking shall him tribute bring."[64]

Decades earlier Shakespeare portrayed a similar scene of royalist revelry in *Hamlet's* most extended meditation on the culture of drunkenness in Denmark—act 1, scene 4. In this scene, by characterizing royal binge drinking as a problem for international politics, Shakespeare anticipated the early seventeenth-century histories of the transmission of the culture of drunkenness from Denmark to England. Shakespeare represented (a) what his countrymen had been saying about Danish drunkenness, (b) what others would soon be saying about English drunkenness, and (c) the logic of social learning by which (a) became (b).

...

It's midnight at the start of the scene—the witching hour when ghosts appear. It would make sense for Shakespeare to follow that exposition with the appearance of King Hamlet's ghost. But that's not what happens. "*A flourish of trumpets and two pieces [go] off,*" reads the stage direction in the second quarto (1.4.6s.d.). Maurice Charney glosses this sound effect:

> There is more cannonading in this play than in any other play of Shakespeare.
> It is, in fact, a conspicuously noisy and active play. This cannonading is
> especially associated with Claudius and his "rouses," or drinking of healths.
> The whole sound effect consists of a roll on the kettle-drums, followed by an
> elaborate trumpet fanfare, and concluded by the firing of the theater cannon or
> "chambers."[65]

Readers today are likely to pay the stage direction little mind, Bruce Johnson writes: "For the modern eye scanning the printed page, the stage direction is so innocuous as to be scarcely noted. Yet what we have here is the sound of trumpet and ordnance suddenly blasting the tense, midnight silence, as represented in the enclosed space of the Elizabethan theatre."[66] Imagine the clamor of a fraternity house on Friday night.

Audiences are asking the same question as Horatio: "What does this mean?" (1.4.7). Hamlet explains that, here at midnight, the king is awake, partying, binge drinking. He's pounding wine. Whenever he finishes a cup, the trumpets and drums clamor:

> The King doth wake tonight and takes his rouse,
> Keeps wassail and the swaggering upspring reels,
> And as he drains his drafts of Rhenish down
> The kettledrum and trumpet thus bray out
> The triumph of his pledge. (1.4.8–12)

The irony of Hamlet's word *wassail*, from the Old English *wes hel*, "be in good health," is that Claudius's wassailing, which comes from a place of merriment, signifies his poor health—his alcoholism, to the extent that Shakespeare understood it as a disease—and contributes to his country's decline.[67] The trumpets "bray[ing] out" his binge turn Claudius into a donkey, or jackass if you like. Imagine his court around him chanting, *Chug! Chug!*

Just as Claudius's lighthearted revelry is embedded within tragedy, the danger of catastrophe lies hidden beneath the carnivalesque atmosphere of fraternities. Shakespeare's Denmark might be envisioned by asking what would happen if a fraternity were to position as president not the most responsible leader but the drunkest brother. If, as Lemon argues, "the audience would know precisely what it meant for a king to be drunk on healths"—he's a lush, a buffoon, a Lord of Misrule, "a king of shreds and patches" (3.4.102)—then we need to think beyond the standard view of Elsinore as a tragic den of corruption, deceit, crime, treason, melancholy, hypocrisy, and isolation.[68] Bringing comedy into the tragedy, as *Hamlet* so powerfully does elsewhere, Claudius's Elsinore shows what happens when the drunken Carlo Buffone of Ben Jonson's *Every Man Out of His Humour*—acted in 1599 by the Lord Chamberlain's Men a year or two before they did *Hamlet*—becomes king.

This Danish custom of heavy drinking is well known in other nations, Hamlet says—at least in the folio edition. It mars Denmark's reputation, troubling Hamlet because he sees his country as virtuous. Others see the Danes as "drunkards." The *-ard* ending embeds the concept designated by the root word, *drunk*, in a person's identity, as in *dullard* or *bastard*. A specific—and minor—habit of the Danes has come to define them in the eyes of others:

> This heavy-headed revel east and west
> Makes us traduced and taxed of other nations:
> They clepe us drunkards and with swinish phrase
> Soil our addition, and indeed it takes
> From our achievements, though performed at height,
> The pith and marrow of our attribute. (1.4.17–22)

The "swinish phrase[s]" are the common early modern comparisons of heavy drinkers to swine, picturing King Claudius now as a pig.

In 1916 Walter Raleigh thought these lines "have little dramatic value, and illustrate Shakespeare's habit of making room in his plays for any topic that is uppermost in his mind."[69] Albert Tolman agreed in 1919: "The passage has no vital relation to the action."[70] That is why, they think, the lines were cut from the quartos. In contrast, Elisabeth Winkler notes that "the common Danish and especially Claudius' (over)indulgence in alcohol have a political facet," making Claudius "a weak and possibly even irresponsible ruler."[71] The passage also challenges the conventional view of Claudius as an evil antagonist. His carousing suggests he should be understood—and performed—with an air of frat-boy frivolity, if not clownish ineptitude.

···

In the folio, Hamlet's reflection on Denmark's international reputation spills into one of the most powerful speeches in the play. Did Shakespeare imagine the "mole of nature" idea (1.4.23–36), and then work backward to the Danish revelry to set it up? Or did he start with the scene of Danish drunkenness and work it up into a philosophical idea? How does our understanding of this passage change when we recognize it is grounded in alcoholism?

With "so oft it chances in particular men" (1.4.23), Shakespeare created an analogy between the binge-drinking state and the socially marked individual. He explains that ancillary aspects of people's births and behaviors can be, in the eyes of others, definitive qualities. Consider my use of frat houses as shorthand for cultures of drunkenness: many different things happen in fraternities, much of it "pure as grace" (1.4.33), but for outside observers binge drinking is often their defining feature. The same happens in individuals, Hamlet says, as those with alcoholism know intimately. "From that particular fault," which often involves a genetic predisposition for which the individual bears no moral responsibility, "since nature cannot choose his origin," our entire identity is often defined—by ourselves and by others (1.4.26–36).

Peter Stallybrass describes the "mole of nature" as a "defect, taint, a 'particular fault' which can corrupt the whole," which Lemon attaches to Claudius's alcoholism, "rendering the subject corrupt, incapacitated, and as a result unable to control his drinking."[72] But that's not quite what Hamlet says. The pathway from "particular fault" to "general censure" is not so direct. Hamlet's reading of American fraternities would not be that their binge drinking is a tragic flaw that may bring these great institutions crashing down. Hamlet sees the transgression impacting not the institution but the interpretation of it by onlookers. Hamlet would say that binge drinking has led cultural commentators to define fraternities too exclusively in terms of a "particular fault," obscuring their many virtues. Here Hamlet sounds like American investigative journalist Alexandra Robbins, whose book *Fraternity: An Inside Look at a Year of College Boys Becoming Men* chronicles a year of interviews with two fraternity guys. "Jake," a freshman pledge, shifts from *aw-shucks* introvert looking for friends to toxic masculinity during his initiation, illustrating the social-learning model of cultures of drunkenness. But Robbins avoids the easy reading of fraternities as swamps of awfulness. "Oliver," a fraternity president fighting to preserve a campus service in the face of fraternities' bad reputation, represents the value fraternities can offer to college boys navigating the uncertainties of American masculinity. Like the "mole of nature" idea, Robbins shows how the public image of cultures of drunkenness is formed from "particular fault[s]," how that image gets in the way of potential virtues of the underlying institutions, and how a Jake can become a Claudius, an Oliver a Hamlet. Like Oliver, Hamlet critiques the culture of drunkenness from the inside. He believes in Denmark's greatness, but sees its virtue eclipsed by a "particular fault" that consumes the attention of outside observers. How many fraternity members must feel the same?

Shakespeare modeled his passage on "The Complaint of Drunkenness" in Nashe's *Pierce Penilesse*:

> A mightie deformer of mens manners and features, is this vnnecessary vice of all other. Let him bee indued with neuer so many vertues, and haue as much goodly proportion and fauour as nature can bestow vppon a man: yet if hee be thirstie after his owne destruction, and hath no ioy nor comfort, but when he is drowning his soule in a gallon pot, that one beastly imperfection, will vtterlie obscure all that is commendable in him: and all his good qualities sinke like lead down to the bottome of his carrowsing cups, where they will lie like lees and dregges, dead and vnregarded of any man.[73]

Like Nashe, Shakespeare emphasized the effect of alcoholism on reputation. Yet Nashe attends to the individual. Shakespeare goes to the level of culture. Claudius may be an alcoholic who is, to quote Nashe, "thirstie after his owne destruction," and here alcoholics may recognize the desire to drink yourself into oblivion. Taking the Shakespearean step and extrapolating to the whole culture, all of Claudius's Elsinore may be "thirstie after [its] owne destruction." Yet modern fraternity members may also recognize, to adapt Nashe to Shakespeare's cultural emphasis, "that one beastly imperfection, will vtterlie obscure all that is commendable in [them]: and all [their] good qualities sinke like lead down to the bottome of [their] carrowsing cups."

...

Hamlet's thoughts on reputation formation flow into some of the most confusing lines in all of Shakespeare's plays.[74] The folio reads:

> the dram of eale
> Doth all the noble substance of a doubt
> To his own scandal. (1.4.36–37)

What is a "dram of eale"? How do you "do . . . a doubt"? Because of these questions, editors often amend the lines to say:

> the dram of evil
> Doth all the noble substance overdaub
> To his own scandal.

A *dram* was originally a small coin. *Dram* came to signify a small amount of liquid, about one-eighth of a fluid ounce. The sense of *dram* as "a small draught of cordial, stimulant, or spirituous liquor" dates to around 1590, about ten years before

Hamlet.[75] Shakespeare used *dram* in that sense in *Romeo and Juliet* (5.1.60), written about two years before *Hamlet*. A "dram of evil" would be a tiny drop, reminiscent of a "mole of nature." In this edit, the dram of evil "overdaub[s]" nobility: blots it out, like "the stamp of one defect" becoming "corruption" in the "general censure." This overdaubing of nobility "scandal[izes]" the dram of evil: discredits it, or "soils its additions," as Hamlet might say. Beyond the benefit of making sense, this edit has the virtue of consistency with the imagery of alcohol and the logic of reputation presented in the scene up to this point. It also carries the prospect of connecting, imagistically, the "dram of evil" with both the "juice of cursed hebona in a vial" that Claudius uses to kill King Hamlet (1.5.62) and the "poisoned cup" that kills Queen Gertrude (5.2.269). Pushed to its utmost limit, the "dram of evil," given its origins in Hamlet's comments on his uncle's binge drinking, holds the possibility that Claudius's alcoholism is what is rotten in the state of Denmark.

...

Shakespeare went out of his way several times to emphasize Claudius's drinking problem. When Guildenstern says Claudius is "marvelous distempered," Hamlet assumes the king is wasted: "With drink, sir?" (3.279–80). When Hamlet plots to kill Claudius only when the king is marred with sin, he plans to do so "when he is drunk asleep" (3.3.89). What kind of drunk is Claudius? An angry drunk? A happy drunk? Hamlet describing the transition from his father to his uncle as "Hyperion to a satyr" (1.2.140) presents Claudius not as an evil tyrant but as a drunken goat, a fool, a clown, a pleasure seeker. To Charney, "The 'wassail' and reeling 'upspring' of Claudius are literally a satyr's revel."[76] Claudius is a party boy elevated to head of state. He is not fit to govern, which is why the ghost of King Hamlet warns, "Let not the royal bed of Denmark be / A couch for luxury" (1.5.82–83). Thus, when ambassadors from Norway appear with news of the utmost importance for foreign relations, Claudius just wants to rage: "At night we'll feast together" (2.2.84). Claudius wants to be Marlowe's Tamburlaine, but ends up Benvolio, the butt of the jokes in the expanded *Doctor Faustus*:

> He took his rouse with stopes of Rhennish wine,
> So kindly yesternight to *Bruno's* health,
> That all this day the sluggard keepes his bed."[77]

Filled with food and wine, Claudius is "the bloat King" (3.4.183)—Falstaff as sovereign.

Why did Shakespeare characterize Claudius as an alcoholic? And Hamlet as emphatically not one? For one thing, it establishes the tension between the two, as Trawick writes, "characterizing Hamlet as a man of restraint and moderation and the King as a man of wanton overindulgence."[78] But what happens if we view Claudius's alcoholism as not metaphorical but literal?

It creates a range of interpretive problems and possibilities that audiences, like families and friends of alcoholics, must ask themselves. The first step is admitting that Claudius has a problem. He is powerless over alcohol. His life has become unmanageable. Perhaps Claudius was drunk when he killed King Hamlet. Perhaps that was a crime of opportunity prompted by an inebriated mind. Such a Claudius evokes Alexander the Great, who, according to Shakespeare's Fluellen, "being a little intoxicates in his prains, did in his ales and his angers, look you, kill his best friend" (*Henry V*, 4.7.31–32). Perhaps the imagery of poison when King Hamlet says, "A serpent stung me" (1.5.36), should be read in light of an earlier toxin, alcohol, working upon Claudius.[79] Perhaps that's why Shakespeare used the imagery of the poison coursing through King Hamlet's body—Claudius "in the porches of [his] ears did pour / The leprous distilment" (1.5.63–64), which then "curd[ed], like eager droppings into milk" (1.5.69)—to later characterize Claudius himself, "like a mildewed ear / Blasting his wholesome brother" (3.4.64–65). The murder in the orchard certainly reads differently if we view Claudius as one who is himself already stung by a serpent. Claudius's intoxication of himself mirrors his intoxication of his brother.[80]

Claudius's drinking habit, as David Houston Wood writes, "goes to the heart of questions pertaining to alcoholism's status as a disability: should society pity the 'drunkard' as the sufferer of a genetic disease? Alternatively, should society blame the individual for his or her weakness? Is it in fact within that person's scope of willpower to amend such a fault, or sin?"[81] Lemon locates these questions in early modern law, quoting Bacon: "If a drunken man commit a felony, he shall not be excused, because his imperfection came by his owne default."[82] By conceiving of Claudius as an alcoholic with a genetic predisposition, Hamlet's "mole of nature" speech, Lemon points out, "offers a theory of drunkenness that exonerates Claudius, condemning not him but, to use the language of the passage, the unfortunate 'chance' that has plagued him with this involuntary defect."[83] If I think about my own case, there were genetic markers for alcoholism, which I didn't know about. There were personality traits that predisposed me to excessive drinking. There were choices I made about how to drink, to which I must be accountable. There was a drinking problem that grew too large to control. And there are ongoing struggles with how to take personal responsibility for the harm I caused loved ones in light of the allure to create excuses by citing conditioning circumstances. Read as an alcoholic, Claudius calls for a similar calculation. He remains the villain of the play, but his villainy refers to—and reads differently in light of—his alcoholism.

Consider Claudius's first guilty-conscience confession, uttered aside after Polonius comments on the divide between private and public selves, if spoken not by a murderous tyrant but by a damaged alcoholic:

> How smart a lash that speech doth give my conscience.
> The harlot's cheek, beautied with plast'ring art,
> Is not more ugly to the thing that helps it
> Than is my deed to my most painted word.
> Oh, heavy burden! (3.1.49–53)

Imagine those lines punctuated with shots of desperation from a flask. Or imagine Claudius as a broken man, brought to his knees for his crushing soliloquy—"Oh, my offense is rank, it smells to heaven" (3.3.36)—barely able to string a sentence together as his pain swirls: "Oh, limèd soul that struggling to be free / Art more engaged!" (3.3.68–69). That might be the best description of the experience of alcoholism I've ever read.

...

In 1918 Howard Mumford Jones thought Hamlet was dead wrong about his uncle's alcoholism: "Nowhere in the play do we see, or hear of, Claudius when he thinks or acts or talks like a drunken man."[84] Yet the way Claudius "thinks or acts or talks" depends on different directors and actors in different stagings. Claudius's alcoholism is best captured not in criticism or historicism but in productions and adaptations that bring to life the cycles of pain in and around any alcoholic. In Mario Kuperman's Brazilian adaptation, *O Jogo da Vida e da Morte* (*The Game of Life and Death*, 1971), "Claudio is permanently drunk," taking shots of *cachaça*, vomiting in front of everyone during the play-within-the-play.[85] In Bill Rauch's 2010 production at the Oregon Shakespeare Festival, a drunk Claudius "prayed not in a church, but before a toilet as he vomited, creating a cheesy alternative meaning to his lines about his rank-smelling offense."[86] Similarly, in Antoni Cimolino's 2015 production at the Stratford Festival, "even when this Claudius tries to pray—the moment in which he usually appears most human—Cimolino presents him as drunk."[87]

Only by spending little time around functioning alcoholics could one complain, along with J. J. M. Tobin, that "Claudius . . . behaves soberly and quite competently but is described by his hostile nephew as politically incompetent, physically ugly, and morally alcoholic and lecherous."[88] Alcoholism and success in a high-powered career are not mutually exclusive. That fusion of contraries gives Claudius complexity of character, separating him from melodramatic villainy.

In the early modern age, *addicted* and *addiction* did not have the medical meaning they do today, as Jose Murgatrod Cree and Lemon have illustrated.[89] The concept was primarily religious, often with positive overtones. At the same time, Lemon elsewhere shows, it is hard to read Falstaff's famous ode to "sherris sack" as anything other than a Shakespearean acknowledgement of alcoholism as a disease.[90] While presenting alcohol as "addict[tion]," the passage suggests genealogical factors ("sons"), imagines a cultural—not merely individual—phenomenon ("thousand"), and conveys the social-learning model explored in *Hamlet* ("teach"): "If I had a thousand sons, the first human principle I would teach them should be to forswear thin potations, and to addict themselves to sack" (*1 Henry IV*, 4.2.110–13).

If Shakespeare understood alcoholism as a disease, the tropes of the modern alcoholic may extend to Claudius. Imagine a weakened Claudius alert with anxiety after Hamlet kills Polonius: "It had been so with us" (3.5.231). Or a helpless man who doesn't understand himself: "My soul is full of discord and dismay" (3.4.263). Imagine an alcoholic contemplating his bottle when commenting on the chaos Hamlet causes:

> Diseases desperate grown
> By desperate appliance are relieved
> Or not at all. (4.3.9–11)

His mood swings uncontrollably to rage as he orders the prince's execution:

> Do it, England,
> For like the hectic in my blood he rages
> And thou must cure me. (4.3.62–64)

In these lines Hamlet is figured as a disease in Denmark, but Hamlet's actions are a response to Claudius's. If we take Claudius's alcoholism seriously, it is possible that the disease in Denmark flows from the disease in him. Here Elsinore is a "culture of intoxication," to use Withington's term, which is startlingly well suited to the imagistic overlaps between alcohol and poison in *Hamlet*.[91]

In these moments, Claudius is less a frat boy and more the tortured, abusive alcoholic of Eugene O'Neill or Tennessee Williams, who depicts family secrets and disease.[92] At the same time, by showing Claudius's alcoholism as first a cultural and then an individual and familial problem, Shakespeare's play is an ominous reminder that tragic individual suffering exists—hidden—within the carnivalesque revelry of American fraternities.

···

When Polonius speaks of youth's excesses, Reynaldo asks, "As gaming, my lord?"; Polonius responds, "Ay, or drinking" (2.1.24–25). Shakespeare then returned to the word used for Claudius's binge drinking to have Polonius imagine Laertes "o'ertook in 's rouse" (2.1.56). The association of drinking with youth highlights how dangerous it is to place a binge drinker as head of state. Yet clearly Claudius is not the only party animal in Elsinore. Alcohol use extends from Claudius and Laertes to the gravediggers ("Fetch me a stoup of liquor" [5.1.53–54]) and Yorrick ("'A poured a flagon of Rhenish on my head once" [5.1.161–62]).

Shakespeare diffusing alcohol throughout Denmark strengthens the likelihood that alcoholism is not an individual problem unique to Claudius but a cultural problem. His drinking is a group activity, and Claudius's court surely feels the pressure of what Lemon calls "compulsory conviviality." As in the Restoration England she describes, "inebriation, through healthing, is a sign of loyalty to king and country."[93] We might imagine Shakespeare's Elsinore filled with the Cavalier poets of the seventeenth century, who registered their loyalty to royalty through toast after toast to the king's health.[94] A culture of drunkenness emanates from Claudius, as with the man Henri Estienne described in 1607, "who hauing taken his preparatiues ouer euening, when all men cry (as the manner is) *The King drinketh*; chanting his Masse the next morning, fell asleepe in his memento: and when he awoke, added with a loud voice, *The King drinketh*."[95]

If all of Elsinore is as drunk as Claudius, perhaps, at the start of the play, the sentinels are uncertain if they see a ghost because they are drunk. That's how a 2001 satire by Eric C. Brown starts out: "*Ber.* [*Belches*] Who's there?"[96] Perhaps those trusted to watch Ophelia were drunk or hungover as she was swallowed by "the weeping brook" (4.5.174). That imagery, with the repetition of "drowned" in the scene

(4.5.163, 164, 182, and 183), emphasizes Ophelia's liquid death. She undergoes the liquefaction Hamlet longs for in the "dew" of his first suicidal soliloquy (1.2.130), while her drowning also points forward to "the drink, the drink" in the final scene (5.2.288).

Similarly, the examples of the gravediggers and Yorrick—his skull in Hamlet's hand—associate drinking with death. That connection deepens when Hamlet then imagines dead and decomposed humans returning to dust, made a plug to "stop a beer barrel" (5.1.191). Yorrick's skull points to the possibility of tragic alcoholism—which the final scene of *Hamlet* takes to its conclusion. And Yorrick's drunkenness brings binge drinking into the court of King Hamlet.

...

Perhaps King Hamlet partied like his brother—a fraternity. Perhaps King Hamlet was drunk when, during parley, he smote the Pollacks on the ice. Perhaps King Hamlet wasn't napping in his orchard: he was passed out.

Associating alcoholism with death and with King Hamlet—in light of Shakespeare placing the "They clype us drunkards" set piece just before the appearance of King Hamlet's spirit—creates the possibility that alcohol is haunting Elsinore. The first recorded use of the word *spirit* to refer to alcohol came from Shakespeare's friend Ben Jonson in 1612, about ten years after *Hamlet* was written.[97] It is not inconceivable that Jonson, Shakespeare, and others used "spirit" in this sense conversationally, perhaps over drinks. In *Othello* Shakespeare wrote of the "invisible spirit of wine" (2.3.258). Richard III asks for wine when he has an "alacrity of spirit" (*Richard III*, 5.2.73). Hamlet's asking if the ghost is "a spirit of health or goblin damned" (1.5.40) recalls Claudius announcing the "jocund health that Denmark drinks." And the "juice of cursed hebona in a vial" (1.5.62) recalls the "dram of evil" in the preceding scene.

I don't think Jonson had King Hamlet's ghost in mind when using this term for alcohol, but these two "spirits" work similarly. The Spirit's description of the poison "cours[ing] through / The natural gates and alleys of the body" (1.5.66–67), overtaking the blood, sounds like alcohol. And viewing King Hamlet's spirit as a symbol of alcohol accords with Hamlet's description:

> The spirit that I have seen
> May be a dev'l, and the dev'l hath power
> T'assume a pleasing shape; yea, and perhaps
> Out of my weakness and my melancholy,
> As he is very potent with such spirits,
> Abuses me to damn me. (2.2.517–22)

Where King Hamlet's Ghost is a "potent . . . spirit," Iago says the English are most "potent in potting" (*Othello*, 2.3.68). Today, as in Shakespeare's time, "potent . . . spirits" can abuse melancholy people and be abused by them, especially in moments of "weakness." Recalling Hamlet's uncertainty about his father's spirit, alcohol can be a devil in disguise.

Coleridge thought Hamlet's "mole of nature" speech flowed nicely into the appearance of the Ghost—Hamlet's contemplative response to Claudius's alcoholism carrying over into his contemplative, not shocked, response to the Ghost, a quality absent from the quartos.[98] But how, more directly, are we to understand the Ghost arising, as it were, out of Claudius's party? In Joan Fitzpatrick's words, "While Claudius consumes white wine, Old Hamlet is released from the mouth of death."[99] Does the unnatural disruption signified by the Ghost's appearance grow, in some way, out of the behavior signified by Claudius's binge drinking?

Yet King Hamlet, like his son, opposes the culture of drunkenness in Denmark, as when he laments "the royal bed of Denmark" becoming "a couch for luxury" (1.5.82–83). Perhaps King Hamlet could drink socially just fine, while Claudius couldn't control himself (that was the situation with my older brother and me, and it strained our relationship). Or maybe King Hamlet was a stick in the mud, turning Gertrude off, turning her to the fun-loving Claudius. Maybe Claudius and Gertrude hooked up in a drunken evening. Maybe that's why Gertrude feels guilty.

···

Alcoholic Gertrudes are popular in performance. In David Giles's 1970 production, Faith Brooks was "increasingly weepy and alcoholic."[100] Such stagings cite Gertrude's fatal drink in act 5 which, given the cluster of ideas associated with alcohol in *Hamlet*—from the performance of masculinity to the possibilities of hidden backstories—reflects Gertrude's increased complexity in the second half of the play.[101] To say that there is no other evidence for alcoholism in Gertrude is really to ask what counts as evidence for alcoholism. Both alcoholics and their families know the swampy difficulty of this question. Campbell Scott and Eric Simonson's 2000 film featured Blair Brown "drinking alone, her hair and manner unkempt."[102] Are these productions projecting Claudius's alcoholism onto Gertrude? If so, is that misogyny, repositioning a man's failings as a woman's? Or, is it empowerment, granting Gertrude complexity of character where Shakespeare did not?

These productions amplify traces of alcoholism in the text while recognizing in Gertrude the lifestyle of the older alcoholic woman of the modern age. This Gertrude is an Elizabeth Taylor: extraordinarily powerful and talented, the woman who has everything, including an addiction that creates a chasm between the public image and the private struggle. In Gregory Doran's 2008 production for the Royal Shakespeare Company, Penny Downie "harrowingly charts Gertrude's decline from high society lady to abject terror and exhausted, alcoholic remorse."[103] In Nicholas Hytner's 2010 production for the National Theatre, Clare Higgins "plays Gertrude as a sensual, raddled alcoholic, drinking to forget her own guilt."[104] One reviewer noted that "alcohol is nourishment to Claudius and Gertrude. They are rarely without shot glass in hand, tipped to lips, although only Gertrude exhibits tipsiness."[105]

Or does Gertrude's fatal drink at the end of the play encourage us to backdate her participation in the culture of drunkenness in Elsinore—an aging sorority sister, not disgusted but enthralled by blackout drinking? Karla Hendrick's Gertrude in Hamilton Clancy's 2014 production was "an alcoholic party girl."[106] Clancy described Hamlet as "a textbook case of adult children of alcoholics": "The ghost of his father is a classic enabler; his message to young Hamlet is essentially 'Don't get mad at your mom.'"[107] The most startling alcoholic Gertrude comes in Ian McEwan's *Nutshell* (2016), told from the perspective of Hamlet in her womb, creating possibilities both for fetal alcohol syndrome and for genetic markers of alcoholism in the prince.[108]

Alcoholic Claudiuses, Gertrudes, and King Hamlets create the possibility of an alcoholic Prince Hamlet, though that goes against Shakespeare's characterization.[109] Most prominently, Hamlet has been alcoholic in Arab adaptations such as Jawad Al-Assadi's *Insū Hāmlit* (1994), directed by Issa Diyab.[110] According to Katherine Hennessey, "The connection between alcohol abuse and Hamlet's decadent passivity would have reinforced a message common among conservative factions in Kuwait, which tout the countrywide ban on the importation of alcohol as evidence of Islamic piety, in self-righteous contrast to (for example) devil-may-care Dubai."[111] If so, these Kuwaiti conservatives view Hamlet's alcoholism as Hamlet views Claudius's in Shakespeare's play. The Hamlet who once opposed a culture of drunkenness in Denmark comes to stand for one in Dubai.

···

To view Denmark as a culture of drunkenness, in the analogy to the American frat house, is to see it filled with people of privilege relatively free from the typical human burdens of work and war. They have money and idle time. The natural human desire for pleasure leads them to long for fellowship and fun. Hormones are raging, everyone looking for sexual partners. That creates a deep concern for one's reputation and a need to stand out from the pack. Acts of excess follow—frivolity, fun, flirting, and fighting—fueled by the alcohol that takes away inhibitions. That's the Elsinore that Hamlet laments, feels estranged from in his period of mourning.

To understand Claudius's villainy—specifically his ambition—through the metaphor of alcoholism is to consider his criminal actions as the habituation of conscious moral choices coming in the context of imposing circumstances, both cultural conventions and individual personality traits. Like the alcoholic, Claudius bears moral responsibility for his actions, though those actions grew into a seemingly autonomous force exerting more control over the situation than Claudius's individual agency. He became diseased and, even if his actions brought that disease into existence, that disease brings about actions that are quite contrary to Claudius's desires. That creates mental stress and shame. His failed attempt to repent is eerily similar to the alcoholic who wants to quit but can't. The vicious cycle continues, expanding outward to ensnare family and friends. With no support system able to intervene, Claudius is powerless to stop.

···

"*A table prepared*," says the stage direction in the final scene (5.2.195). The table has indeed been set by the imagery of alcohol throughout the play. "*Trumpets, drums*" (5.2.195s.d.)—the sounds signifying the culture of drunkenness throughout the play—proclaim coming catastrophe. The tragedy of alcoholism in *Hamlet* culminates in the poisoned cup.[112]

Filled with liquor, the "chalice for the nonce" (4.4.159) is lethal even before Claudius poisons it. His order, "Set me the stoups of wine upon that table" (5.2.238), recalls the association of alcohol and death in the previous scene—through the repetition of the gravedigger's word *stoup*—and the liquid imagery flowing throughout the play, from the *dew* in Hamlet's opening soliloquy to Ophelia's death. Then the rouse accompanied with cannon fire in Claudius's final toast recalls his antics that set off Hamlet's "dram of evil" speech:

> If Hamlet give the first or second hit,
> Or quit in answer of the third exchange,
> Let all the battlements their ordnance fire.
> The King shall drink to Hamlet's better breath
> And in the cup an union shall he throw
> Richer than that which four successive kings
> In Denmark's crown have worn. Give me the cups,
> And let the kettle to the trumpet speak,
> The trumpet to the cannoneer without,
> The cannons to the heavens, the heaven to earth:
> Now the King drinks to Hamlet. (5.2.239–49)

Shakespeare is asking audiences to remember Claudius's binge drinking as the catastrophe approaches. "*Flourish. Drum [and] trumpets. A piece goes off,*" after Hamlet's first hit on Laertes (5.2.256s.d.). Like the cascading swell of drums, trumpets, and cannons, Claudius's alcoholism amplifies into a culture of drunkenness that then turns tragic. For a bit, he might be the happy drunk of the second scene of the play. "Give me drink," he says (5.2.258), bustling around the stage. His words recall the "jocund health" that inaugurated the play's symbolism of alcohol: "Here's to thy health. Give him the cup" (5.2.259).

Then Gertrude joins Denmark's culture of drunkenness: "The Queen carouses to thy fortune, Hamlet" (5.2.265). Or maybe a production like Thomas Bradic's from 1992 builds up to this moment: "After watching her take a stiff drink simply to survive the chatter of Polonius, it's not surprising when she insists on her inadvertently fatal quaff as she watches her son fight Laertes. Nowadays, one could picture this queen checking into Betty Ford or saying to herself: 'My name is Gertrude, and I am an alcoholic.'"[113] Gertrude "carours[ing]" brings her into the cloud of tragedy cast around alcohol. She is no longer Ophelia-like, an innocent bystander—the random person walking down the street struck by a drunk driver on his way home from Hawaiian night at a frat house.

Claudius becomes the helpless drunk recognizing the effects of his actions on others. "Gertrude, do not drink," he exclaims (5.2.267). This was a key moment for Imogen Stubbs in Trevor Nunn's 2004 Royal Shakespeare Company production: "'I will, my lord, I pray you pardon me' (5.2.244) really said 'Don't humiliate me by telling the whole court you think I'm an alcoholic!'"[114]

"It is the poisoned cup," Claudius says to himself (5.2.269). *The cup is poisoned*: that is the conceit Shakespeare's treatment of alcohol has been building to throughout the play. Hamlet abstains: "I dare not drink yet, madam" (5.2.270). He remains outside the culture of drunkenness.

Alcohol has been killing Denmark from the inside, as it does to Gertrude. "The drink, the drink! O my dear Hamlet," she cries. "The drink, the drink—I am poisoned" (5.2.288–89). Laertes then becomes the alcoholic having a moment of clarity: "The foul practice / Hath turned itself on me" (5.2.296–97). He admits the exact nature of his wrongs—"Thy mother's poisoned. . . . The King, the King's to blame" (5.2.298–99)—and makes amends. Hamlet stabs Claudius, then feeds the king his own poisoned liquor: "Drink of this potion" (5.2.304). Claudius dying from alcohol poisoning symbolizes the tragic quality of the culture of drunkenness in Denmark. Laertes's acerbic commentary imagines Claudius having ordered a drink—"He is justly served" (5.2.305)—then glosses the alcoholic who drinks himself to death: "It is a poison tempered by himself" (5.2.306).

Two moments punctuate the tragedy of alcohol in the play. First, an overwhelmed Horatio reaches for the poisoned cup: "Here's yet some liquor left" (5.2.319). Symbolically, Horatio is poised to become the next victim of Denmark's culture of drunkenness—the alcoholic drinking to cope with loss and depression. As ever, Hamlet stands against alcohol: "Give me the cup" (5.2.321). In Lemon's astute gloss, "The survival of Horatio depends entirely on his abstinence."[115] With any alcoholic, there will be Horatios who survive the path of destruction and Hamlets, Ophelias, and Gertrudes taken down by it. If, in act 1, Shakespeare obliquely connected alcohol with the "potent . . . spirit," that figure is reiterated in Hamlet's final moments: "The potent poison quite o'ercrows my spirit" (5.2.331).

Second, the folio concludes with uncharacteristically precise stage directions, indicating the play's end on the early modern stage. Just before Hamlet dies, the folio reads, "*March afar off, and shout within*" (5.2.294s.d.). Perhaps Shakespeare demanded these sound effects because he had woven together a thread of concepts throughout the play—alcohol, drums, cannons, and tragedy. "Go, bid the soldiers shoot," Fortinbras declares (5.2.381), entering the cluster of symbols surrounding binge drinking in *Hamlet*. Polish dissident Janusz Glowacki envisioned Elsinore's drunkenness continuing in *Fortinbras Gets Drunk* (1985).[116] As for Shakespeare's original text, the folio stage direction reads, "*Exeunt marching, after the which a peal of ordnance are shot off*" (5.2.350). Those cannon shots ringing out through the cold night air of the Elizabethan playhouse could only recall, for an early modern audience, the cannons repeatedly shot as Claudius downed his drinks earlier in the play. Those cannons closing the play convey how much of this tragedy can be traced back to Claudius's alcoholism and the culture of drunkenness in Denmark.

JEFFREY R. WILSON is a faculty member in the Writing Program at Harvard University, where he teaches the "Why Shakespeare?" section of the university's first-year writing course. He is author of three books, *Shakespeare and Trump* (2020), *Shakespeare and Game of Thrones* (2021), and *Richard III's Bodies from Medieval England to Modernity: Shakespeare and Disability History* (forthcoming). His work has appeared in journals such as *College Literature, Genre,* and *Modern Language Quarterly* and been featured in public venues including National Public Radio, Literary Hub, Zocalo Public Square, and MLA's *Profession.* On Twitter, @DrJeffreyWilson.

Acknowledgments

I would like to thank Michael Cranston, Rebecca Lemon, Jeremy Lopez, Julia Reinhard Lupton, Victoria Silver, and Reavant Singh for comments and conversations about the ideas presented in this essay.

Notes

1   All citations of Shakespeare's plays refer to Greenblatt, *Norton Shakespeare.* Unless otherwise noted, references to *Hamlet* are to the combined text.

2   According to Albert E. Egge: "The word [*rouse*] is common in all the Scandinavian languages in the form *rus,* which means 'a carouse, a fit of intoxication.' For example in Danish, *at tage sig en rus* or *at faa sig en rus,* 'to indulge in a spree'; *at sove rusen ud,* 'to sleep off one's debauch, sleep oneself sober.' The word must have been borrowed from the Danish" ("Note on Shakespeare," 244).

3   Johnson, *Hamlet,* 144n3.

4   Davies, *Dramatic Miscellanies,* 3.11.

5   Marlowe, *Tamburlaine the Great,* G3.

6   Bloom, "Manly Drunkenness," 31.

7   Srigley, "'Heavy-Headed Revel East and West.'"

8   Stow, *Annales of England,* 1436.

9   Stow, *Annales, or a Generall Chronicle of England,* 887.

10   Trawick, *Shakespeare and Alcohol,* 17.

11   There is a textual inconsistency in the earliest editions: *too sullied* in quarto editions, *too solid* in folio. The folio version is more resonant with the liquid imagery in my reading.

12   See Holl, "'Now 'mongst This Flock of Drunkards.'"

13   Trawick, *Shakespeare and Alcohol,* 50. Beyond Trawick's appendix, see Thomas, "Shakespeare's Alcoholics"; *Boozy Bard;* and Dalrymple, "Shakespeare on Alcohol."

14   Greenblatt, *Will in the World,* 70.

15   Greenblatt, *Will in the World,* 70. But see Matusiak, "Was Shakespeare 'Not a Company Keeper'?"

16   Greenblatt, *Will in the World,* 387.

17   See Earnshaw, "Falstaffian State"; Kezar, "Shakespeare's Addictions"; Smyth, "'It Were Far Better Be a Toad, or a Serpent, Then a Drunkard'"; and Fitzpatrick, *Food in Shakespeare.*

18   See Wood, "'Fluster'd with Flowing Cups'"; and Lemon, "Incapacitated Will."

19   See Nguyen, "Dressed in Drunk Hope"; Lemon, "Sacking Falstaff"; and Romanelli, "Sour Beer at the Boar's Head."

20   McBride, "Natural Drink for an English Man," 180–81.

21   See esp. Parolin, "'Poor Creature Small Beer'"; Sebek, "'Wine and Sugar of the Best and the Fairest'"; and Raber, "Fluid Mechanics."

22   Raber, "Fluid Mechanics," 76.

23   See Malone, *Writing under the Influence;* Jamison, *Recovering;* Klepuszewski, "Drink and Alcohol Literature"; Klepuszewski, "'From Jubilation to Despair'"; and Klepuszewski, "'Delightful Logic of Intoxication.'"

24   On the performance tradition, see Bevington, *Murder Most Foul.* The books cited are Greenblatt, *Hamlet in Purgatory;* Cutrofello, *All for Nothing;* and Lewis, *Hamlet and the Vision of Darkness.*

25   See Wechsler and Wuethrich, *Dying to Drink;* DeSantis, *Inside Greek U.;* Biddix, et al., "Influence of Fraternity and Sorority Involvement"; Hechinger, *True Gentlemen;* and Robbins, *Fraternity.*

26   See Hughey, "Paradox of Participation: Nonwhites in White Sororities and Fraternities"; Joyce, "Perceptions of Race and Fit"; and Gillon, Beatty, and Salinas, "Race and Racism in Fraternity and Sorority Life."

27   Chauvin, "Social Norms and Motivations."

28   Wechsler, Kuh, and Davenport, "Fraternities, Sororities, and Binge Drinking"; Larimer et al., "Individual in Context."

29   McCready, "Relationships between Collective Fraternity Chapter Masculine Norm Climates and the Alcohol Consumption of Fraternity Men."

30   Withington, "Intoxicants and Society in Early Modern England," 632.

31   Withington, "Introduction," 15.

32   See Capone et al., "Fraternity and Sorority Involvement."

33   Durkin, Wolfe, and Clark, "College Students and Binge Drinking"; Park, Sher, and Krull, "Risky Drinking in College Changes"; Capece and Lanza-Kaduce, "Binge Drinking among

College Students"; DeMartino, Rice, and Saltz, "Applied Test."

34 Sudhinaraset, Wigglesworth, and Takeuchi, "Social and Cultural Contexts of Alcohol Use."

35 Bloom, "Manly Drunkenness," 25.

36 Shephard, *Meanings of Early Modern Manhood,* 94.

37 Byrd, "Binge Drinking in and out of College."

38 Lemon, "Compulsory Conviviality in Early Modern England," 390.

39 See Sher, Bartholow, and Nanda, "Short- and Long-Term Effects of Fraternity and Sorority Membership on Heavy Drinking"; McCabe et al., "Selection and Socialization Effects of Fraternities and Sororities on U.S. College Student Substance Use"; and McCabe, Veliz, and Schulenberg, "How Collegiate Fraternity and Sorority Involvement Relates to Substance Use."

40 I take this point from Britland, "Circe's Cup."

41 Borsari, Hustad, and Capone, "Alcohol Use in the Greek System."

42 Rich, *Allarme to England*, Fiii.

43 Foulweather, *Wonderfull, Strange, and Miraculous Astrologicall Prognostication*, B3.

44 Jonson, "Ode."

45 Rowlands, "Drunkard."

46 Nashe, *Pierce Penilesse*, C3.

47 Seymour, *Remarks*, 2.148.

48 Sutherland, *Principles of Criminology*, 6.

49 Young, *Englands Bane*, D2.

50 Withington, "Intoxicants and Society," 656.

51 Gascoigne, *Delicate Diet*, Cii.

52 Nashe, *Pierce Penilesse*, C4.

53 Tlusty, *Bacchus and Civic Order*, 3.

54 Bloom, "Manly Drunkenness," 25.

55 Barckley, *Discourses on the Felicities of Man*, 25–26.

56 Rich, *Martial Conference*, H3.

57 Beaumont and Fletcher, *Captaine*, 57.

58 Camden, *Remaines*, 17.

59 Peacham, *Complete Gentleman*, 194.

60 Camden, *Annales*.

61 Howell, "To My Lord Viscount S. from Hamburgh."

62 Lemon, "Compulsory Conviviality," 384.

63 *England's Royall Conquest*, quoted from McShane, "Roaring Royalists and Ranting Brewers," 75.

64 *England's Triumph*, quoted from McShane, "Roaring Royalists," 79.

65 Charney, "Hamlet without Words," 459.

66 Johnson, "*Hamlet*: Voice, Music, Sound," 261.

67 The etymology of *wassail* appears in Drayton, *Poly-Olbion*, 153–54; and Slatyer, *History of Great Britanie*, 165.

68 Lemon, "Compulsory Conviviality," 402.

69 Raleigh, *Shakespeare's England*, 17.

70 Tolman, "Shakespeare Studies," 87–88.

71 Winkler, "Alimentary Metaphors and Their Political Context," 97.

72 Stallybrass, "'Well Grubbed, Old Mole,'" 11; Lemon, "Incapacitated Will," 113.

73 Nashe, *Pierce Penilesse*, Fr.

74 See Haley, "'Cause of This Defect.'"

75 *Oxford English Dictionary*, 2nd ed., s.v. "dram," n. 1, *OED Online*, def. 3 (accessed August 13, 2021).

76 Charney, "Hamlet without Words," 460.

77 Marlowe, *Doctor Faustus*, E3.

78 Trawick, *Shakespeare and Alcohol*, 18.

79 On the imagery of poison as the dominant metaphor of the play, see Mahalik, "Rising Gorge."

80 As Withington notes, "Robert Cawdrey listed 'intoxicate' as 'poisoned' in his 1604 dictionary of 'hard words'" ("Cultures of Intoxication," 13).

81 Wood, "'Fluster'd with Flowing Cups.'"

82 Lemon, "Incapacitated Will," 106, quoting Bacon, *Elements*, 34.

83 Lemon, "Incapacitated Will," 113.

84 Jones, *King in Hamlet*, 60.

85 Kuperman, *O jogo da vida e da morte*. See Resende, "Shakespeare on the Screen." Thanks to Mark Thornton Burnett for this reference. See also Burnett, "*Hamlet* and the Moment of Brazilian Cinema."

86 Kolkovich, "Review of *Hamlet*, dir. Bill Rauch," 225. Thanks to Elizabeth Kolkovick for this reference.

87 Fischer, "Ranking the Plays at Stratford Festival 2015." Thanks to Joseph Kidney for this reference.

88 Tobin, *Hamlet*, 33.

89 See Cree, "Protestant Evangelicals and Addiction in Early Modern English"; and Lemon, *Addiction and Devotion in Early Modern England*.

90 Lemon, "Sacking Falstaff."

91 Withington, "Cultures of Intoxication."

92 See Wedge, "Mixing Memory with Desire."

93 Lemon, "Compulsory Conviviality," 406.

94 See Brown, "Sons of Beer and Sons of Ben"; Kublesek, "Wine for Comfort"; and McShane, "Roaring Royalists and Ranting Brewers."

95 Estienne, *Apology for Herodotus*, 189.

96 Brown, "'Your Only Emperor for Diet,'" 10.

97 *Oxford English Dictionary*, 2nd ed., s.v. "spirit," n., def. 21.b.

98 Coleridge, *Lectures on Shakespeare*, 151.

99 Fitzpatrick, *Food in Shakespeare*, 106.

100 Giles, *Hamlet*; O'Connor, *Ian McKellen*, 86.

101 I take this point on the political significance of gendered binge drinking from Owen, "Drink, Sex, and Power in Restoration Comedy."

102   Scott and Simonson, *Hamlet*; Henderson, "Artistic Process," 84.

103   Doran, *Hamlet*; Spencer, "David Tennant."

104   Hytner, *Hamlet*; Spenser, "Hamlet, National Theatre, Review."

105   Breuer, "HD Hamlet."

106   Clancy, *Hamlet*; Collins-Hughes, "Hanging in a Park with Danish Royalty."

107   Shakespeare in the Parking Lot, "Bryant Park Inaugurated a New Shakespeare Program."

108   McEwan, *Nutshell*. Thanks to Varsha Panjwani for this reference.

109   See Gledhill, "Was Hamlet a Drunkard?"; Thomas and Strassberger, *Hamlet, Prince of Denmark*; and Hill, *Hamlet*.

110   Al-Assadi and Diyab, *Insū Hāmlit*. Al-Assadi's play is available in Litvin, Arab, and Carlson, *Four Arab Hamlet Plays*.

111   Hennessey, *Shakespeare on the Arabian Peninsula*, 274.

112   Drunkenness is connected to the catastrophe in Shakespeare's main source, Saxo Grammaticus's *Historiae Danicae*. Amleth exacts his revenge by getting his uncle and his followers blackout drunk, then setting fire to the palace. See McGlone, "Poisoned Chalice."

113   Bradac, *Hamlet*; Shirley, "Splendid Prince."

114   Nunn, *Hamlet*; Stubbs, "Gertrude," 38. Thanks to Varsha Panjwani for the Nunn reference.

115   Lemon, "Compulsory Conviviality," 401.

116   Glowacki, "*Fortinbras Gets Drunk*."

Works Cited

Al-Assadi, Jawad, and Issa Diyab, dirs. *Insū Hāmlit (Forget Hamlet)*. Kuwait: Arabian Gulf Theatre Troupe, 2009.

Bacon, Francis. *The Elements of the Common Lawes of England*. London, 1630.

Barckley, Richard. *Discourses on the Felicities of Man*. London, 1598.

Beaumont, Francis, and John Fletcher. *The Captaine*. In *Comedies and Tragedies*, edited by James Shirley. London, 1647.

Bevington, David. *Murder Most Foul: Hamlet through the Ages*. Oxford: Oxford University Press, 2011.

Biddix, J. Patrick, Malinda Matney, Eric Norman, and Georgianna Martin. "The Influence of Fraternity and Sorority Involvement: A Critical Analysis of Research (1996–2013)." *ASHE Higher Education Report* 39, no. 6 (2014).

Bloom, Gina. "Manly Drunkenness: Binge Drinking as Disciplined Play." In *Masculinity and the Metropolis of Vice, 1550–1650*, edited by Amanda Bailey and Roze Hentschell, 21–44. New York: Palgrave Macmillan, 2010.

The Boozy Bard: Shakespeare on Drinking. Chichester: Summersdale, 2005.

Borsari, Brian, John T. P. Hustad, and Christy Capone. "Alcohol Use in the Greek System, 1999–2009: A Decade of Progress." *Current Drug Abuse Reviews* 2, no. 3 (2009): 216–55.

Bradac, Thomas F., dir. *Hamlet*. Santa Ana, CA: Shakespeare Orange County, 1992.

Breuer, Joann Green. "HD Hamlet—Determined Relevance." *Arts Fuse*, December 11, 2010. artsfuse.org/18140/fuse-theater-review-hd -hamlet-determined-relevance.

Britland, Karen. "Circe's Cup: Wine and Women in Early Modern Drama." In *A Pleasing Sinne: Drink and Conviviality in Seventeenth-Century England*, edited by Adam Smyth, 109–26. Cambridge: Brewer, 2004.

Brown, Cedric C. "Sons of Beer and Sons of Ben: Drink as a Social Marker in Seventeenth-Century England." In *A Pleasing Sinne: Drink and Conviviality in Seventeenth-Century England*, edited by Adam Smyth, 3–20. Cambridge: Brewer, 2004.

Brown, Eric C. "'Your Only Emperor for Diet': Hamlet and the Dangers of Perilous Eating and Drinking." *Mississippi Review* 29, no. 3 (2001): 9–17.

Burnett, Mark Thornton. "*Hamlet* and the Moment of Brazilian Cinema." In *"Hamlet" and World Cinema*, 92–120. Cambridge: Cambridge University Press, 2019.

Byrd, Kaitland M. "Binge Drinking in and out of College: An Examination of Social Control and Differential Association on Binge Drinking Behaviors between College Students and Their Non-college Peers." *Sociological Spectrum* 36, no. 4 (2016): 191–207.

Camden, William. *Annales*, translated by Abraham Darcie. Vols. 3 and 5. London, 1625.

Camden, William. *Remaines, concerning Britaine*. 2nd ed. London, 1614.

Capece, Michael, and Lonn Lanza-Kaduce. "Binge Drinking among College Students: A Partial Test of Akers' Social Structure-Social Learning Theory." *American Journal of Criminal Justice* 38, no. 4 (2013): 503–19.

Capone, Christy, Mark D. Wood, Brian Borsari, and Robert D. Laird. "Fraternity and Sorority Involvement, Social Influences, and Alcohol Use among College Students: A Prospective Examination." *Psychology of Addictive Behaviors* 21, no. 3 (2007): 316–27.

Charney, Maurice. "Hamlet without Words." *ELH* 32, no. 4 (1965): 457–77.

Chauvin, Chantel D. "Social Norms and Motivations Associated with College Binge Drinking." *Sociological Inquiry* 82, no. 2 (2012): 257–81.

Clancy, Hamilton, dir. *Hamlet*. New York: Drilling Company, 2014.

Coleridge, Samuel Taylor. *Lectures on Shakespeare (1811–1819)*, edited by Adam Roberts. Edinburgh: Edinburgh University Press, 2016.

Collins-Hughes, Laura. "Hanging in a Park with Danish Royalty." *New York Times*, May 28, 2014. www.nytimes.com/2014/05/29/theater /the-drilling-company-presents-hamlet-in -bryant-park.html.

Cree, Jose Murgatroyd. "Protestant Evangelicals and Addiction in Early Modern English." *Renaissance Studies* 32, no. 3 (2017): 446–62.

Cutrofello, Andrew. *All for Nothing: Hamlet's Negativity*. Cambridge, MA: MIT Press, 2014.

Dalrymple, Theodore. "Shakespeare on Alcohol." *British Medical Journal* 342 (2011). doi.org/ 10.1136/bmj.d1789.

Davies, Thomas. *Dramatic Miscellanies*. London, 1784.

DeMartino, Cynthia H., Ronald E. Rice, and Robert Saltz. "An Applied Test of the Social Learning Theory of Deviance to College Alcohol Use." *Journal of Health Communication: International Perspectives* 20, no. 4 (2015): 479–90.

DeSantis, Alan D. *Inside Greek U.: Fraternities, Sororities, and the Pursuit of Pleasure, Power, and Prestige*. Lexington: University Press of Kentucky, 2007.

Doran, Gregory, dir. *Hamlet*. Stratford: Royal Shakespeare Company, 2008.

Drayton, Michael. *Poly-Olbion*. London, 1612.

Durkin, Keith F., Timothy W. Wolfe, and Gregory A. Clark. "College Students and Binge Drinking: An Evaluation of Social Learning Theory." *Sociological Spectrum* 25, no. 3 (2005): 255–72.

Earnshaw, Steven. "The Falstaffian State." In *The Pub in Literature: England's Altered States*, 45– 68. Manchester: Manchester University Press, 2000.

Egge, Albert E. "A Note on Shakespeare." *Modern Language Notes* 23, no. 8 (1908): 244–45.

Estienne, Henri. *Apology for Herodotus*. London, 1607.

Fischer, Mike. "Ranking the Plays at Stratford Festival 2015." *Tap Milwaukee*, August 4, 2015. archive.jsonline.com/entertainment/arts /ranking-the-plays-at-stratford-festival-2015 -b99550305z1-320614672.html.

Fitzpatrick, Joan. *Food in Shakespeare: Early Modern Dietaries and the Plays*. Aldershot: Ashgate, 2007.

Foulweather, Adam [Thomas Nashe]. *A Wonderfull, Strange, and Miraculous Astrologicall Prognostication for This Yeere 1591*. London, 1591.

Gascoigne, George. *A Delicate Diet, for Daintiemouthde Droonkardes*. London, 1576.

Giles, David, dir. *Hamlet*. London: British Broadcasting Corporation, 1970.

Gillon, Kathleen E., Cameron C. Beatty, and Cristobal Salinas Jr. "Race and Racism in Fraternity and Sorority Life: A Historical Overview." *New Directions for Student Services*, no. 165 (2019): 9–16.

Gledhill, Bobbie. "Was Hamlet a Drunkard?" *Proceedings of the Russellian Society* 2 (1986): 1–13.

Glowacki, Janusz. "*Fortinbras Gets Drunk* (1985)." In *Hunting Cockroaches and Other Plays*, 131–216. Evanston, IL: Northwestern University Press, 1990.

Greenblatt, Stephen. *Hamlet in Purgatory*. Princeton, NJ: Princeton University Press, 2001.

Greenblatt, Stephen. *Will in the World: How Shakespeare Became Shakespeare*. New York: Norton, 2004.

Haley, David. "'The Cause of This Defect': The Dram of Eale." In *A Certain Text: Close Readings and Textual Studies on Shakespeare and Others*, edited by Linda Anderson and Janis Lull, 29–49. Cranbury, NJ: Associated University Presses, 2002.

Hechinger, John. *True Gentlemen: The Broken Pledge of America's Fraternities*. New York: Public Affairs, 2017.

Henderson, Diana E. "The Artistic Process: Learning from Campbell Scott's *Hamlet*." In *A Concise Companion to Shakespeare on Screen*, edited by Diana E. Henderson, 77–95. Malden, MA: Blackwell, 2006.

Hennessey, Katherine. *Shakespeare on the Arabian Peninsula*. New York: Palgrave Macmillan, 2018.

Hill, Dominic, dir. *Hamlet*. Glasgow: Citizens Theatre, 2014.

Holl, Jennifer. "'Now 'mongst This Flock of Drunkards': Drunk Shakespeare's Polytemporal Theater." *Borrowers and Lenders* 11, no. 2 (2018). borrowers.uga.edu/783933 /show.

Howell, James. "To My Lord Viscount S. from Hamburgh." In *Epistolae Ho-elianae*, 181–82. 2nd ed. London, 1650.

Hughey, Matthew W. "A Paradox of Participation: Nonwhites in White Sororities and Fraternities." *Social Problems* 57, no. 4 (2010): 653–79.

Hytner, Nicholas, dir. *Hamlet*. London: National Theatre, 2010.

Jamison, Leslie. *The Recovering: Intoxication and Its Aftermath*. New York: Little, Brown, 2018.

Johnson, Bruce. "*Hamlet*: Voice, Music, Sound." *Popular Music* 24, no. 2 (2005): 257–67.

Johnson, Samuel, ed. *Hamlet*. In vol. 8 of *The Plays of William Shakespeare*, 127–316. London, 1765.

Jones, Howard Mumford. *The King in Hamlet.* Austin: University of Texas Press, 1918.

Jonson, Ben. "Ode." In *Pancharis the First Booke,* edited by Hugh Holland, A10. London, 1603.

Joyce, S. Brian. "Perceptions of Race and Fit in the Recruitment Process of Traditionally, Predominantly White Fraternities." *Oracle: The Research Journal of the Association of Fraternity/Sorority Advisors* 13, no. 2 (2018): 29–45.

Kezar, Dennis. "Shakespeare's Addictions." *Critical Inquiry* 30, no. 1 (2003): 31–62.

Klepuszewski, Wojciech. "'The Delightful Logic of Intoxication': Fictionalising Alcoholism." *Acta Neophilologica* 52, nos. 1–2 (2019): 97–118.

Klepuszewski, Wojciech. "Drink and Alcohol Literature: Two Critical Perspectives." *Hungarian Journal of English and American Studies* 24, no. 2 (2018): 375–87.

Klepuszewski, Wojciech. "'From Jubilation to Despair': Representations of Drink in British and Irish Literature." *Beyond Philology* 14, no. 2 (2017): 85–102.

Kolkovich, Elizabeth Zeman. "Review of *Hamlet,* dir. Bill Rauch." *Shakespeare Bulletin* (Ashland, OR) 29, no. 2 (2011): 223–28.

Kublesek, Marika. "Wine for Comfort: Drinking and the Royalist Exile Experience, 1642–1660." In *A Pleasing Sinne: Drink and Conviviality in Seventeenth-Century England,* edited by Adam Smyth, 55–68. Cambridge: Brewer, 2004.

Kuperman, Mario, dir. *O jogo da vida e da morte (The Game of Life and Death).* Futura Films, 1971.

Larimer, Mary E., Britt K. Anderson, John S. Baer, and G. Alan Marlatt. "An Individual in Context: Predictors of Alcohol Use and Drinking Problems among Greek and Residence Hall Students." *Journal of Substance Abuse* 11, no. 1 (2000): 53–68.

Lemon, Rebecca. *Addiction and Devotion in Early Modern England.* Philadelphia: University of Pennsylvania Press, 2018.

Lemon, Rebecca. "Compulsory Conviviality in Early Modern England." *English Literary Renaissance* 43, no. 3 (2013): 381–414.

Lemon, Rebecca. "Incapacitated Will." In *Staged Transgression: Performing Disorder in Early Modern England,* edited by Rory Loughnane and Edel Semple, 104–19. New York: Palgrave Macmillan, 2013.

Lemon, Rebecca. "Sacking Falstaff." In *Culinary Shakespeare: Staging Food and Drink in Early Modern England,* edited by David B. Goldstein and Amy L. Tigner, 113–31. Pittsburgh, PA: Duquesne University Press, 2016.

Lewis, Rhodri. *Hamlet and the Vision of Darkness.* Princeton, NJ: Princeton University Press, 2017.

Litvin, Margaret, Joy Arab, and Marvin Carlson, eds. *Four Arab Hamlet Plays.* New York: Martin E. Segal Theatre Center Publications, 2016.

Mahalik, Christa. "The Rising Gorge: Poison, *Hamlet,* and Sin." *Apothecary's Chest: Magic, Art and Medication* 39, no. 1 (2009): 49–57.

Malone, Aubrey. *Writing under the Influence: Alcohol and the Works of Thirteen American Authors.* Jefferson, NC: McFarland, 2017.

Marlowe, Christopher. *Doctor Faustus.* London, 1616.

Marlowe, Christopher. *Tamburlaine the Great.* London, 1590.

Matusiak, Christopher. "Was Shakespeare 'Not a Company Keeper'? William Beeston and MS Aubrey 8, fol. 45v." *Shakespeare Quarterly* 68, no. 4 (2017): 351–73.

McBride, Charlotte. "A Natural Drink for an English Man: National Stereotyping in Early Modern Culture." In *A Pleasing Sinne: Drink and Conviviality in Seventeenth-Century England,* edited by Adam Smyth, 181–91. Cambridge: Brewer, 2004.

McCabe, Sean Esteban, John E. Schulenberg, Lloyd D. Johnston, Patrick M. O'Malley, Jerald G. Bachman, and Deborah D. Kloska. "Selection and Socialization Effects of Fraternities and Sororities on U.S. College Student Substance Use: A Multi-cohort National Longitudinal Study." *Addiction* 100, no. 4 (2005): 512–24.

McCabe, Sean Esteban, Philip Veliz, and John E. Schulenberg. "How Collegiate Fraternity and Sorority Involvement Relates to Substance Use during Young Adulthood and Substance Use Disorders in Early Midlife: A National Longitudinal Study." *Journal of Adolescent Health* 62, no. 3 (2018): S35–43.

McCready, Adam M. "Relationships between Collective Fraternity Chapter Masculine Norm Climates and the Alcohol Consumption of Fraternity Men." *Psychology of Men and Masculinities* 20, no. 4 (2019): 478–90.

McEwan, Ian. *Nutshell.* New York: Knopf Doubleday, 2016.

McGlone, Kathleen. "The Poisoned Chalice: Wine as a Vehicle of Death in *Women Beware Women, The Tragedy of Mariam,* and *Hamlet.*" *Mediaevalia* 30, no. 1 (2009): 105–22.

McShane, Angela. "Roaring Royalists and Ranting Brewers: The Politicization of Drink and Drunkenness in Political Broadside Ballads from 1640 to 1689." In *A Pleasing Sinne: Drink and Conviviality in Seventeenth-Century England,* edited by Adam Smyth, 69–88. Cambridge: Brewer, 2004.

Nashe, Thomas. *Pierce Penilesse.* London, 1592.

Nguyen, Brooke. "Dressed in Drunk Hope: Alcoholism in Shakespeare's Macbeth."

Magnificat: A Journal of Undergraduate Nonfiction, 2012. Commons.marymount.edu /49irs.49pear/dressed-in-drunk-hope -alcoholism-in-shakespeares-macbeth.

Nunn, Trevor, dir. *Hamlet*. London: Old Vic, 2004.

O'Connor, Garry. *Ian McKellen: A Biography*. New York: St. Martin's, 2019.

Owen, Susan J. "Drink, Sex, and Power in Restoration Comedy." In *A Pleasing Sinne: Drink and Conviviality in Seventeenth-Century England*, edited by Adam Smyth, 127–42. Cambridge: Brewer, 2004.

Park, Aesoon, Kenneth J. Sher, and Jennifer L. Krull. "Risky Drinking in College Changes as Fraternity/Sorority Affiliation Changes: A Person-Environment Perspective." *Psychology of Addictive Behaviors* 22, no. 2 (2008): 219–29.

Parolin, Peter. "'The Poor Creature Small Beer': Princely Autonomy and Subjection in *2 Henry IV*." In *Culinary Shakespeare: Staging Food and Drink in Early Modern England*, edited by David B. Goldstein and Amy L. Tigner, 21–39. Pittsburgh, PA: Duquesne University Press, 2016.

Peacham, Henry. *The Complete Gentleman*. London, 1622.

Raber, Karen. "Fluid Mechanics: Shakespeare's Subversive Liquors." In *Culinary Shakespeare: Staging Food and Drink in Early Modern England*, edited by David B. Goldstein and Amy L. Tigner, 75–96. Pittsburgh, PA: Duquesne University Press, 2016.

Raleigh, Walter. *Shakespeare's England: An Account of the Life and Manners of His Age*. 2 vols. Oxford: Clarendon, 1916.

Resende, Aimara da Cunha. "Shakespeare on the Screen: Brazilian Cinema and TV." *Actes des congrès de la Société française Shakespeare* 33 (2015). Doi.org/10.4000/50irs.50peare.3574.

Rich, Barnabe. *Allarme to England*. London, 1578.

Rich, Barnabe. *A Martial Conference*. London, 1598.

Robbins, Alexandra. *Fraternity: An Inside Look at a Year of College Boys Becoming Men*. New York: Dutton, 2019.

Romanelli, Christina. "Sour Beer at the Boar's Head: Salvaging Shakespeare's Alewife, Mistress Quickly." *Humanities* 8, no. 1 (2019). Doi.org/ 10.3390/h8010006.

Rowlands, Samuel. "Drunkard." In *Looke to It, for Ile Stab Ye*, C3. London, 1604.

Scott, Campbell, and Eric Simonson, dirs. *Hamlet*. Hallmark, 2000.

Sebek, Barbara. "'Wine and Sugar of the Best and the Fairest': Canary, the Canaries, and the Global in Windsor." In *Culinary Shakespeare: Staging Food and Drink in Early Modern England*, edited by David B. Goldstein and

Amy L. Tigner, 41–56. Pittsburgh, PA: Duquesne University Press, 2016.

Seymour, E. H. *Remarks, Critical, Conjectural, and Explanatory upon the Plays of Shakespeare*. London, 1805.

Shakespeare, William. *Hamlet*. In *The Norton Shakespeare*, edited by Stephen Greenblatt, 1764–1854. 3rd ed. New York: Norton, 2016.

Shakespeare, William. *Henry V*. In *The Norton Shakespeare*, edited by Stephen Greenblatt, 1533–1612. 3rd ed. New York: Norton, 2016.

Shakespeare, William. *Othello*. In *The Norton Shakespeare*, edited by Stephen Greenblatt, 2073–2158. 3rd ed. New York: Norton, 2016.

Shakespeare, William. *Richard III*. In *The Norton Shakespeare*, edited by Stephen Greenblatt, 555–648. 3rd ed. New York: Norton, 2016.

Shakespeare in the Parking Lot. "Bryant Park Inaugurated a New Shakespeare Program with the Drilling Company's Shakespeare in the Parking Lot Production of 'Hamlet' May 15–31, 2014." www.shakespeareintheparkinglot.com /bryant_park.htm (accessed August 9, 2021).

Shephard, Alexandra. *The Meanings of Early Modern Manhood in Early Modern England*. Oxford: Oxford University Press, 2003.

Sher, Kenneth J., Bruce D. Bartholow, and Shivani Nanda. "Short- and Long-Term Effects of Fraternity and Sorority Membership on Heavy Drinking: A Social Norms Perspective." *Psychology of Addictive Behaviors* 15, no. 1 (2001): 42–51.

Shirley, Don. "Splendid Prince, Worthy Production of 'Hamlet.'" *Los Angeles Times*, August 10, 1992. www.latimes.com/archives/la-xpm-1992 -08-10-ca-4861-story.html.

Slatyer, William. *The History of Great Britanie*. London, 1621.

Smyth, Adam. "'It Were Far Better to Be a Toad, or a Serpant, Then a Drunkard': Writing about Drunkenness." In *A Pleasing Sinne: Drink and Conviviality in Seventeenth-Century England*, edited by Adam Smyth, 193–210. Cambridge: Brewer, 2004.

Spencer, Charles. "David Tennant: Thrills Abound in Doctor Who *Hamlet*." *Telegraph*, August 6, 2008. www.telegraph.co.uk/culture/theatre /drama/3557930/David-Tennant-thrills -abound-in-Doctor-Who-Hamlet.html.

Spenser, Charles. "Hamlet, National Theatre, Review." *Telegraph*, October 8, 2010. www .telegraph.co.uk/culture/theatre/theatre -reviews/8050155/Hamlet-National-Theatre -review.html.

Srigley, Michael. "'Heavy-Headed Revel East and West': Hamlet and Christian IV of Denmark." In *Shakespeare and Scandinavia: A Collection of*

Nordic Studies, edited by Gunnar Sorelius, 168–92. Newark: University of Delaware Press, 2002.

Stallybrass, Peter. "'Well Grubbed, Old Mole': Marx, Hamlet, and the (Un)fixing of Representation." *Cultural Studies* 12, no. 1 (1998): 3–15.

Stow, John. *The Annales of England*. London, 1605.

Stow, John. *The Annales, or a Generall Chronicle of England*. London, 1615.

Stubbs, Imogen. "Gertrude." In *Performing Shakespeare's Tragedies Today: The Actor's Perspective*, edited by Michael Dobson, 29–40. Cambridge: Cambridge University Press, 2006.

Sudhinaraset, May, Christina Wigglesworth, and David T. Takeuchi. "Social and Cultural Contexts of Alcohol Use: Influences in a Social-Ecological Framework." *Alcohol Research* 38, no. 1 (2016): 35–45.

Sutherland, Edwin. *Principles of Criminology*. 4th ed. Washington, DC: Lippincott, 1939.

Thomas, Ambroise, and Thaddeus Strassberger, dirs. *Hamlet, Prince of Denmark*. St. Paul: Minnesota Opera, 2013.

Thomas, Raymond D. *Shakespeare's Alcoholics, and Some Observations concerning "the Subtle Blood of the Grape."* White Plains, NY: Alcohol Facts, 1949.

Tlusty, B. Ann. *Bacchus and Civic Order: The Culture of Drink in Early Modern Germany*. Charlottesville: University Press of Virginia, 2001.

Tobin, J. J. M., ed. *Hamlet*, by William Shakespeare. Boston: Wadsworth Cengage, 2012.

Tolman, Albert H. "Shakespeare Studies: Part IV. Drunkenness in Shakespeare." *Modern Language Notes* 34, no. 2 (1919): 82–88.

Trawick, Buckner B. *Shakespeare and Alcohol*. Amsterdam: Rodopi, 1978.

Wechsler, Henry, George Kuh, and Andrea E. Davenport. "Fraternities, Sororities, and Binge Drinking: Results from a National Study of American Colleges." *NASPA Journal* 33, no. 4 (1996): 260–79.

Wechsler, Henry, and Bernice Wuethrich. *Dying to Drink: Confronting Binge Drinking on College Campuses*. New York: Rodale, 2002.

Wedge, George F. "Mixing Memory with Desire: The Family of the Alcoholic in Three Mid-century Plays." *Dionysos: The Literature and Addiction TriQuarterly* 1, no. 1 (1989): 10–18.

Winkler, Elisabeth. "Alimentary Metaphors and Their Political Context in Shakespeare's Plays." In *The Pleasures and Horrors of Eating: The Cultural History of Eating in Anglophone Literature*, edited by Marion Gymnich and Norbert Lennartz, 95–108. Göttingen: Bonn University Press, 2010.

Withington, Phil. "Intoxicants and Society in Early Modern England." *Historical Journal* 54, no. 3 (2011): 631–57.

Withington, Phil. "Introduction: Cultures of Intoxication." *Past and Present*, no. 222, suppl. 9 (2014): 9–33.

Wood, David Houston. "'Fluster'd with Flowing Cups': Alcoholism, Humoralism, and the Prosthetic Narrative in Othello." *Disability Studies Quarterly* 29, no. 4 (2009). dsq-sds.org /article/view/998/1182.

Young, Thomas. *Englands Bane: or, The Description of Drunkennesse*. London, 1617.

The Addicted Self
Habit and Addiction in Early Modern Minds

JOSE CREE

Abstract   This article explores the formation and characterization of early modern addiction through the interactions of mind, body, and will, focusing particularly on the work of the sixteenth-century Christian philosopher Pierre de La Primaudaye. In La Primaudaye's writings addiction is a wholly internalized behavior, the product of repeated interactions within the mind. Intended for the purpose of cultivating virtuous behaviors, these interactions could become corrupted, resulting in negative addictions formed between overwhelming passions, a clouded judgment, and an inflexible will. The specific types of addiction a person inclined toward were determined by a host of variables, including temperament, age, and gender. As this article reveals, in early modern accounts of addicted behavior young men were associated with lust and old men with contemplation, while women were considered more vulnerable to all addictions, virtuous and sinful. The image of addiction that emerges from this examination is one not of a disease or a disorder, but of a natural function of the body that could on occasion be led astray.
Keywords   Pierre de La Primaudaye, early modern, addiction, gender

One of the central themes in addiction narratives—both past and present—is the self. The autonomous self and the constrained self, the self that pursues either vice or virtue, the self that is dedicated or given over to particular pursuits. It is notable that when the verb *to addict* first appeared in English, it was commonly used reflexively, with direct reference to selfhood. A 1534 translation of Desiderius Erasmus warned against letting children "addict them selves to any voluntary purposed living," and Richard Taverner in 1540 praised the man who "hath addicted himself to the service of god."[1] Yet despite an apparent shared connection to selfhood, modern and early modern understandings of addiction were markedly different. While modern addiction narratives tend to focus on the relationship between the addict and the object of their addiction, the absence of both the noun *addict* and the adjective *addictive* from seventeenth-century vocabulary suggests a markedly different relationship existed between addiction and the self—perhaps a relationship focused less on the dynamic between addict and addictive object and more on the internalized processes that occur within the self.[2]

ENGLISH LANGUAGE NOTES

60:1, April 2022 DOI 10.1215/00138282-9560221

In early modern use, the object of the addiction was most often a type of behavior rather than a substance—people were described as having addictions to study, poetry, or drinking, rather than to tobacco, alcohol, or chocolate—and as a result these early uses of the term were of little interest to scholars of substance addiction. Instead, scholars like Roy Porter, Jessica Warner, and Harry G. Levine debated the point at which the term *addict* first became associated with a medicalized alcohol addiction model, with Porter dismissing Shakespeare's use of the word with the warning that "we must beware anachronism and the fallacious discovery of bogus forerunners."[3] However, in more recent years scholars have begun to recognize that premodern addiction is a topic of value in its own right. In 2008 Deborah Willis set out to explore the role of an emerging early modern addiction discourse in Christopher Marlowe's *Doctor Faustus*, noting that "it is a discourse that has affinities with, but also crucial differences from, our own contemporary ideas about addiction."[4] More recently Rebecca Lemon's work has explored the role of addiction as an expression of devotion or, increasingly over the early modern period, as disease, as revealed in religious, legal, literary, and political texts.[5] Finally, my own work has examined the origins of the term *addict* in the writings of sixteenth-century Protestant reformers.[6] These works have laid the foundation for a new understanding of early modern addiction, setting out a concept that is at once markedly different yet profoundly similar to our own use of the term.[7]

Within this emerging field, scholarship to date has largely focused on what the expression of early modern addiction looked like—the externality of addiction in all its complex and variable forms. However, in this article I want to shift inward and explore the roles played by the inner workings of the self in the formation of addiction. In it I set out to understand how contemporaries understood addiction to form within the self via the processes of the mind, and how addiction related to contemporary ideas about habit, free will, virtue and vice, pleasure, and disposition. I put forward a model in which addictions are normal, habitual, everyday behaviors, where the noun *addict* is not needed because every person has addictions, and where the "pull" of addiction comes not from the addictive qualities of the object but from the internal disposition of the subject in relation to external phenomena. In other words, this chapter develops an addiction model rooted in early modern descriptions of the mind, and early modern accounts of human behavior. Since the language surrounding mind, heart, brain, and soul is often problematic, with terms used differently by different early modern writers, I have attempted to avoid confusion by using *mind* to encompass the heart, soul, and brain when speaking in general terms, and have referred to specific parts only when the distinction is relevant and specified by the authors themselves.

My analysis of the addicted self relies primarily on Pierre de La Primaudaye's *Academie françoise*, which consists of four lengthy volumes of moral, natural, and Christian philosophy, written and published in France between 1578 and 1608. All four volumes appeared in English translation as a single publication in 1618. Dana Jalobeanu calls the work "eclectic and massive," and Anne Lake Prescott describes it as a "four-part quasi-encyclopaedia . . . on how a Christian might lead a good life."[8] La Primaudaye's sources for the *Academie françoise* are various. Aristotle is referenced more than 150 times in the work, and Plato and Socrates are not far behind. Parts of it follow Pliny's *Historia naturalis*, but—according to Jalobeanu—also reveal the clear influence of Seneca's *Naturales quaestiones*.[9] Despite this, La Primaudaye is often highly critical of classical philosophers. Jalobeanu refers to the work as being "not only a school of wisdom, but also a battlefield," in which the enemies are "the 'Epicures and Atheists.'"[10] On La Primaudaye's side is the "true Christian philosopher," backed up by scripture; La Primaudaye's 159 references to Aristotle pale in comparison to his mentions of Saint Paul (216), and Jesus (447). In other words, the concept of addiction depicted within the *Academie françoise*—and its relationship to mind, body, and action—does not represent the work of any single school but rather a diverse collection of knowledge gathered together under a broad Christian banner.

La Primaudaye's work was chosen as the focus of this article for three reasons. First, it deals extensively with the subject matter: of addiction, habitual behavior, virtue and vice, disposition, and the interactions between these different functions and elements. Second, it echoes established ideas and concepts, "gathering into one educational text varied evidence from other books," rather than contributing anything radical or new. As Prescott puts it, "Encyclopaedias are not meant to be original."[11] While the format is ostensibly a dialogue, in practice the different voices rarely (if ever) disagree; their role is to break up the flow of information, not to introduce controversy. Third, the book was widely read and popular across Europe but particularly in England. Jalobeanu writes that it "went through a large number of editions in French, English and Italian" and that it "might have been an important source of 'facts' and 'stories' for the late Elizabethan and early Jacobean drama."[12] Cis Van Heertum writes that the work "had a considerable reputation, both in France and, judging from the number of English editions, also in England."[13] It would not be unreasonable to claim that La Primaudaye's work was relevant, representative, and influential, within a certain segment of European intellectual culture.

The Will

In early modern accounts, addiction, like all human action, was determined by the will. The will, according to La Primaudaye, was "that power of desiring"; it was the part of the soul that decided whether to pursue a particular course of action or behavior. La Primaudaye believed that the will was a free agent that could not be forced or limited. "Our Will is at liberty and free, and cannot be constrained . . . otherwise it should not be a Will." Even if a person were prevented from carrying out their will, "yet their Will, if we consider the matter well, is neither hindered, forced or constrained. For that keeps it not from willing still that which it pleases."[14] While the will was guided by reason, La Primaudaye writes, "that always she hath her liberty to make choice of which reason she please, out of all those that are set before her" (*TFA*, 2.41). Nevertheless, according to La Primaudaye, the will operated within certain limitations, which restricted or hampered its ability to choose freely. First, in his view the will, like all the functions of the soul, only had the ability to pursue good. La Primaudaye wrote that "there are two actions of will, whereof the first is that inclination to good by which it embraces the same, and the second is the turning aside from evil" (*TFA*, 2.34). Second, the will could deal only in absolutes: "The actions thereof are to Will, and not to Will" (*TFA*, 2.41). This restriction meant that the will could not determine the strength of an addiction; it could only decide within each instance whether to pursue it or not.

In essence, while La Primaudaye regarded the will as immediately responsible for all human behavior, he did not see it as an independent agent but rather as a yes/no switch between mind and action. According to him, there were three other factors that determined which actions were put forward by the mind for consideration by the will. He wrote that "the Philosophers made three chief principles and beginnings that affect men's actions, namely, powers; habits, or qualities; & affections, or passions" (*TFA*, 2.68; punctuation changed for clarity). Habits "are gotten by a long and continual custom of doing good or evil" and are strengthened through repetition (*TFA*, 2.68). The affections—a concept similar to emotion, but one that included desire—introduced the capacity for vice through their ability to overrule reason. The third category—powers—included disposition/inclination and provided a means of explaining the impact of a wide variety of internal and external qualities on human behavior. I consider each of these in turn.

Habit

Habit is of particular importance to understanding early modern addiction, because addiction was associated specifically with habitual behaviors rather than one-off acts; throughout all four books La Primaudaye uses the term *addict* exclusively to describe repeated actions. He made the relationship between addiction and habit explicit in a chapter titled "Of Four Things to Be Considered in the Will," in which he argues that habit was not a person's behavior but the processes that occurred within the mind to produce that behavior. He describes how the series of actions within the mind that result in a judgment can be over swiftly, or they can linger and repeat:

> Now if these actions be sudden, and pass lightly, so that the mind doth not stay in them, nor acquaint it self with them, the bare & simple name of action belongs to them. But if the mind doth one and the same thing often, muses much upon it, calls it often to memory, and accustoms itself thereunto, so that it is in a manner imprinted in it, and thereby the mind becomes prompt and ready in regard of the long continuance therein, then do these actions take the name of habit. (*TFA*, 2.41)

When the actions of the mind were brief or rare, the judgment was passed to the will, and a desire was formed, expressed, and extinguished. However, when the same judgment was reached repeatedly it became a habit: the will addicted itself to whatever the judgment recommended, and the actions of the mind changed to make it easier to keep reaching that judgment. In other words, even if the addiction began as an act of volition, the nature of habit made it increasingly difficult for the will to choose otherwise. As La Primaudaye explains: "Habit . . . is bred by the often repeating and reiterating of the same things. Whereby the mind is made more fit and apt to perform those exercises, unto which they have addicted themselves, and wherein they have continued" (*TFA*, 2.41). The difference between habit and addiction is clear in the grammar La Primaudaye used: the noun *habit* described a process that existed in the mind, while the verb *addict* indicated the action that proceeded from it.

The purpose of habit was to make the pursuit of good easier. "How hard soever it be to our flesh to follow after a virtuous, honest, and sober life, yet custom will make it easy to overpass" (*TFA*, 2.42). However, a bad habit could form in much the same way as a good one, and once in place it became increasingly easy for the will to pursue vice. What habit could not explain was, if the will could choose only good, how were sinful behaviors pursued in the first place? To explore this, we must examine the other functions that La Primaudaye believed informed the will.

Affections

Affections were feelings that affected the mind, and their purpose, according to La Primaudaye, was to push the heart toward pleasure; to "prick it forward to the desire of pleasure, and . . . minister pleasure unto it" (*TFA*, 2.36). The affections played a fundamental role in determining human action, particularly when that action was considered morally reprehensible; they were the internal force that had the ability to overpower the soul's innate propensity for good. However, all things being correct, the affections were supposed to be governed by reason and understanding, so that any impulse to sin could be overruled before it became an action. Furthermore, like the other elements of the heart and soul, their natural purpose was virtuous. For sinful addictions to form, two things must happen. First, the natural virtuous affection must become corrupted and turn instead toward vice. Second, the corrupt affection must be strong enough to overpower reason and judgment.

La Primaudaye wrote that "the natural affections of the heart . . . should be no sin at all unto men, but a benefit given them of God in the perfection of their nature" (*TFA*, 2.36). After all, "the affections proceed from the heart, [which] is a seat of that love which we ought to bear as well towards God, as towards men, which comprehends the whole law of God and all justice" (*TFA*, 2.36). However, the affections were strongly influenced by inclination, and corrupt inclinations could lead the affections astray. If affection was the feeling of pleasure that the heart pursues, inclination was the force determining which particular behaviors a person found pleasurable; inclination (or disposition) was not a fixed quality but was influenced by a huge variety of internal and external variants, and these were not always a force for good. "Now if these inclinations be well guided, they are goodly seeds of virtues, but if they be not well ordered and ruled, they corrupt and degenerate, yea they turn into the vices that are contrary to those virtues" (*TFA*, 2.41). This could occur due to excess—such as severity turning the virtue of justice into the vice of cruelty—or through sin, as when "the inclinations and natural affections of our soul . . . are turned into vices & into their seeds, through that corruption which sin brings unto them" (*TFA*, 2.41).

However, even when inclination drove an affection toward vice it should still not result in sinful action, because the will should listen first and foremost to reason and understanding. La Primaudaye explains that whereas the affections reside in the heart, the faculties of knowing—reason, understanding, and judgment—

inhabit the brain, "for God hath lodged the understanding & reason in the brain of man, as it were in a high tower, in which it ought to reign as a Queen and Princess" (*TFA*, 2.11).[15] The "Will doth not follow after or refuse any thing, which the Judgment hath not first determined to be good or evil: and the Judgment decrees nothing before it hath taken advice of Reason" (*TFA*, 2.28). Understanding "determines and judges what is true and what false, what good and what evil. Then doth the Will choose that which is good, and refuses the evil" (*TFA*, 2.28). However, while the normal motion of the affections was gentle enough to be easily ruled, they had the capacity to become agitated. Some affections "are so violent, that they altogether trouble the soul, even in such a vehement manner, that they drive her from the seat of judgement" (*TFA*, 2.28). La Primaudaye likened these violent affections to a furnace throwing out thick, blackening smoke:

> The mind, reason and memory may be troubled by the affections of the heart, which resembles a fiery furnace, & is like to a thick smoke ascending out of a great fire which would dim the eyes & make them as it were blind. And when the light of the mind is thus darkened, reason cannot discourse so well, nor judgement judge so uprightly, nor memory retain so firmly, or bring forth so readily that which it hath kept. (*TFA*, 2.35)

Nor were just reason and judgment affected: "The Will is much more troubled by this fire of affections that heats and kindles it, whereby it is made a great deal more untoward to follow the counsel & advise of reason. . . . And when these two principal parts & powers of the soul are thus troubled and moved, it is no marvel if man forget God & himself, and if with all his soul and body he turn aside from that which he ought to follow after" (*TFA*, 2.35). Strong affections could cloud judgment and understanding and turn the will away from reason. It is important to note that La Primaudaye considered the will an active participant in the pursuit of sin; affections could cloud judgment and make the will ignore reason, but ultimately the will was still making the choice which it—wrongly—believed to be the right one. "If it so fall out, that the will give place to the appetite, it is always with her consent, and that because she agrees rather unto the sensual appetite then unto Reason" (*TFA*, 2.34).

Disposition

As discussed, there were three factors that, according to La Primaudaye, contributed to human action: habit, affection, and power. Habit pushed for the repetition of established behaviors, while affection and the motions of the heart introduced the capacity for sin. There was considerable overlap between these two categories, since "when the actions of an affection are grown to be habits, then are they called either virtues or vices, according as they are well or ill done" (*TFA*, 2.42). In general, the affections pushed the heart toward pleasure. However, the type of behavior that an individual found pleasurable differed from person to person, as determined by their powers, or disposition. La Primaudaye wrote that "concerning powers, they come to us by nature, and are effective principles of all actions both good & bad, yea by them we know in children, during their young years, the signs and tokens of some virtue or vice, that will reign most in them afterwards, which we commonly call, Inclination or Disposition" (*TFA*, 2.68). The basis for understanding this category of powers is humoral theory, on which the concept of inclination or disposition is based.

The humoral system, the dominant medical theory throughout the early modern period, was based on the belief that the body contained four humors—blood, phlegm, black bile, and yellow bile—which existed in a perfect balance unique to the individual. Humoral theory was holistic, and the humors corresponded with other qualities (hot, cold, wet, dry), seasons (spring, summer, autumn, winter), elements (earth, wind, air, fire), and many more, effectively blurring the lines between the body, the mind, and the physical world. It was understood that a person's humoral state dictated not just the physical condition of their body but also their temperament: whether sanguine, melancholic, phlegmatic, or choleric. Each temperament came with particular personality traits and corresponded with specific affections and behaviors. To give specific examples: "When there is excess of the phlegmatic humour in men, their natures are commonly slothful, they shun labour and give themselves to bodily pleasures. . . . And if there be an excess of choleric humour, their natures are easily provoked and stirred up to wrath" (*TFA*, 2.68). If the sanguine "complexion be not moderated and well guided, it will easily pass measure in every affection, so that it will fall into foolish and unlawful loves, into excessive and unmeasurable joys, and into prodigality instead of following liberality" (*TFA*, 2.41).

The humors "may be seeds and provocations, either to virtues or to vices, according to that correspondence which is between the bodies & the soul, and the temperature of the one with the affections of the other" (*TFA*, 2.41). This correspondence could be influenced by a huge range of internal and external variables including "the composition, complexion and disposition of mans body, whether it be sound, or whether it be sick. Also the Age, strength, or weakness, the perfection or imperfection thereof, common custom, . . . time and place" (*TFA*, 2.29). While there were an almost unlimited number of variables that could affect disposition and inclination, I want to discuss three in this article: consumption, age, and morality.

One striking example of the variability of disposition is the effect of consumption. Unsurprisingly, writers made connections between intoxicating substances and behavioral changes; La Primaudaye writes that an excess of wine "makes men quarrellers, wranglers, rash, incensed, furious, dice-players, adulterers, homicides, in a word addicted to all vice, and dissolution" (*TFA*, 3.80). However, animal-derived products could also alter behavior because disposition could be passed on through consumption. As *Aristotle's Manual of Choice Secrets*—a book on midwifery—explains: "Take this for a Rule, That whatever any Creature is addicted unto, they stir up the same quality in the Man or Woman that Eats them. And therefore Partridges, Quails, Sparrows, &c. being extremely addicted to Venery, work the same effect in those Men and Women that Eat them."[16] Similarly, an anonymous 1677 work explained that the emperor Tiberius was "excessively addicted" to drinking "by reason of his Nurse who suckled him; who her self was an excessive and unmeasurable drinker."[17] Disposition could be altered by the consumption of both intoxicants and animal products, creating short- and long-term changes in human behavior.

Another notable factor in determining disposition was age, and La Primaudaye describes the implications of this in detail. There were six distinct ages—infancy, childhood, youth, adolescence, virility, and old age—and in each, inclination and capacity for pleasure differed. In adolescence, La Primaudaye writes, "the inclination to pleasures, and the eschewing of labour, which are natural in man, commonly begin then to assault him with such violence, that if young men be not well followed, they quickly turn to vice" (*TFA*, 1.52). Adolescents were considered particularly susceptible to corporeal pleasures and could become "like beasts [that] seek for nothing but to satisfy their lustful desires" (*TFA*, 1.52). In contrast, during old age "the natural power and strength of man begins to decline & fade away," but "the desire of contemplation and knowledge increases as much as the pleasures of their body decrease" (*TFA*, 1.52). Youthful addiction to pleasure and vice was a common trope, described in considerable detail in works like Thomas Gouge's *Young Man's Guide*. His chapters included titles such as "Sheweth the Vices Whereunto Young Men Are Addicted. One Is Rash and Hasty Anger," and "Of Drunkenness, Which Is Another Vice, Whereunto Young Men Are Addicted."[18] In contrast, biographies of famous men often comment on their youthful addiction to contemplative pursuits, indicating they had the strength and virtue to overcome the natural inclinations of their age. In Anthony Wood's book of famous people educated at Oxford, he often commented on the young age at which their addiction began: "JOHN RYCKS [was] much addicted in his Youth to Piety and Learning," and "JOHN HILSEY . . . [was] much addicted from his Childhood to Learning and Religion."[19] Marcus Manilius wrote his biographies of astronomers in a similar style, including such figures as "JOHANNES PIERIUS VALERIANUS . . . being but yet young and much addicted to Astronomical Studies" and "TYCHO BRAHE . . . even from his Childhood being addicted to Astronomical Studies."[20] Throughout early modern print there are strong associations between youth and excess, and age and contemplation, indicating a common trope that arguably carries through to the present day.

The final variable I want to discuss is moral status, a quality La Primaudaye considered innate and linked directly with human behavior. He wrote that the type of pleasure a person inclined toward was determined in part by their moral status; whether they were vile and base, prudent and wise, or somewhere in between. La Primaudaye sketched out a hierarchy of pleasures from the lowest bodily pleasure to the highest spiritual one. He began at the bottom with touch, "the basest & most abject of all," followed by taste—"a little more honest and less contemptible, and yet is it brutish enough"—followed by smell, hearing, and finally sight, "because the eyes are of the nature of the fire, which comes nearest to the celestial nature" (*TFA*, 2.47). Above corporeal pleasures were those of the fancy, "namely the getting and possessing of silver, of riches, of power, of honours, and of glory," and above those were the various pleasures of the soul: "Those that are proper to the spirit and mind, are purest and best of all among which that delight that is in contemplation is the chiefest" (*TFA*, 2.47). According to La Primaudaye, corporeal and spiritual addictions were mutually exclusive, and he noted that those "that are addicted to the service of their bellies . . . care nothing for the food of their minds." Conflict could occur between people with different addictions, since "such men as are addicted to these other more base and earthly pleasures, mock and deride them that condemn their delights, and make so great account of these spiritual and heavenly pleasures" (*TFA*, 2.48).

La Primaudaye noted another key difference between corporeal and spiritual pleasures. The pleasures of the body were wearisome and unsustainable, requiring long recovery periods. The glutton, drunkard, or wanton (lustful person) tired quickly, and could not sustain the pursuit of their pleasure for long periods, yet were also left unfulfilled, since corporeal pleasures "commonly bring with them more irksomeness & loathing then joy & pleasure: leaving many times behind them a long & shameful repentance" (*TFA*, 2.47). Once they had recovered from this weariness, they returned immediately to their addiction, since "for the doing whereof he needs no external aid, but only that all lets and impediments should be removed and taken out of the way" (*TFA*, 2.48). In contrast, since the mind is constantly active, "the spirit needs no space of time wherein to intermit his pleasures" and is continually occupied by the pursuit of its pleasure (*TFA*, 2.48). Since addictions of the fancy—ambition, covetousness, greed—do not weary the soul, "the more she hath, the more her delight increases, and becomes insatiable" (*TFA*, 2.48). This was even more true of the pleasures of reason, "because the spirit is not weary or tired, but is recreated and refreshed" (*TFA*, 2.48). As a result, the only way to end a bad addiction of the mind was to "so change the matters about which it is to be employed, that they be good and honest"—essentially, to replace one addiction with another (*TFA*, 2.48). On the other hand, a good addiction—since good addictions are always of the mind—was easy to maintain once it was established.

Humoral theory provides a framework for understanding differences in human behavior, and for linking those differences to a host of internal and external factors. Disposition—which was influenced by temperament, age, climate, diet, health, and more—determined both the types of affection someone was prone to and the types of behavior they were inclined toward. However, it is important to remember that an inclination toward a particular behavior did not necessarily result in an addiction. Following La Primaudaye's argument, to form an addiction, either a disposition must be accepted by the faculties of the mind (reason, understanding, and judgment), or—in the case of sinful addictions—it must generate an affection strong enough to overpower the mind. An illustration of this can be found in an anecdote told about the Greek philosopher Socrates. According to the story, recounted by Cicero, the physiognomist Zopyrus once accused Socrates of having a long list of vices, including addiction to women. Socrates's disciples mocked and ridiculed Zopyrus for his absurd claim until Socrates himself came to his defense, confessing that he was in fact naturally inclined to the vices listed by Zopyrus but did not act on those inclinations. Cicero writes of the incident that "it is possible that these defects may be due to natural causes; but their eradication and entire removal, recalling the man himself from the serious vices to which he was inclined, does not rest with natural causes, but with will, effort, training."[21]

Women

One aspect that is notably scarce in La Primaudaye's discussion of addiction is women. Although he regarded women as "flesh of the flesh of man, blood of his blood, and bone of his bones, even as it were his own body, and a second self," at certain points in the book La Primaudaye makes it clear that the inclinations and affections of women differed from those of men (*TFA*, 2.2). He writes that "women are commonly sooner driven into choler [anger, irritability] then men," that women "are by nature more changeable by will, and more frail in counsel," and that "this sex is frail, spiteful, and given to revenge" (*TFA*, 1.29, 45, 47).

So in what ways did women differ from men when it came to addiction? First, and somewhat surprisingly, given his other statements, La Primaudaye did not consider the souls of women to be inferior. He writes that "women (as Plato saith) have a soul as well as we, and as quick a spirit, yea oftentimes a more excellent spirit than we, we must not think them incapable of the goodly reasons of Philosophy, wherein many of them have gone beyond many Philosophers" (*TFA*, 1.47). While the quality of a woman's soul and spirit was equal to a man's, and she had the capacity for excellent reasoning, her will was more easily swayed by the will of others. "Generally the weaker that thing is, which discourses and doubts, the easier may a man put and add unto it, what he will," "and therefore youth is easier to be persuaded than old folks, sick than sound, women than men" (*TFA*, 2.8).

The weakness of the female will was a common trope in early modern writing. A 1555 work of erotic fiction by Oliver Oldwanton claimed to offer proof "that women are never so much addict or bent to their own will and opinion, but that by wisdom and good policy, they may easily be broken thereof."[22] Oldwanton not only considered the female will weak but also believed that this weakness made it easier for their addictions to be broken. However, the same weakness supposedly made women more susceptible to addictions in the first place. In a work translated in 1613 the French Catholic friar Sébastien Michaelis wrote that "this sex hath this property, to be exceedingly addicted unto something, be it good, or be it bad: so that if a woman addict her self to well doing, she is more servant in it then a man; and so contrariwise, if she abandon her self to evil, she is more obstinate to persist in the same then a man is."[23] As Michaelis explains, this was the reason why "sober and virtuous women . . . are they that cast the first stones against Sorcerers, and cry louder then the rest to have them burnt: so contrariwise, Sorceresses are more obstinate, and more addicted unto witchcrafts, and do with less remorse of conscience plunge themselves into the most execrable facts that may be, than men."[24]

It is clear that La Primaudaye and many of his contemporaries regarded women as more susceptible to addiction, as tending to form stronger addictions, but also as being more likely to break their addictions. There is a contradiction here, since addictions are habitual behaviors that become more entrenched over time; how can a woman's will be at once too weak to resist repeatedly choosing affection over reason, yet also strong enough to break a long-established addiction on a whim? These contradictions are not resolved within La Primaudaye's work, and it seems likely that his discussions on the topic of female addiction were written not with any thought to consistency but based on an ideological belief in an innate male right to supremacy.

This conclusion is borne out by La Primaudaye's further writing on the topic of female behavior and subservience. In his description of the male spirit La Primaudaye explained that the will takes input from both the mind—reason and understanding—and the heart—the affections. Ideally (in men), while the affections and natural inclinations had their say, both should ultimately be governed by reason, which in turn guided the will. Women had all these faculties as well; they had the capacity for reason, which informed their will, and they had their own inclinations and affections, being "given to revenge" and "sooner driven into choler." However, La Primaudaye argued that women should ignore their own reason and affections and instead exclusively follow those of their husbands. He writes that "a woman should rule and govern her self in all things, by the wisdom and good pleasure of her husband; because he is her head, and she is his body" and that "a wife must have no proper and peculiar passion or affection to her self, but must be partaker of the pastimes, affairs, thoughts and laughters of her husband" (*TFA*, 4.13, 1.48). This subservience of the female will to the male was not something dictated by reduced capacity; even when a woman was more capable than her husband, she should submit her will to his because that was his right. La Primaudaye writes, "For although there may be diverse women found, that are wiser then some men . . . [yet they must] in all their actions give their husbands that preeminence of superiority which of right belonged unto them" (*TFA*, 4.13). Where a woman's own inclinations contrasted with those of her husband, according to La Primaudaye, she should abandon her own passions and instead adopt the inclinations, pleasures, habits, and addictions of her husband.

Conclusions

In La Primaudaye's work addiction can be understood as an action resulting from habit—individuals addict themselves to forms of habitual behaviors, both positive and negative. A positive addiction is a natural process, part of the normal functioning of a virtuous mind; the affections, reason, understanding, and disposition combine to repeatedly propose a positive action, and the will repeatedly chooses to follow that action. It is notable that the most frequent addiction referred to in early modern English print is not drunkenness or vice but the virtuous pursuit of study, suggesting writers of the time saw strong associations between addiction and positive behaviors.[25] A negative addiction occurs when the affections overwhelm the other faculties, misleading the will into choosing the pursuit of vice. In La Primaudaye's work everyone has addictions, and all behaviors are potentially addictive.

In the introduction I claimed that La Primaudaye's writing can be regarded as representative of a particular section of European intellectual culture, and indeed many of the ideas discussed in this article are echoed throughout the work of his contemporaries. In his 1682 *Warning to Drunkards* Owen Stockton emphasized the relationship between addiction and habit, writing that "a drunkard is one that is given, addicted, accustomed to the sin of drunkenness, one that is frequently drunk. Noah was once overtaken with drunkenness, but he was no drunkard, he was not addicted and accustomed to this sin."[26] As with modern understandings of the concept, early modern addiction was something created through repetition.

In La Primaudaye's work the will is always a free agent—however much affections may have clouded its judgment—which chooses the pursuit of addiction, whether virtuous or sinful. Stockton echoes this argument, writing that "drunkenness is not a sin of infirmity, but a wilful and presumptuous sin."[27] Similarly, Jeremy Taylor writes that "every one that hath a vicious habit, chooses his sin cheerfully, acts it frequently, is ready to do it in every opportunity, and at the call of every temptation . . . the habit is not contracted, nor can it remain but by our being willing to sin."[28] Like La Primaudaye, Taylor critiqued the "extremely dangerous and destructive" false doctrine of the Roman schools, which believed that a habit "is so natural, that it is no way voluntary . . . and therefore it can have in it no blame."[29] Yet despite this view of free will, La Primaudaye and his contemporaries agreed that the will could fall under increasing pressure as an addiction or habit grew in strength. As such, the language of constraint can often be found alongside discussions of addiction in early modern writing. Taylor wrote that God orders us to "be not enslaved to [sinful habit], under the power of it, of such a lost liberty that we cannot resist the temptation."[30] Owen Stockton, voicing the hypothetical objections of reluctant reformers, wrote, "But I have such inclinations to drinking, and have been so long addicted to this sin, and am so enslaved to it, that I think it is in vain to pray for help against it."[31]

Early modern writers recognized that individuals could feel enslaved by their own addictions and that this feeling was amplified the longer a habit existed. They also recognized how hard it could be to break an addiction. Stockton called addiction to drunkenness "an enticing, bewitching sin, which is very hardly left by those that are addicted to it," and Taylor wrote that the reforming drunkard "is daily tempted, and the temptation is strong, and his progression is slow; he marches upon sharp-pointed stones, where he was not used to go, and where he hath no pleasure."[32] However, while there remained an uneasy balance between the undoubted freedom of the will and the forces that acted on it, ultimately addiction only had the power to amplify and reiterate chosen behaviors, not to overthrow the will completely.

There are clear parallels between the issues discussed by La Primaudaye and debates about addiction today. The disease model of addiction, which frames addiction as an illness rather than a choice, effectively removes free will from the addict; it positions the addict as medically unwell rather than morally depraved. In recent years there has been a movement away from the disease model of addiction—in some circles at least—toward a model that assigns the addict a greater degree of choice. Gene Heyman argues that addiction is a choice, not an illness, and that being an addict means repeatedly and willingly making choices that are not in the addict's own best interests.[33] In an article titled "Addiction Is Not a Disease," the psychiatrist Tim Holden writes that "addiction is self-acquired" and argues that "calls to destigmatize addiction remove any sense of personal responsibility," resulting in "a steady erosion of individual responsibility and loss of any concept of personal blame for bad choices."[34] However, despite the apparent similarity of these debates, there are also fundamental differences in the underlying concept of addiction that it is important not to overlook. Too often historical accounts of addiction are framed in terms of *addicts* and *addictive* objects, when in fact this makes little sense in an early modern setting where every person is an addict and every behavior potentially addictive. As this article has shown, early modern addiction must be understood in the context of early modern concepts of the mind, which reveal that—in its proper state at least—addiction in early modern Europe was regarded by many not as a disease or a failure of the will, but as the normal output of a properly functioning human body.

JOSE CREE studies medical humanities at the University of Sheffield. Her thesis, "The Invention of Addiction in Early Modern England," examines the changing meanings of *addiction* across the early modern period, from the translation of classical ideas through to the emergence of a modern addiction model.

Acknowledgments

This article is adapted from the fourth chapter of my thesis, which was funded by the White Rose College of Arts and Humanities and is available at White Rose eTheses Online, etheses.whiterose.ac.uk/22933.

Notes

1   Erasmus, *Ye Dyaloge Called Funus*; Taverner, *The Principal Lawes Customes and Estatutes of England*.

2   The noun *addict* was first recorded in 1899 and the adjective *addictive* in 1891, according to the *Oxford English Dictionary*, 3rd ed., s.v. "addict," n.

3   Porter, "Drinking Man's Disease," 392; Levine, "Discovery of Addiction"; Warner, "'Resolv'd to Drink No More.'"

4   Willis, "*Doctor Faustus* and the Early Modern Language of Addiction."

5   Lemon, "Scholarly Addiction"; Lemon, *Addiction and Devotion in Early Modern England*.

6   Cree, "Protestant Evangelicals and Addiction in Early Modern English," 446.

7   See also Cook, *Alcohol, Addiction, and Christian Ethics*, which begins with biblical and classical forms of addiction (Augustine, Aquinas) and includes a section on early modern addiction.

8   Prescott, "Pierre de la Primaudaye's French Academy," 158; Jalobeanu, "Idolatry, Natural History, and Spiritual Medicine," 218–19.

9   Jalobeanu, "Idolatry, Natural History, and Spiritual Medicine," 218.

10   Jalobeanu, "Idolatry, Natural History, and Spiritual Medicine," 219–20.

11   Prescott, "Pierre de la Primaudaye's French Academy," 160.

12   Jalobeanu, "Francis Bacon's Natural History," 202.

13   Van Heertum, "Pierre de la Primaudaye," 316.

14   La Primaudaye, *The French Academie*, 2.35 (hereafter cited as *TFA*, followed by book and chapter numbers; the text is not paginated).

15   This claim is not uncontroversial, however. La Primaudaye notes that "we may see in many places of the Scripture, and in their writings and exhortations that follow the doctrine and style thereof, that the heart is often taken for the seat of the mind, of the understanding and of reason, as well as for the affections of the soul" (*TFA*, 2.36).

16   Aristotle [pseud.], *Aristotle's Manual of Choice Secrets*.

17   *Heraclitus Christianus*.

18   Gouge, *Young Man's Guide*.

19   Wood, *Exact History*.

20   Manilius, *Sphere of Marcus Manilius*.

21   Cicero, *De Fato*.

22   *Lyttle Treatyse*.

23   Michaelis, *Admirable History*.

24   Michaelis, *Admirable History*.

25   This is based on a collocation analysis of the EEBO-TCP corpus performed on CQPweb that found that *study* appeared as a collocate 322 times. The next in order of frequency are *pleasures* (191), *religion* (184), and *service* (164). For context, *drunkenness* appears as a collocate just 78 times.

26   Stockton, *Warning to Drunkards*.

27   Taylor, *Vnum necessarium*; Stockton, *Warning to Drunkards*.

28   Taylor, *Vnum necessarium*.

29   Taylor, *Vnum necessarium*.

30   Taylor, *Vnum necessarium*.

31   Stockton, *Warning to Drunkards*.

32   Taylor, *Vnum necessarium*.

33   Heyman, *Addiction*.

34   Holden, "Addiction Is Not a Disease."

Works Cited

Aristotle [pseud.]. *Aristotle's Manual of Choice Secrets, Shewing the Whole Mystery of Generation*, translated by J. P. London, 1699. Early English Books Online, Text Creation Partnership, Phase II. name.umdl.umich.edu/A25811.0001 .001 (accessed August 31, 2018).

Cicero, Marcus Tullius. *De Fato*, translated by H. Rackham. Information Philosopher. www .informationphilosopher.com/solutions /philosophers/cicero/de_fato_english.html#11 (accessed August 31, 2018).

Cook, Christopher C. H. *Alcohol, Addiction, and Christian Ethics*. Cambridge: Cambridge University Press, 2006.

Cree, Jose Murgatroyd. "Protestant Evangelicals and Addiction in Early Modern English." *Renaissance Studies* 32, no. 2 (2018): 446–62.

Erasmus, Desiderius. *Ye Dyaloge Called Funus*. London, 1534. Early English Books Online, Text Creation Partnership, Phase I. name .umdl.umich.edu/A00329.0001.001 (accessed June 24, 2021).

Gouge, Thomas. *The Young Man's Guide through the Wilderness of This World to the Heavenly Canaan Shewing Him How to Carry Himself Christian-Like in the Whole Course of His Life*. London, 1676. Early English Books Online, Text Creation Partnership, Phase I. name.umdl.umich.edu /A41668.0001.001 (accessed August 31, 2018).

Heyman, Gene. *Addiction: A Disorder of Choice*. Cambridge, MA: Harvard University Press, 2009.

Holden, Tim. "Addiction Is Not a Disease." *Canadian Medical Association Journal* 184, no. 6 (2012): 679.

Jalobeanu, Dana. "Francis Bacon's Natural History and the Senecan Natural Histories of Early Modern Europe." *Early Science and Medicine* 17, no. 1–2 (2012): 197–229.

Jalobeanu, Dana. "Idolatry, Natural History, and Spiritual Medicine: Francis Bacon and the Neo-Stoic Protestantism of the Late Sixteenth Century." *Perspectives on Science* 20, no. 2 (2012): 207–26.

La Primaudaye, Pierre de. *The French Academie Fully Discoursed and Finished in Foure Bookes*, translated by Thomas Bowes, R. Dolman, and William Phillip. London, 1618. Early English Books Online, Text Creation Partnership, Phase I. name.umdl.umich.edu/A05105.0001 .001 (accessed August 31, 2018).

Lemon, Rebecca. *Addiction and Devotion in Early Modern England*. Philadelphia: University of Pennsylvania Press, 2018.

Lemon, Rebecca. "Scholarly Addiction: *Doctor Faustus* and the Drama of Devotion." *Renaissance Quarterly* 69, no. 3 (2016): 865–98.

Levine, Harry G. "The Discovery of Addiction: Changing Concepts of Habitual Drunkenness in America." *Journal of Studies on Alcohol* 39, no. 1 (1978): 143–74.

A Lyttle Treatyse Called the Image of Idlenesse Conteynynge Certeyne Matters Moued betwene Walter Wedlocke and Bawdin Bacheler, translated by Oliver Oldwanton. London, 1555. Early English Books Online, Text Creation Partnership, Phase II. name.umdl.umich.edu /A14893.0001.001 (accessed August 31, 2018).

Manilius, Marcus. *The Sphere of Marcus Manilius Made an English Poem with Annotations and an Astronomical Appendix*, translated by Edward Sherburne. London, 1675. Early English Books Online, Text Creation Partnership, Phase I. name.umdl.umich.edu/A51768.0001.001 (accessed August 31, 2018).

Michaelis, Sébastien. *The Admirable History of the Posession and Conuersion of a Penitent Woman*, translated by W. B. London, 1613. Early English Books Online, Text Creation Partnership, Phase I. name.umdl.umich.edu/A07467.0001 .001 (accessed August 31, 2018).

Porter, Roy. "The Drinking Man's Disease: The 'Pre-history' of Alcoholism in Georgian Britain." *British Journal of Addiction* 80, no. 4 (1985): 385–96.

Prescott, Anne Lake. "Pierre de la Primaudaye's French Academy: Growing Encyclopaedic." In *The Renaissance Computer: Knowledge Technology in the First Age of Print*, edited by Neil Rhodes and Jonathan Sawday, 155–66. London: Routledge, 2000.

Stockton, Owen. *A Warning to Drunkards Delivered in Several Sermons to a Congregation in Colchester*. London, 1682. Early English Books Online, Text Creation Partnership, Phase II. name .umdl.umich.edu/A61655.0001.001 (accessed August 31, 2018).

Taverner, Richard. *The Principal Lawes Customes and Estatutes of England Which Be at This Present Day in vre*. London, 1640. Early English Books Online, Text Creation Partnership, Phase I. name.umdl.umich.edu/A22779.0001.001 (accessed August 31, 2018).

Taylor, Jeremy. *Vnum necessarium. Or, The Doctrine and Practice of Repentance. Describing the Necessities and Measures of a Strict, a Holy, and a Christian Life*. London, 1655. Early English Books Online, Text Creation Partnership, Phase II. name.umdl.umich.edu/A95515.0001 .001 (accessed August 31, 2018).

Van Heertum, Cis. "Pierre de la Primaudaye's *The French Academie*: The Source Text for *Houwelycschen Staet ende Houwelycschen Voorwaerde* (1644)." *Quaerendo* 19, no. 4 (1989): 314–18.

Decades later a British colonial administrator named William Alexander Pickering remembered the *Nerbudda* incident as the first time that Taiwan had occupied the minds of Britons since an infamous event over a century earlier. This, Pickering wrote, was when London had been visited by "an impostor named George Psalmanazar, who professed to be a Japanese convert from the island [of Taiwan], and who published in Latin a wonderful and fictitious account of its model government, flourishing towns, and civilised population."[3] Although he linked the two events, Pickering overlooked the key point of connection between them. For Psalmanazar's imposture—his elaborate performance as a Taiwanese aristocrat, which took place between the years 1703 and 1712—was, no less than the *Nerbudda* incident, sustained under the influence of opium.

This essay explores Psalmanazar's life, writing, and reception in an effort to understand what Rebecca Lemon has called the "paradox of addiction" in early modern Europe: addiction's status as "a simultaneously devotional and compulsive practice" that was "lauded and condemned" depending on context.[4] Two elements of Psalmanazar's life highlight this paradox while also pointing to a key inflection point in the second half of the eighteenth century, as addiction evolved into a concept centered on compulsive substance use while slowly shedding its older, more "positive" associations with devotion and piety.[5]

First, though he was a fake world traveler, Psalmanazar was a genuine cosmopolitan: he was born in southern Europe; traveled through Italy, Germany, and the Low Countries; and settled in a diverse area of East London, where he developed relationships with everyone from a young Samuel Johnson to communities of Portuguese and Moroccan Jews. Both his performance as an Asian sojourner in continental Europe and this later life as a multilingual scholar in a globalizing London relied on Psalmanazar's unusually fluid identity. Stripped of the normal accoutrements of personhood, the man known as Psalmanazar (his true name and nationality were never revealed) became a kind of vessel, a living Russian doll in which were nested a succession of different identities—and addictions. Psalmanazar thus exemplifies the "confused cosmopolitanism" of the concept of addiction in eighteenth-century Europe—an emerging association of addiction with foreign lands, racialized bodies, and exotic customs.[6]

Second, Psalmanazar was a supposed reformed addict who, in fact, continued to use his drug of choice on a daily basis. He claimed to have traded one set of early modern addictions (the vices typical of all humans, who, he wrote, were "by Nature . . . wholly addicted to Sensible Things and Pleasures") for an "addiction" to religious study.[7] Yet, by his own admission, the opiate dependence of Psalmanazar's youth continued throughout his life's second phase as a sober religious scholar. What had changed was the *mode* in which Psalmanazar's drug of choice was used: no longer in the service of "vanity" or "extravagance" but instead in the service of pious scholarship and Enlightenment principles of moderation.

In her book *Performing China*, Chi-ming Yang identifies two "epistemological crises . . . at the heart" of Psalmanazar's life as an impostor—a life that included meeting with Isaac Newton and other members of the Royal Society of London and being credited by Jonathan Swift as an inspiration for *A Modest Proposal*.[8] One of these crises, Yang writes, involved "the performance of virtue as a means of indexing commercial relations between Europe and Asia."[9] In other words, Psalmanazar exploited Britons' fear of and fascination with Asian societies as reputed sources of both enormous wealth and moral depravity. Another was Psalmanazar's canny attention to the religious anxieties of his era. By positioning himself as a convert to Anglicanism who had fled Taiwan due to the corrupt influence of missionaries from the Society of Jesus, Psalmanazar opened another front in an increasingly paranoid fear of Jesuit conspiracies among a key subset of London's elite—including his first sponsor, the bishop of London.[10]

Psalmanazar's performances of addiction mark a third epistemological crisis. In tracing his changing addictions, we can identify a moment when the "paradoxical" early modern model of addiction began to transform into something closer to the "modern addictions" of the nineteenth and twentieth centuries. Part of what makes Psalmanazar so distinctive and important in this regard is that his addictions were not just memorialized in writing but *publicly performed*. The most salient fact about Psalmanazar's life, after all, was that he was a brilliant actor playing a series of roles. Psalmanazar thus literally *embodied* the changing personae of the addict over a period of six decades, from 1703 to 1763.

Importantly, however, Psalmanazar's influence continued after his own final curtain call. Although little more than a historical footnote today, Psalmanazar was well known in the eighteenth and nineteenth centuries. His two major published works appeared sixty years apart. His *Historical and Geographical Description of Formosa* (1704) claimed to offer an authentic ethnographic account of Formosan society but was a complete fabrication. In contrast, Psalmanazar's posthumous *Memoirs* (1764) was a vivid confession of his deceit and a redemptive account of his religious rebirth as a pious scholar. The *Memoirs* appeared a year after his death, with publication directions specified in his will ("I desire it may be sold to the highest bidder . . . [and] in the plain and undisguised manner in which I have written it").

In this second phase of his life, Psalmanazar described himself as "an obscure Layman, who had spent a great Part of his latter Years in Privacy and Retirement, and who . . . was in no way addicted or bigotted to either Party or Opinion."[11] But despite his claims to obscurity, it was *this* persona that would secure his lasting reputation throughout the following decades. Summaries of Psalmanazar's life (often fixating on his friendship with Samuel Johnson, who supposedly called him "the best man he had ever known") appeared in dozens of publications in at least five languages during the nineteenth century.[12] These included everything from dictionary entries and tourist guidebooks to influential publications such as *Curiosities of Literature* (1807), a widely read essay collection by Isaac D'Israeli, friend of Lord Byron and father of the future prime minister Benjamin D'Israeli.[13] Psalmanazar was of particular fascination to Joseph Cottle, the publisher of Samuel Taylor Coleridge and Robert Southey and a personal friend of Thomas De Quincey (1785–1859), who, as the author of *Confessions of an English Opium-Eater*, played a key role in shaping perceptions of addiction in the nineteenth-century English-speaking world.[14] Psalmanazar's deeply ambiguous relationship with both addiction and his own identity, I propose in the final section of this essay, helps elucidate the origin of one of the most influential genres of modern confessional writing: the addiction and recovery memoir.

Cosmopolitan Addictions

Psalmanazar's posthumous autobiography, *Memoirs of ****: Commonly Known by the Name of George Psalmanazar, a Reputed Native of Formosa* (1764), is self-indulgent and sprawling, describing everything from his struggles with "an inveterate itch" to his attempts to find work as a painter of ornamental fans.[15] Yet it is silent about the basic facts of his life. Even in death, Psalmanazar refused to reveal his real name, his age, or his country of birth. All the reader learns is that he started out as a teenage runaway from a provincial city in a Catholic country in "the southern parts" of Europe (*M*, 70).

After a stint at a Jesuit academy, the young Psalmanazar (presumably during the late 1690s) set off for Rome and became dependent on the alms of travelers. He noticed that when he claimed to be a pilgrim from faraway Ireland, his fellow travelers looked more kindly on him. This short-lived stint as an Irish Catholic ended when Psalmanazar encountered an *actual* Irish Catholic, forcing him to adopt an identity less likely to be revealed as false. He began to claim that he was a Japanese convert to Catholicism and, eventually, that he had been born and raised on Formosa (Taiwan), an island that supposedly belonged to the emperor of Japan.

The choice of Taiwan proved a canny one. For the island—though nominally under the control of China's Qing Dynasty by the time Psalmanazar published his *Description of Formosa* (1704)—was a place that was easy to create fictions about. Earlier in the seventeenth century, the Dutch had established a base of operations centered at Fort Zeelandia. But the conquest of key ports by Zheng Chenggong (known to Europeans as Koxinga), a powerful Ming Dynasty loyalist fleeing the Qing conquest of mainland China, effectively cut off European contact with the island in 1662.[16] For the Kangxi emperor of China, the great enemy of Koxinga, Taiwan was a "barbaric, distant island, unworthy of obedience," and a "place beyond the sea . . . no bigger than a ball of mud."[17] Even after Koxinga and the Southern Ming met their final defeat by the Qing (Taiwan was formally annexed into the Qing Empire in May 1684), the island remained almost entirely cut off from European trade and peripheral to Qing interests.[18] It would remain so, in large part, until the time of the Opium Wars.

Within this vacuum Psalmanazar was free to create a patchwork of proto-Orientalist fables based on travel accounts from Japan, China, the Indian Ocean, and even Mesoamerica, with some apparent borrowings from Thomas More's *Utopia* thrown in as well. A recurring feature of these accounts was the belief that the societies of "the Indies" were "addicted to idolatry" and other vices, from wanton sexuality to narcotic drugs.[19] In seventeenth-century England the concept of an "addiction" to idols or idolatry seems to have been most frequently applied either to Catholics or to Old Testament exegesis.[20] But an increasing number of texts also applied the concept of addiction to the societies of Asia, summarizing the outlandish accounts of Dutch and Portuguese merchants like Engelbert Kaempfer and Jesuit missionaries such as Luís Frois and Matteo Ricci.[21] By the time Thomas Dyche's *New English Dictionary* appeared, in 1735, the shift in the connotations of "addiction" had become obvious. Out of nineteen appearances of the word *addicted* or *addict* in Dyche's *Dictionary*, nearly 40 percent (seven) refer to supposed addiction to superstition and idolatry among what Dyche calls "the Eastern nations," ranging from Java and Pegu to Persia and Turkey.[22]

Psalmanazar's account of Formosans drew deeply from these accounts. He described a society that was utopian in some respects, with a well-run state and inhabitants possessing "a sharp natural wit" and remarkable skill in languages (after all, if he was going to portray himself as a Formosan scholar worthy of patronage, it helped his case to make his Formosans highly intelligent). But it was also one unrestricted by European conventions of morality. In his detailed discussion of Formosan religious practice, which reads like an early modern Protestant fever dream of Catholic excess, Psalmanazar described devious "Priests . . . who so explain all sorts of Omens, that they can never be convicted of Lying in what they Say: For either they pretend that their God is well-pleas'd . . . or that in the same Instant when they saw such an Omen the Soul of some of his Relations was Transform'd into a Star," and the like.[23] He described a notable Formosan who was "much Addicted to this kind of Superstition," and who was condemned to death as a result of his attempt to outsmart these sinister priests.[24]

Formosans also engaged in human sacrifice to their "Idols," Psalmanazar claimed, and offered "Foreigners" access to "Virgins or Whores, to be made use of at their Pleasure, with Impunity."[25] Psalmanazar noted that "Parents never beat" Formosan children, even to "deter them from the Vices to which they are addicted."[26] The use of exotic intoxicants even blended with cannibalism: at funerals, he claimed, "the Friends of the Deceas'd flock together, and bring with 'em Store of Man's Flesh, and several intoxicating Liquors."[27]

"His Darling Opium"

In Psalmanazar's telling, then, the Formosans joined the other peoples of Asia as a society beset by troubling addictions. When it came time to *perform* this Formosan identity, however, Psalmanazar faced a problem. He was, after all, positioning himself as a *reformed* heathen, newly converted to the Anglican faith.[28] Therefore he could not embody the signature addictions to idolatry, superstition, or cannibalism that European audiences had come to expect of a man from the far eastern edge of the known world.

In their place Psalmanazar substituted another emerging stereotype of Asians: addiction to opium. During the early modern period a profound shift took place in how Europeans thought and wrote about mind-altering drugs.[29] Many such substances, from hemlock to hellebore to opium, had long-standing traditions of use attested in both classical authorities like Pliny and herbal medical practices of unlicensed healers. Yet, beginning in the final decades of the sixteenth century, it became increasingly common to associate mind-altering drugs with foreign lands, especially the lands of "the Indies" or "the Turks."[30] Tobacco was a catalyst for this "exotification" of drugs.[31] As has been well documented by historians and literary scholars, tobacco remained closely associated among sixteenth-century Europeans with what Peter Mancall summarized as "exotic, savage, and demonic forces," despite or perhaps even because of its rapid rise to popularity.[32]

It is striking, however, that a substance that appears to be native to western and central Europe, with a record of use in Europe dating back to the Neolithic, would join tobacco as an iconic drug of "the Indies." This was opium (the latex of

Papaver somniferum) along with the drugs derived from it, known since the fifteenth century as "opiates." As Francis Bacon put it, tobacco had "in our age . . . immoderately grown into use," because "it affects men with a secret kind of delight, insomuch that they who have once inured themselves unto it can hardly afterwards leave it." Yet despite its self-evident novelty, tobacco was for Bacon *not* an entirely new class of drug. Instead, Bacon grouped it together with what he called "simple Opiates." After all, Bacon reasoned, tobacco's bewitching, compulsive quality "troubles the Head, as Opiates do." Indeed, Bacon speculated that yet another new import from the Indies, the "Herb . . . of the Turks . . . which they call *Caphe* [coffee]," must be "of the same nature with *Opiates*," since it was said to enlarge the Turks' "Courage" and "Wit" but, when taken in too large doses, would, like opium and tobacco, "disturb the mind."[33]

For European medical experts of Bacon's generation and beyond, opium was a strange hybrid of ancient and modern, domestic and foreign. True, it had been used continuously since the time of the ancient Greeks. But it was widely believed that Asian medical traditions placed special emphasis on opiates and, moreover, that Asian bodies *processed* opiates in a distinctive fashion. As Bacon put it: "The *Greciani* [Greeks] attributed much, both for health and for prolongation of life, [to] Opiates, but the *Arabians* much more, insomuch that their *grand Medicines* (which they called the *gods Hands*) had *Opium* for their Basis and principal ingredient."[34] Bacon clearly had intimate experience with opiates, probably having used them himself (for instance, he mentioned the "exceeding strong" effects of "three grains" use).[35] But he was wary of what he believed to be the drug's strikingly different effects on Europe and Asian bodies.[36] "The Turks find Opium, even in a reasonable good quantity, harmless and comfortable," Bacon wrote, "insomuch that they take it before their Battel to excite courage: but to us, unless it be in a very small quantity, and with good Correctives, it is mortal."[37]

Subsequent authorities throughout the seventeenth century offered similar judgments. John Ray, for instance, noted that what he called "wild Poppy" was well known to classical authorities and was native to northern Alpine valleys.[38] But Ray emphasized that it was "the Turks, Persians, and other Oriental peoples" who "used it at present to regenerate the spirits" and make themselves "truly inebriated."[39]

In fact, opium was a plant native to Europe.[40] The story of how a European medicinal plant with a legacy of use stretching back several millennia was reconstituted as an emblematic product of Asia is a tangled one. But what is clear is that by the time Psalmanazar developed his persona, circa 1700, opium—especially *immoderate* and *habitual* opium use—had already been widely linked to Asia in medical and popular writings.[41] By this time the traditional poppy-derived medicines, such as poppy-water, syrup of poppy, and mithridate, had been joined by an enormous range of "branded" remedies. One list assembled by the London physician John Radcliffe (1730) described, among others: "Dr. Goddard's Hypnotick Extract; Paregorick Extract; Somniferous Liniment; Pacific Decoctions; Powder of Haly, both Venice and London Treacle; Lohoch of Poppy; Nepthent Opiate; Starkey's Pills; Liquid Laudanum with Quinces."[42] Cesare Zarotti, a Venetian physician, complained about this profusion of new opiate remedies as early as the 1650s. Above all, Zarotti was frustrated by the "stupid" notions that circulated about the effects of opiates. Was opium, as some said, used "in the Indies" to "excite venery" and create "cheerfulness of spirit"?[43] Or was it, "as so many authoritative Greeks" of the past claimed, a cold and "frigid" drug that did exactly the opposite? Or indeed, as other travelers of Zarotti's time had begun to assert, was opium a drug of war used by the soldiers of the Ottoman Empire to cultivate a fierce fighting spirit?[44]

In general, the effects of the opium poppy appear to have been widely known in seventeenth- and early eighteenth-century England. In a murder trial from 1695, a London man was found guilty of a "most cruel" crime that involved a man killing his wife with "Opium in a drinking Potion," which he had supposedly described to her simply as "something that should make her rest." In his defense, the man alleged "that it was not Opium, but that it was two Spoonfuls of Poppy-water." The jury found him guilty of murder by poisoning nonetheless: at least in the mind of the jury and court, it would appear, an "opiate" like poppy-water was not functionally different from opium itself. Both were capable of inducing death.[45]

Habitual opiate taking also began to appear as a legal defense in the early decades of the eighteenth century. In a 1711 criminal case involving a theft from an East India Company warehouse in London's docklands, the suspect attempted to establish that his crimes occurred when "he had been under an Indisposition of Mind." He did so by calling to the stand both a physician, Dr. Cromp, and an unnamed apothecary who testified about the suspect's opium dependence. The number of "Drops of Opium he took when he was not well," it was reported, "might do him an Injury" and was "more than he would have him or any other person take." The jury once again declared the suspect's guilt.[46] In a 1727 trial of a man accused of highway robbery, by contrast, the suspect's use of opium was mentioned in the context of what the court recorder called, echoing the language of Psalmanazar, "Extravagancies" and "extravagant Expressions." The jury, in this case, was persuaded that the suspect was not in his right mind and therefore could not be declared guilty.[47]

Meanwhile, medical writers were still debating what they thought was a starkly different effect on Asian versus European bodies that had been noted decades earlier by Francis Bacon and Garcia de Orta. In 1696 the London physician Gideon Harvey offered up one variant on this climactic theory of opium's effects in his description of what he called "half Venoms, or demi-poisons." These, Harvey wrote, "are such as vehemently disturb the brain and heart . . . such are Mandrake, Henbane, Hemlock, Datura Seeds, which latter are only energic and effectual in the Indies, and not in other Climats, as Opium is a demi-poison here, being taken in a small Dose, and not in Turky, though in a greater doth become a whole poison."[48]

In his *Memoirs* Psalmanazar noted that his most important guidebook for his use of opium had been John Jones's *Mysteries of Opium Reveal'd* (1701). Jones offered a highly positive account of opium that portrayed a drug used widely, openly, and with substantial benefit to health and "industry."[49] It caused "a most agreeable, pleasant and charming Sensation," which was "gentle" and "sweet."[50] Indeed, the drug was so gentle, Jones claimed, that it could be used as a kind of morning stimulant, "if the Person keeps himself in Action, Discourse or Business." For Jones, the drug was indeed a spur of "Alacrity, and Expediteness in Dispatching and Managing of Business."[51]

Jones was also adamant that opium was "exciting to Venery," even making the bizarre speculation that "all Animal Seed, especially of the more Salaceous Creatures, is an Opiate in some degree" due to their supposed properties as an aphrodisiac and "Hypnotick."[52] Yet, Jones admitted, most were ignorant of opium's supposedly aphrodisiac properties "in these Western Parts of the World."[53] Ray's account of opium stated the matter more plainly. Opium, he wrote, was used by the Chinese, Persians, and Indians "to excite them to venery" such that they could "make offerings to Venus throughout an entire night."[54] Summarizing a widespread medical consensus, Ray added: "On account of their diversity of temperaments," opium "stimulates venerey" *exclusively* among "peoples of the East." By contrast, Ray wrote, "among those of the Western, or Northern countries, it curbs the same" and should be used only in moderation.[55]

As Susan Stewart has noted, Psalmanazar's "hyperbolic intensity" in parts of his *Description of Formosa* (such as his excited account of Formosan child sacrifice) was weighed against his need to make the account plausible: "a balance between the novel and the comprehensible."[56] Opium happened to fall into precisely this space between novelty and familiarity. The drug was familiar enough to his audience yet also a distinctive marker of foreignness, specifically of Asian identity, when used in what Psalmanazar called an "extravagant," sexualized, and generally "immoderate" fashion.

By demonstrating his prodigious use of opium alongside his sexual "gallantry," therefore, Psalmanazar was not just adding another picturesque detail to his persona. He was, in a sense, *pharmacologically performing* the truthfulness of his claims. If high doses of opium were fatal to Europeans, as many medical experts claimed, then Psalmanazar's enormous dosages would help prove that he *wasn't* European. This helps explain a curious fact of Psalmanazar's attempts to wean himself off his addiction, described in greater detail below: even as he decreased his dosage, Psalmanazar admitted, he felt compelled to add a substitute in the form of a bitter liquid so that it would seem to onlookers that his opiate use remained sky-high.

In the final decades of his life, however, Psalmanazar believed that he had found a way to "tame" this immoderate impulse through the same methods that had led him to God: an obsessive devotion to study, especially of religious texts. Psalmanazar studied himself out of addiction to "extravagance"—but also into a *new* addiction to studying itself. Along the way, he continued to habitually use opiates. Yet this use, too, became reframed as an aid to a life of pious scholarship, not as an idol to vanity.

Spiritual Addictions

The specter of childhood sexual abuse runs through Psalmanazar's *Memoirs*, from the unnamed evils committed by his onetime mentor, Mr. Innes, to his enormous and never fully explained sense of shame. Psalmanazar writes of his early teenage years as an itinerant traveler in Europe: "Thus did I find my affairs grow from bad to worse . . . and glad would I have been to have returned home to my mother; but the thought of my present condition would not permit me to think on it, and perhaps, I could have preferred any death to so great a mortification as it would have been both to her and me" (*M*, 150).

The closest Psalmanazar comes to directly confronting the sexual danger he lived under when "very young" was to mention the "procuresses, who wander about the streets . . . and pick up all the likely fellows they meet with, in order to make a lewd trade of them" (*M*, 151). Psalmanazar admitted to having "now and then been invited and led by them in a seeming hospitable manner, to some charitable ladies to receive, as was pretended, some token of their generosity" but in reality to perform sexual favors. Psalmanazar insisted that an "itch" he suffered from protected him from "criminal commerce with any of the sex," although he admitted that "I have reason to believe I should easily have yielded at any hazard" (*M*, 151). Later, when working as a servant for the owner of a "grand coffee-house" in Aix-la-Chapelle, Psalmanazar again skits along the edge of admitting to some form of sexual abuse, writing that his master sometimes sent him to bring "cooling liquors" to gatherings of the "beau monde." These nearly had "fatal consequences to me . . . which I shall forbear mentioning, merely for the ill impression it might be apt to make" (*M*, 155). Although he never describes exactly what "it" was, Psalmanazar blessed "the divine mercy which kept me back from it" and was thankful that "another man [his employer] kept, much older and fitter for the business," went in his stead (*M*, 156).

The entirety of the years between age twenty and thirty-two, Psalmanazar lamented, were "a sad blank" due to his "shameful, idle, and scandalous way of living . . . which would rather disgust than inform, or even divert a sober reader" (*M*, 252). Psalmanazar was referring here both to his "gallantry with the fair sex" and to "that vast quantity of laudanum I have been known to take for above these forty years" (*M*, 231, 56). But of course, Psalmanazar *did* describe the years he dismissed as a "blank." He did so not to "divert" his reader, he implied, but to offer up a cautionary tale. The young adulthood that Psalmanazar repeatedly described as one ruined by shame, vanity, and extravagance would, he seemed to hope, make up for his final years spent in contemplation of the redemption found in sober living and religious faith (*M*, 119, 231).

It was, in short, a memoir of addiction and recovery.

As Lemon has noted, the concept of addiction was often associated with religious devotion in sixteenth and early seventeenth-century English writings. Pious individuals were frequently said to be "addicted to prayer."[57] The poet John Taylor, in his 1628 ode to a "little black dogg . . . called Drunkard," wrote of his "Adiction to the Proverb, Love me and love my Hound."[58] Psalmanazar made his midlife renewal of faith into the key plot point of his own story. Like all things in life, it was an act done in a highly dramatized and performative way. Psalmanazar had, from the beginning of his entry into London in early 1704, portrayed himself as a convert to Anglicanism. To this day, one of the only surviving archival sources relating to Psalmanazar is in Lambeth Palace Library. Sandwiched amid lawsuits, property disputes, and correspondence in a miscellany of church paperwork are a handful of papers in which Psalmanazar has sketched, in crude ink drawings, a dozen or so of the stock figures of Formosan society, from the "Vice Roy" to the "Country bumpkin." The individual responsible for depositing them in the library was likely the bishop of London, who emerged as Psalmanazar's most important patron in London.

But as Yang puts it, Psalmanazar's initial religious conversion was a "performative work" that hinged on the paradoxical role of "denying worldly artifice while indulging in public spectacle." It was not until the 1730s, when Psalmanazar came across William Law's *Serious Call to a Devout and Holy Life* (1729), that he began to rebuild his identity around a newly acquired protoevangelical form of Christian faith. This included an intense interest in biblical studies that led him to master Hebrew. A biographer of Psalmanazar, Michael Keevak, has argued that the former impostor effectively traded in one exoticized identity for another, switching from a performance of Formosan identity to a new persona as an expert in Jewish history, well versed in Hebrew, who spent time amid London's close-knit Jewish community.[59] Keevak notes that according to the sole contemporary description of Psalmanazar's "singular" clothing style, he resembled "the famous wandering Jew."[60]

Psalmanazar's specific religious beliefs remain somewhat elusive. Yet what comes across very clearly in his *Memoirs* is his fervent desire to be thought of as a devoted scholar of religion whose identity, in a sense, was subsumed in the study of religious texts. In his "History of the Jews" (1747), an entry in *The Universal History*, a collaborative encyclopedia project in which he participated, Psalmanazar dwelled on the ethical benefits of an obsessive devotion to the uncorrupted text. He criticized the Samaritans as "guilty of the most flagrant forgery in corrupting their pentateuch in many places."[61] Conversely, he praised the prophet Ezra's devotion to preserving the authenticity of holy texts, writing that Ezra's followers were "wholly addicted to the reading, and thoroughly versed in sacred writings."[62]

Psalmanazar ultimately used his long-standing performance of addiction to legitimize what Yang has called his "performance of virtue" as well. Throughout his life Psalmanazar nurtured several simultaneous addictions. There were the opiates he used on a daily basis—but there was also his addiction to "devotion" and to "study." Psalmanazar's *Memoirs* make the point clearly: his opiate usage, Psalmanazar sought to explain, had been transformed into another helper on his path toward a devout and godly life.

Enlightenment Origins of the Addiction Memoir

In his movement from a man addicted to vices (opium, "vanity," "extravagance") to one addicted to study, Psalmanazar drew on a trope already very familiar from centuries of devotional literature. In many ways his journey exemplified the early modern meanings of addiction, in all their multiplicity. But it would be a mistake to see Psalmanazar's memoirs as simply following a template laid out beforehand by works that likely influenced their writing, such as Augustine's *Confessions*, Bunyan's *Pilgrim's Progress*, and Law's *Serious Call to a Devout and Holy Life*, which Psalmanazar specifically mentioned as an inspiration (*M*, 217). Psalmanazar's unflinching yet strangely complacent depiction of his own substance use and of his other addictions fundamentally changed the character of this confessional form.

There were, in short, elements of Psalmanazar's addictions that were strikingly new. Foremost among them was the highly public nature of his *Memoirs*. They were written with a significant amount of introspection about his emotional and intellectual life but also with an eye toward a large audience. It is a telling detail that Psalmanazar's will requested that he be buried in an anonymous common shroud, with no grave marker and no ceremony—but also demanded that his auto-biography be auctioned off to the highest bidder and published widely.[63]

In so doing, Psalmanazar helped lay down some important characteristics of an important modern literary genre: the addiction-and-recovery memoir. In his history of writers on drugs, *The Road to Excess*, Marcus Boon describes the addiction memoir as rising into prominence after World War I, following origins in prewar works such as Léon Daudet's *La lutte* (1907).[64] However, Thomas De Quincey is probably the figure most commonly associated with the origins of the addiction memoir, if not as a coherent genre, then at least as a kind of recurring reference point for later writers exploring similar themes.[65] As the author of *Confessions of an English Opium-Eater*, De Quincey also appears as a central figure in historical accounts of the perception of opiate addiction as a social problem. David Courtwright has argued that public accounts of habitual use of opiates rise into prominence in the 1830s, the decade immediately following De Quincey's *Confessions*.[66] Likewise, Carolyn Eastman links a new perception of opium as a "public health problem" in the 1820s to "the publication of Thomas de Quincey's addiction memoir."[67]

The wide readership and far-reaching impact of De Quincey's *Confessions* certainly justifies its central importance as a literary account of addiction. And De Quincey was likely the first English-language writer to elevate the introspective examination of compulsive drug use to the central focus of a published work. On the other hand, De Quincey's experience of addiction was in fact relatively common—not just in the England of the 1820s but in the literary world of the generation before his birth. Psalmanazar's memoir hints at a largely forgotten eighteenth-century London in which opiate use was widespread, though increasingly stigmatized.

Psalmanazar framed his initial return to opiate dependence in terms familiar from the contemporary recovery languages of "tapering" and "relapse." He describes how "Divine Providence was pleased to bless" him with a "contrary turn of mind," that made him "abhor all my former follies" (*M*, 61). Committed to "a thorough change," Psalmanazar began to slowly reduce his "usual dose," which he described as ten to twelve teaspoons of his own special preparation of laudanum, "morning and night, and very often more" (*M*, 59). Over the course of six months he slowly tapered this amount down by half an ounce per day. However, Psalmanazar admitted that his "foolish vanity" led him to *pretend* to continue using his enormous former dosage, "conceal[ing] my reduction" by adding "some other bitter tincture . . . to appear as still taking my usual quantity." It was a tacit admission of a central fact of Psalmanazar's opiate use: it was part of his performance of "singularity," a central element of his larger addiction to "extravagance" (*M*, 59–60).

Predictably, Psalmanazar began to find that even a reduction during half a year still led to what are today known as withdrawal symptoms. Psalmanazar calls them "affecting and discouraging inconveniences, such as a great lassitude and uneasiness of the mind, an indolence and incapacity for study, a dislike of every thing I read or wrote, to solitude and application" (*M*, 60). In effect, his effort to conquer his damaging addiction (to opiates) was sabotaging his parallel work to cultivate a "positive" addiction to study.

Psalmanazar's account would thus seem to be one of the earliest—and indeed perhaps *the* earliest—accounts of drug addiction that pays sustained attention to the interior life of the addict, including such tropes as relapses, psychological withdrawal symptoms, and recovery through faith. But did it have an influence on later accounts of addiction such as De Quincey's *Confessions of an English Opium-Eater?*

One thing is certain: Psalmanazar was a recurring figure in the periodicals of late eighteenth-century and nineteenth-century Britain and beyond. In the widely read *London Magazine* (the same journal that first serialized De Quincey's *Confessions*) Psalmanazar merited mention in both 1763 and 1764. The latter article summarized the more scandalous details from his confessions ("[to] living on raw flesh . . . he soon habituated himself").[68] In its June 1820 issue, just over a year before De Quincey's *Confessions* first appeared in its pages, the *London Magazine* again rehashed the lore relating to "this extraordinary man."[69] By 1849 Peter Cunningham's popular *Handbook of London* was directing tourists to, among other things, the former lodgings of George Psalmanazar on Ironmonger Row.[70] "Vanity was indeed the ruling passion of this singular man," mused one biographer later in the nineteenth century. "This is curiously illustrated in connection with his use of opium, to which he was so far addicted at one point as to consume enormous quantities." Now steeped in the outlook of the Victorian-era temperance movement, the author attacked Psalmanazar's "maintenance" regime of continued low-dose opiate dependence, calling it a "pernicious notion, which, perhaps, is without a parallel."[71]

De Quincey himself made direct reference to Psalmanazar, albeit in passing: he referred to "the somewhat harmless forgeries of Psalmanazer."[72] In the preface to *Confessions of an English Opium-Eater*, De Quincey also wrote that most confessions written in English to that date ("that is, spontaneous and extra-judicial confessions") had been created either by those suffering from the "defective sensibility of the French" or by "demireps, adventurers, or swindlers."[73] With this last category, De Quincey may, too, have had in mind Psalmanazar.

And then there are the less direct connections. In May 1818 a high De Quincey was "every night . . . transported into Asiatic scenes." De Quincey wrote, "A young Chinese seems to me an antediluvian man renewed." But he was also "terrified by the modes of life" there, by "mystic sublimity" and "the unimaginable horror . . . [of] these dreams of oriental imagery . . . tropical heat and vertical sunlights."[74] There were, of course, many precedents for De Quincey's "dreams of oriental imagery." But in its intensely hyperbolic contrasts and its focus on "antiquity," there is perhaps also something distinctly Psalmanazarian. During this period and the subsequent three years, as De Quincey was writing *Confessions of an English Opium-Eater*, he corresponded with and borrowed money from Joseph Cottle, who would later write extensively about Psalmanazar.[75] Cottle's long-standing interest in opiate addiction predated his relationship with De Quincey. He had long been deeply concerned by his friend Coleridge's "long, very long . . . habit" of taking up to a pint of laudanum per day. In this, Cottle wrote, Coleridge "exceed[ed] the quantity which Psalmanazar ever took, or any of the race of opium consumers on record."[76]

As the problems of "morphinism" and other forms of opiate addiction became pressing social concerns in the middle decades of the nineteenth century, Psalmanazar's story was increasingly portrayed less as a picaresque, proto-Romantic tale and more as a cautionary case study of drug dependence. An 1843 pharmacy textbook remembered Psalmanazar as a famous exemplar of opiate addiction, or what the author called "long-protracted indulgence." Four such figures were named: first, "a Turk of the name of Mustapha Shatar" who, when living in Smyrna, was said to consume 180 grains of opium a day. Second, De Quincey, who "is affirmed to have consumed, at one time, eight thousand drops of laudanum daily." Third, "the poet Coleridge." And finally, Psalmanazar.[77] A 1865 article in *Temple Bar* magazine keyed in on Psalmanazar's "account of the reasons which made him during forty years of his life an opium-eater . . . De Quincey's exploits in this line have generally been regarded as unparalleled; but if what is here stated be correct, then De Quincey but did what another had done before him."[78]

Conclusion

Psalmanazar helps us rethink addiction history in several important ways. First, his *Memoirs* offer an underappreciated reference point and forerunner for the genre of the addiction and recovery memoir before De Quincey. A striking aspect of this earlier vision of opium addiction was its grounding in what I have called the "confused cosmopolitanism" of eighteenth-century travel accounts and pharmacological texts. Psalmanazar's cosmopolitan and globally oriented account of addiction is, to my mind, more reflective of the lived reality of opiate addiction in his era than is the long-standing focus on addiction among a relatively small subset of the Romantic-era intelligentsia.[79] Yet among this group, too, Psalmanazar had a genuine influence. As we have seen, Psalmanazar was a recurring figure in late eighteenth and early nineteenth-century periodicals, was known to De Quincey and Southey, and seems to have exerted a real influence over the Romantic-era publisher and writer Joseph Cottle.

As Carl Fisher notes, there was an increasing polarization of discourse around addiction in the early nineteenth century. Crusaders for temperance framed compulsive substance use as plainly demonic, while, conversely, Romantic-influenced scientists and writers like Humphry Davy, Coleridge, and Southey began to think of compulsive substance use as potentially unlocking a mystical transcendence of the material realm.[80] Psalmanazar reveals a figure who was in many ways at the geographic and temporal heart of the Enlightenment—someone who knew Newton and Johnson and who directly influenced Swift and Buffon—and who struggled with this emerging polarization of the concept of addiction.[81] Opium addiction for Psalmanazar was both a pathway to the exotic Indies and a self-invented form of "maintenance," taken at home and used in solitary labors. It was both part of his downfall and part of his rebirth as a Christian scholar. Throughout it all, however, Psalmanazar thought about addiction in a fundamentally introspective, personal, spiritual framework. It may well be in this respect that his influence on the addiction memoir is most apparent.

The performances that comprised Psalmanazar's life dramatized a key moment in the formation of the modern concept of addiction. Much recent work on the history and science of addiction can be generalized as an effort to move away from reductive definitions of addiction that assume a simplistic binary of immoderate consumption versus total renunciation. On a surface level, Psalmanazar's self-portrayal as a reformed sinner reflecting on the evils of his past would seem to fit into just such a simplistic binary. But the truth is far more interesting: by Psalmanazar's telling, his *struggle* with opiate addiction ended, yet his *reliance* on opiates didn't. He simply developed a lifestyle, an outlook, and a method that, from his perspective, transformed a damaging compulsion into a benign habit. In this respect, Psalmanazar may well have been more ahead of his time—or, at least, in closer dialogue with twenty-first-century scientific and popular writings on drug use—than many in the generations that followed him.

BENJAMIN BREEN is associate professor of history at the University of California, Santa Cruz, where he teaches classes on early modern Europe, the history of science, environmental history, and world history.

Notes

1 Mao, *Qing Empire and the Opium War*, 442; Tsai, *Maritime Taiwan*, 67–68. Ta-hung-ah's name (達洪阿) is transliterated as Dahonga in some accounts.

2 Mao, *Qing Empire and the Opium War*, 442.

3 Pickering, *Pioneering in Formosa*, 46.

4 Lemon, *Addiction and Devotion*, 156.

5 As Lemon notes, we should be wary of assuming a simplistic "shift from sixteenth-century devotion to eighteenth-century compulsion" (*Addiction and Devotion*, x), since the two meanings of the term overlapped throughout the early modern period. Yet Psalmanazar's reception in the nineteenth century (especially his links with De Quincey and the Romantics) seems to me to place him in a distinctive liminal position. He was a prime example of the ambiguous early modern concept of addiction. Yet his literary celebrity in the decades bookending 1800 influenced the emerging "modern" concept of addiction as a wholly negative compulsive practice. On conceptions of addiction in the nineteenth century, see Courtwright, *Dark Paradise*, chap. 2; Foxcroft, *Making of Addiction*; and Berridge, "Morality and Medical Science."

6 Several excellent studies of the global circulation of people, objects, and ideas in the early modern period provide context for Psalmanazar's reception by European audiences primed for stories of foreign exotica but unable to fact-check claims about them. See, e.g., Bethencourt, *Cosmopolitanism in the Portuguese-Speaking World*; Games, *Web of Empire*; Mokhberi, *Persian Mirror*; Pimentel, *The Rhinoceros and the Megatherium*; and Schmidt, *Inventing Exoticism*.

7 Psalmanazar, *Description of Formosa*, 66.

8 Swift acknowledged the precedent of "the famous *Psalmanaazaar*, a Native of the Island of Formosa, who came from thence to London above twenty years ago; and in Conversation told my Friend, that in his Country when any young Person happened to be put to death, the Executioner sold the Carcase to Persons of Quality as a prime Dainty" (*Modest Proposal*, 14).

9 Yang, *Performing China*, 78.

10 On Psalmanazar's negotiations of credibility and religious identity, see Yang, *Performing China*, 94–95; Keevak, *Pretended Asian*, 37–40; and Breen, "No Man Is an Island."

11 Psalmanazar, *Essays on the Following Subjects*, 4–5.

12 Thrale, *Anecdotes of the Late Samuel Johnson*, 68.

13 D'Israeli, "Literary Forgeries." D'Israeli later enlarged his account of Psalmanazar into a fairly lengthy biographical sketch reprinted in the numerous subsequent editions of his best-selling essay collection. On D'Israeli's relationship with Byron, see Cline, "Unpublished Notes on the Romantic Poets." Psalmanazar's cosmopolitan literary afterlife included references in such publications as Boucher de la Richarderie, *Bibliothèque universelle des voyages*, 289; *Göttingische Anzeigen von gelehrten Sachen*, 1189; *New-York Review and Atheneum Magazine*, 411.

14 See Cottle's lengthy, multipart essay on "the life and character of Psalmanazar" in Cottle, *Malvern Hills*, 433–60.

15   Psalmanazar, *Memoirs*, 150, 246 (hereafter cited as *M*).

16   On Koxinga and the Dutch loss of Taiwan, see Andrade, *Lost Colony*, 68–82.

17   Po, *Blue Frontier*, 96, 123.

18   Po, *Blue Frontier*, 123–24. On the misinformation and communication gaps that characterized European accounts of maritime Asia in the seventeenth century, see Winterbottom, *Hybrid Knowledge*, esp. 28–34.

19   For instance, the chronicler Samuel Purchas, drawing on Portuguese and Dutch accounts in his summary of Chinese religiosity, described the Chinese as "much addicted to idols" (*Hakluytus Posthumus*, 483).

20   Byfield, *Principle of All Principles*, 47 (the Papists "are so addicted to Idolatry"); Williams, *Brief Discourse*, 12 (the ancient Israelites "border'd upon Nations violently addicted to Idolatry"). Matthew Henry's widely read commentary on the Old Testament (which first appeared in partial form in 1707) even inserted the term into a verse from Deuteronomy about Pharaonic Egypt (29:16). Whereas the King James Bible had simply read, "For ye know how we have dwelt in the land of Egypt," Henry's translation elaborated: "You know we have dwelt in the land of Egypt, *a country addicted to idolatry*" (*Exposition*, 718; emphasis added).

21   Kaempfer, *History of Japan*, 53. Summarizing such accounts, the English traveler Thomas Herbert wrote that "the Japanians are exceedingly addicted" to "Manadas," a Spanish term meaning "herd" but used by Herbert to mean a collection of idols (*Some Years Travels*, 373).

22   See Dyche's entries "Religions of Asia," "Metempsychosis," "Ombiasses," "Santons," "Magi," and "Zabians." Dyche's other uses of *addicted* include three references to addiction to study and other references to addictions to gambling, hunting foxes, women, and "the things of this world" (*New General English Dictionary*, s.v. "secularity").

23   Psalmanazar, *Description*, 249.

24   Psalmanazar, *Description*, 250.

25   Psalmanazar, *Description*, 164–65.

26   Psalmanazar, *Description*, 287.

27   Psalmanazar, *Enquiry into the Objections*, "Addenda to Page 25."

28   Psalmanazar describes how, in the first months of his imposture, he pretended to read from a holy book of Formosan scripture, complete with evening prayers, but this seems not to have continued once he met a Scottish chaplain named William Innes, with whom he converted and traveled to London.

29   Breen, *Age of Intoxication*, chap. 5.

30   On the social history of drug consumption in seventeenth-century England, see Withington, "Where Was the Coffee"; and Withington, "Intoxicants."

31   But see also the enormous range of other "Indies drugs" detailed in Wallis, "Exotic Drugs and English Medicine."

32   Mancall, "Tales Tobacco Told," 656.

33   All quotations in this paragraph are from Bacon, *The History Natural and Experimental of Life and Death*, 29. This is a translation from Bacon's Latin original, which first appeared as Bacon, *Historia Vitae et Mortis*. Bacon, in turn, apparently drew on the accounts of the Portuguese physicians Garcia de Orta (*Colóquios*, "Colóquio 41: Do Amfiam") and Cristóbal Acosta (*Aromatum*, 21–22), with Acosta claiming, for example, that opium was "of great use in Asia and Africa" but harmful to European bodies unless used in moderation (22; my translation).

34   Bacon, *History of Life and Death*, 29.

35   Bacon, *History of Life and Death*, 28.

36   Here Bacon drew on the Hippocratic assumption that climate and geography directly influenced the efficacy of medicines. This belief persisted throughout the eighteenth century and interacted in complex ways with European imperialism, on which see Seth, *Difference and Disease*; and Harrison, "Tender Frame of Man."

37   Bacon, *History of Life and Death*, 29.

38   Interestingly, recent archaeological finds indicate that the opium poppy, *Papaver somniferum*, was cultivated in the northern Alps at least as early as the Late Neolithic (ca. 5000–4000 BCE) and may even have been first domesticated in this region. See Tolar et al., "Plant Economy at a Late Neolithic Lake Dwelling," 218; Martin, "Plant Economy and Territory Exploitation," 70; and Salavert et al., "Opium Poppy in Europe."

39   Ray, *Catalogus Plantarum Angliae*, 222 ("Turcae, Persae, aliaeque gentes Orientales eo hodie utuntur ad spiritus recreandos").

40   Salavert et al., "Opium Poppy in Europe."

41   On the "exoticization" of opium in this period, see Breen, *Age of Intoxication*, chap. 6, and for the parallel case of coffee, see Cowan, *Social Life of Coffee*.

42   Radcliffe, *Radcliffe's Practical Dispensatory*, 452.

43   Zarotti, *Medica Martialis*, 237–38; my translation.

44   Zarotti, *Medica Martialis*, 238.

45   Trial of Edmund Allen, July 3, 1695, in Hitchcock et al., *Old Bailey Proceedings*, ref. no. t16950703-19.

46   Trial of Thomas Abram, December 5, 1711, in Hitchcock et al., *Old Bailey Proceedings*, ref. no. t17111205-31.

47 Opium reappeared in the Old Bailey court records in 1740, when two victims of an accused pickpocket named Elizabeth Briggs speculated that she had "grated something" into a "hot Pint" of beer ("I believe it was Opium") that "was enough to turn my Head" (trial of Elizabeth Briggs, February 27, 1740, in Hitchcock et al., *Old Bailey Proceedings*, ref. no. t17400227-21).

48 Harvey, *Treatise of the Small-Pox*, 51.

49 Although Jones was at pains to emphasize that opium was a familiar drug, he too linked opium to Asia, writing of newly created "great Fields of Poppy in Turky" as well as of importers from Persia and the East Indies that carried "vast quantities" of the drug into London's marketplaces (*Mysteries of Opium*, 13).

50 Jones, *Mysteries of Opium*, 20.

51 Interestingly, Jones's example was not a man of business but a woman, "a certaine serene Person . . . who found her self every way better disposed for Business, and more enabled to bear the Fatigues thereof" (*Mysteries of Opium*, 21).

52 Jones, *Mysteries of Opium*, 191.

53 Jones, *Mysteries of Opium*, 358.

54 Ray, *Catalogus Plantarum Angliae*, 223 ("Chinenses utuntur ad excitandam Venerem . . . ut per totam noctem Veneri litent . . . Apud Persas et Indos ad eosdem usus").

55 Ray himself wondered if this was true but admitted that he had not been able to test it experimentally (*Catalogus Plantarum Angliae*, 233: "orientalibus, ob diversitatem temperamentorum, venerem stimulare existimat, in aliis vero, ut occidentalibus aut septentrionalibus, eandem fraenare").

56 Stewart, *Crimes of Writing*, 48, 51.

57 Lemon, *Addiction and Devotion*, 8–9.

58 Taylor, *Dog of War*, n.p.

59 In his memoirs he describes learning Hebrew by conversing with Jews from Germany, Poland, Hungary, Spain, Portugal, Italy, and Morocco and disparagingly compares the Hebrew pronunciations of "some of them whom I met with by chance in the Portuguese synagogue" with the "antient pronunciation" he observed from "conversing with some Morocco Jews" (*M*, 227–28).

60 Keevak, *Pretended Asian*, 115.

61 Psalmanazar, *Universal History*, 232.

62 Stewart, *Crimes of Writing*, 59.

63 His last will and testament is reproduced in *M*, 2–7.

64 Boon, *Road of Excess*, 69.

65 Sometimes De Quincey's *Confessions* are instead described as an early entry in the related genre of the "recovery memoir." See, e.g., Wilson, *Guilty Thing*, 233.

66 Courtwright, *Forces of Habit*, 95.

67 Eastman, *Strange Genius*, 276.

68 *London Magazine*, "Some Account."

69 *London Magazine*, "Table-Talk."

70 Cunningham, *Handbook of London*, 249.

71 De Costa, "George Psalmanazar, Impostor and Saint," 32.

72 De Quincey, *Posthumous Works*, 117.

73 De Quincey, *Confessions*, viii.

74 De Quincey, *Confessions*, 117–18.

75 De Quincey to Cottle, August 2, 1821, MSS 72/192 z:65, Bancroft Library, University of California, Berkeley. Cottle's biographical sketch of Psalmanazar won praise from Southey, who wrote to him on February 26, 1826, that "I very much admire the manner, and the feeling, with which you have treated Psalmanazar's story" (Cottle, *Reminiscences of Samuel Taylor Coleridge and Robert Southey*, 245).

76 Cottle, *Early Recollections*, 169.

77 Dunglison, *General Therapeutics*, 364–65.

78 *Temple Bar*, "George Psalmanaazaar," 390.

79 For a recent effort to expand such studies into a larger examination of the "addiction aesthetic," see Colman, *Drugs and the Addiction Aesthetic*.

80 Fisher, *War Within*. Davy's discovery of the intoxicating properties of nitrous oxide fascinated both Coleridge and Southey, the latter of whom wrote to his brother, Thomas Southey: "Davy has actually invented a new pleasure for which language has no name. . . . I am going for more this evening—it makes one so strong & so happy! so gloriously happy!" (Southey, *Collected Letters of Robert Southey*). On the ways that Davy's compulsive use of nitrous oxide "led him away from materialism" and toward a pseudospiritual sense of "revelation," see Golinski, *Experimental Self*, 31–33.

81 On Psalmanazar's Enlightenment connections, such as Buffon's apparent belief in the credibility of his account of Taiwan, see Breen, "No Man Is an Island"; and Chien, "Psalmanazar Affair."

Works Cited

Acosta, Cristóbal [Cristóvão da Costa]. *Aromatum et medicamentorum in orientali india nascentium*. Antwerp, 1582.

Andrade, Tonio. *Lost Colony: The Untold Story of China's First Great Victory over the West*. Princeton, NJ: Princeton University Press, 2011.

Bacon, Francis. *Historia Vitae et Mortis. Sive, Titulus Secondus in Historia Naturali et Experimentali ad Condendam Philosophiam*. London, 1623.

Bacon, Francis. *History Natural and Experimental of Life and Death: or, of the Prolongation of Life*. London, 1669.

Bacon, Francis. *Sylva Sylvarum, or, A Natural History in Ten Centuries: Whereunto Is Newly Added the History Natural and Experimental of Life and Death.* London, 1670.

Berridge, Virginia. "Morality and Medical Science: Concepts of Narcotic Addiction in Britain, 1820–1926." *Annals of Science* 36, no. 1 (1979): 67–85.

Bethencourt, Francisco, ed. *Cosmopolitanism in the Portuguese-Speaking World.* Leiden: Brill, 2017.

Boon, Marcus. *The Road of Excess: A History of Writers on Drugs.* Cambridge, MA: Harvard University Press, 2002.

Boucher de la Richarderie, G. *Bibliothèque universelle des voyages.* Paris, 1808.

Breen, Benjamin. *The Age of Intoxication: Origins of the Global Drug Trade.* Philadelphia: University of Pennsylvania Press, 2019.

Breen, Benjamin. "No Man Is an Island: Early Modern Globalization, Knowledge Networks, and George Psalmanazar's Formosa." *Journal of Early Modern History* 17, no. 4 (2013): 391–417.

Byfield, Adoniram. *The Principle of All Principles concerning Religion.* London, 1624.

Chien, Hung-yi. "The Psalmanazar Affair and the Birth of Taiwan Studies in Europe: A Reassessment of the Historic Hoax." *International Journal of Taiwan Studies* 3, no. 1 (2020): 112–36.

Ching-Hwang, Yen. "Ch'ing Changing Images of the Overseas Chinese (1644–1912)." *Modern Asian Studies* 15, no. 2 (1981): 261–85.

Cline, Clarence Lee. "Unpublished Notes on the Romantic Poets by Isaac D'Israeli." *Studies in English* 21 (1941): 138–46.

Colman, Adam. *Drugs and the Addiction Aesthetic in Nineteenth-Century Literature.* Basingstoke: Palgrave Macmillan, 2019.

Cottle, Joseph. *Early Recollections: Chiefly Relating to the Late Samuel Taylor Coleridge, during His Long Residence in Bristol.* Vol. 2. London, 1837.

Cottle, Joseph. *Malvern Hills, with Minor Poems, and Essays.* Vol. 2. London, 1829.

Cottle, Joseph. *Reminiscences of Samuel Taylor Coleridge and Robert Southey.* London, 1847.

Courtwright, David T. *Dark Paradise: A History of Opiate Addiction in America.* Cambridge, MA: Harvard University Press, 2001.

Cowan, Brian. *The Social Life of Coffee: The Emergence of the British Coffeehouse.* New Haven, CT: Yale University Press, 2008.

Cree, J. M. "Protestant Evangelicals and Addiction in Early Modern English." *Renaissance Studies* 32, no. 3 (2018): 446–62.

Cunningham, Peter. *Handbook of London: Past and Present.* London, 1849.

De Costa, B. F. "George Psalmanazar, Impostor and Saint." *National Repository,* July 1877, 32.

De Quincey, Thomas. *Confessions of an English Opium-Eater.* 1822; repr. Boston, 1873.

De Quincey, Thomas. *The Posthumous Works of Thomas De Quincey,* edited by Alexander H. Japp. Vol. 1. London, 1891.

D'Israeli, Isaac. "Literary Impostures." In vol. 1 of *Curiosities of Literature.* London, 1807.

Dunglison, Robley. *General Therapeutics and Materia Medica.* Vol. 2. London, 1857.

Dyche, Thomas. *A New General English Dictionary.* London, 1735.

Eastman, Carolyn. *The Strange Genius of Mr. O: The World of the United States' First Forgotten Celebrity.* Chapel Hill: University of North Carolina Press, 2020.

Fisher, Carl Erik. *The Urge: Our History of Addiction.* New York: Penguin, forthcoming.

Foxcroft, Louise. *The Making of Addiction: The "Use and Abuse" of Opium in Nineteenth-Century Britain.* Aldershot: Ashgate, 2007.

Games, Alison. *The Web of Empire: English Cosmopolitans in an Age of Expansion, 1560–1660.* Oxford: Oxford University Press, 2009.

Golinski, Jan. *The Experimental Self: Humphry Davy and the Making of a Man of Science.* Chicago: University of Chicago Press, 2016.

Göttingische Anzeigen von gelehrten Sachen. Vol. 93. Göttingen, 1809.

Harrison, Mark. "'The Tender Frame of Man': Disease, Climate, and Racial Difference in India and the West Indies, 1760–1860." *Bulletin of the History of Medicine* 70, no. 1 (1996): 68–93.

Harvey, Gideon. *A Treatise of the Small-Pox and Measles Describing Their Nature, Causes, and Signs.* London, 1696.

Henry, Matthew. *An Exposition of the Old and New Testament.* 6 vols. London, 1790.

Herbert, Thomas. *Some Years Travels into Divers Parts of Africa and Asia the Great.* London, 1677.

Hitchcock, Tim, et al. *The Old Bailey Proceedings Online, 1674–1913.* www.oldbaileyonline.org (accessed May 12, 2021).

Jones, John. *The Mysteries of Opium Reveal'd.* London, 1701.

Kaempfer, Engelbert. *The History of Japan,* translated by J. G. Scheuchzer. Vol. 3. Glasgow: MacLehose and Sons, 1906.

Keevak, Michael. *The Pretended Asian: George Psalmanazar's Eighteenth-Century Formosan Hoax.* Detroit: Wayne State University Press, 2004.

Lemon, Rebecca. *Addiction and Devotion in Early Modern England.* Philadelphia: University of Pennsylvania Press, 2018.

London Magazine. "Some Account of the Learned Mr. George Psalmanazar." November 1764, 592–94.

London Magazine. "Table-Talk." June 1820, 647.

Mancall, Peter C. "Tales Tobacco Told in Sixteenth-Century Europe." *Environmental History* 9, no. 4 (2004): 648–78.

Mao, Haijian. *The Qing Empire and the Opium War: The Collapse of the Heavenly Dynasty*, translated by Joseph Lawson, Craig Smith, and Peter Lavelle. Cambridge: Cambridge University Press, 2016.

Martin, Lucie. "Plant Economy and Territory Exploitation in the Alps during the Neolithic (5000–4200 cal BC): First Results of Archaeobotanical Studies in the Valais (Switzerland)." *Vegetation History and Archaeobotany* 24, no. 1 (2015): 63–73.

Mokhberi, Susan. *The Persian Mirror: Reflections of the Safavid Empire in Early Modern France.* Oxford: Oxford University Press, 2019.

New-York Review and Atheneum Magazine. Vol. 2. New York, 1826.

Orta, Garcia de. *Colóquios dos simples e drogas he cousas medicinais da Índia.* Goa, 1563.

Pickering, William Alexander. *Pioneering in Formosa: Recollections of Adventures among Mandarins, Wreckers, & Head-Hunting Savages.* London, 1898.

Pimentel, Juan. *The Rhinoceros and the Megatherium: An Essay in Natural History*, translated by Peter Mason. Cambridge, MA: Harvard University Press, 2017.

Po, Ronald C. *Blue Frontier: Maritime Vision and Power in the Qing Empire.* Cambridge: Cambridge University Press, 2018.

Psalmanazar, George. *An Enquiry into the Objections against George Psalmanaazaar of Formosa.* London, 1710.

Psalmanazar, George. *Essays on the Following Subjects: I. On the Reality and Evidence of Miracles . . . Written Some Years Since . . . by an Obscure Layman in Town.* London, 1753.

Psalmanazar, George. *An Historical and Geographical Description of Formosa, an Island Subject to the Emperor of Japan.* London, 1704.

Psalmanazar, George. *Memoirs of ****: Commonly Known by the Name of George Psalmanazar, a Reputed Native of Formosa.* London, 1764.

Psalmanazar, George, et al. *An Universal History, from the Earliest Account of Time.* Vol 10. London, 1747.

Purchas, Samuel. *Hakluytus Posthumus, or, Purchas His Pilgrimes.* Vol. 12. Glasgow: MacLehose and Sons, 1906.

Radcliffe, John. *Radcliffe's Practical Dispensatory.* London, 1730.

Ray, John. *Catalogus Plantarum Angliae et Insularum Adjacentium.* London, 1677.

Rosenthal, Richard J., and Suzanne B. Faris. "The Etymology and Early History of 'Addiction.'" *Addiction Research and Theory* 27, no. 5 (2019): 437–49.

Sala, Angelus. *Opiologia: or, A Treatise concerning the Nature, Properties, True Preparation and Safe Use and Administration of Opium*, translated by Thomas Bretnor. London, 1618.

Salavert, Aurélie, Lucie Martin, Ferran Antolín, and Antoine Zazzo. "The Opium Poppy in Europe: Exploring Its Origin and Dispersal during the Neolithic." *Antiquity*, no. 364 (2018). www.cambridge.org/core/journals/antiquity/article/opium-poppy-in-europe-exploring-its-origin-and-dispersal-during-the-neolithic/2EF55CA05436425F48982EF9C405B849.

Schmidt, Benjamin. *Inventing Exoticism: Geography, Globalism, and Europe's Early Modern World.* Philadelphia: University of Pennsylvania Press, 2015.

Seth, Suman. *Difference and Disease: Medicine, Race, and the Eighteenth-Century British Empire.* New York: Cambridge University Press, 2018.

Southey, Robert. Letter to Thomas Southey, July 12, 1799. In *The Collected Letters of Robert Southey, Part Two.* romantic-circles.org/editions/southey_letters/part_two/html/lettereed.26.421.html (accessed January 20, 2021).

Stewart, Susan. *Crimes of Writing: Problems in the Containment of Representation.* Oxford: Oxford University Press, 1991.

Swift, Jonathan. *A Modest Proposal for Preventing the Children of Poor People from Being a Burden to Their Parents or the Country.* London, 1730.

Taylor, John. *A Dog of War, or, The Trauels of Drunkard, the Famous Curre.* London, 1628.

Temple Bar. "George Psalmanaazaar." July 1865, 385–98.

Thrale, Hester Lynch. *Johnsoniana: Anecdotes of the Late Samuel Johnson.* London, 1884.

Tolar, Tjaša, Stefanie Jacomet, Anton Velušček, and Katarina Cufar. "Plant Economy at a Late Neolithic Lake Dwelling Site in Slovenia at the Time of the Alpine Iceman." *Vegetation History and Archaeobotany* 20, no. 3 (2011): 207–22.

Tsai, Shih-Shan Henry. *Maritime Taiwan: Historical Encounters with the East and the West.* New York: Sharpe, 2009.

Vries, Jan de. *The Industrious Revolution: Consumer Behaviour and the Household Economy, 1650 to the Present.* Cambridge: Cambridge University Press, 2008.

Wallis, Patrick. "Exotic Drugs and English Medicine: England's Drug Trade, c. 1550–c. 1800." *Social History of Medicine* 25, no. 1 (2012): 20–46.

Williams, John. *Brief Discourse concerning the Lawfulness of Worshipping God*. London, 1694.

Wilson, Frances. *Guilty Thing: A Life of Thomas De Quincey*. New York: Macmillan, 2016.

Winterbottom, Anna. *Hybrid Knowledge in the Early East India Company World*. London: Springer, 2016.

Withington, Phil. "Intoxicants and the Invention of 'Consumption.'" *Economic History Review* 73, no. 2 (2020): 384–408.

Withington, Phil. "Where Was the Coffee in Early Modern England?" *Journal of Modern History* 92, no. 1 (2020): 40–75.

Yang, Chi-ming. *Performing China: Virtue, Commerce, and Orientalism in Eighteenth-Century England, 1660–1760*. Baltimore: Johns Hopkins University Press, 2011.

Zarotti, Cesare. *M. Valerii Martialis Epigrammatum, Medicae, aut Philosophicae Considerationis Enarratio*. Venice, 1657.

A Primer for Rebellion
Indian Cannabis and Imperial Culture
in the Nineteenth Century

UTATHYA CHATTOPADHYAYA

Abstract   This essay explores how the British imperial archive of cannabis addiction in
the mid-nineteenth century was shaped by ideas of religious devotion, ordinary leisure,
and anxieties arising from revolt and rebellion. It asks how cannabis was discursively
constituted as ubiquitous in India and subsequently cast as a conduit to anti-imperial violence in narratives of imperial counterinsurgency. In colonial India, British imperial strategies of knowing the plant's intoxicating power indexed together several devotional and
laboring bodies, among whom the figure of the Indian rebel occupied a unique globally
legible location. Revisiting the popular reportage and writing on the Indian Rebellion,
this essay argues that cannabis was materialized through the rebel's body as the ratio-
nale for victory, loss, and disorder to ultimately inform and reveal how the reproduction
of race and gender shaped the insurgent and counterinsurgent logic of cannabis use
under empire.
Keywords   cannabis, imperialism, India, the Indian Rebellion, bhang

In February 1858, a few months before the British Crown formally took over the
reins of its Indian territories, and at the height of the bloody British counterinsurgency against the rebellion, the *Belfast News-Letter* in Ireland published a tiny but
widely circulated missive from India. This anonymous letter, first carried by Calcutta's pro-Britain *Friend of India,* had made its way around the world through the
webbed networks of printed periodical culture. The periodical as a genre of publication, in Isabel Hofmeyr's words, "convened a miniature empire on every page."[1]
Together with newspapers and pamphlets but also often unlike them, periodicals
were populated through the exchange of news items, multiple republications of
extracts and letters, abridged quotations, and syndicated opinion pieces. Despite
the proliferation of telegraph and fee-bound wire transfers, periodicals remained
central to imperial culture, bound up with the temporality of maritime networks
as ships carried bundles of publications from one part of the world to another.
This snippet, which went from colonial India to colonial Ireland, announced the
following:

ENGLISH LANGUAGE NOTES
60:1, April 2022 DOI 10.1215/00138282-9560243
© 2022 Regents of the University of Colorado

> No Hindoostanee ever attacks Europeans without having *primed* himself with bhang. The manufacture of bhang can be controlled by the government. Why should it not for the future be absolutely suppressed and the manufacture made as penal as active rebellion? No other drug will supply its place, because no other possesses at once invigorating and stupefying qualities. It produces little or no revenue and is utterly abhorred by the respectable classes of the community.[2]

This declaration was curious for a number of reasons. One, it effectively put bhang production at par with treasonous rebellion by demanding equivalent penalties for both. Two, it declared bhang consumption ubiquitous and agentive in violence against European power. Three, it captured the dilemma of explaining bhang's perceived dichotomous role as stimulant and calmative, while also enclosing it as a unique and exceptional substance. Finally, it highlighted the double-edged position of bhang as a potential, yet failing, object of colonial revenue extraction as well as a subject of moral disdain among the Indian elite. Taken together, this is indicative of most, if not all, the intersections of imperial power and Indian social life since the nineteenth century that cannabis lay at the heart of. Cannabis was indeed a revenue object in India that was more systematically enveloped into the British state apparatus after the 1850s. European doctors, pharmacologists, pharmacists, botanists, and chemical examiners had struggled to classify cannabis within a triadic template of intoxicating property, chemical composition, and potential medical use. For most of the nineteenth century they labored to produce a glossary of words for cannabis in South Asian languages. While historians of medicine have often examined the struggle to understand Indian cannabis through European science, the other set of associations announced by the missive—between rebellion, violence, and bhang— have so far escaped thorough scrutiny.

Bhang, in historical scholarship on South Asian drugs, has largely been used as a nominal term. Scholars use it as a taxonomic word to refer to one of the three main cannabis commodities that Britain subjected to its revenue apparatus. The other two, ganja and charas, were cannabis commodities produced from the flowering top and resin from both the stalk and flowers of the hemp plant, respectively. Bhang was commonly made from cannabis leaf. Scholarly references to bhang, while useful for cataloging the vernacular, nonetheless limit our understanding of the cultural and material locations of the actual substance denoted by the term. *Bhang* has traversed multiple Indian languages as a category, and as *bang, bangi,* or *bangue,* also became a referent in Swahili, Persian, English, and Portuguese. It is widely used in northern, western, and central regions of the South Asian subcontinent. In the Hindi-speaking north, the term indexed not one but several habitations of the cannabis leaf. Depending on context and usage, it could refer to either a loose dusty cannabis commodity, or solely the cannabis leaves, or the entire cannabis plant, or a set of confectionary drinks made primarily of milk and boiled cannabis leaf that were differentiated by culinary combinations of nuts, spices, and cream.

The European encounter with bhang before the nineteenth century was limited to the interests of naturalists and collectors of tropical drugs. It was one among the large field of natural medicines that elicited the curiosity of Portuguese, French, and English writers since the seventeenth century.[3] By the late nineteenth century, however, the dominant framing of cannabis in the imperial archive was a homogeneous substance that catalyzed madness among Indians.[4] Historians of drugs have, so far, challenged fallacious British presumptions and emphasized instead the strongly divergent views on cannabis among British administrators and doctors.[5] However, in focusing on medicine, asylums, and temperance politics, present scholarship has ignored what the writer of the missive to Belfast implicitly acknowledges—that bhang, at a midcentury moment of crisis for the legitimacy of British supremacy in India, was effectively at par with rebellion in global imperial culture. Bhang was cast as the "primer"—the preface to rebellion that added capacity, ability, and masculinity to the Indian rebel.

In the mid-nineteenth century, narratives of Indian cannabis charted imperial geographies spanning the smallest towns in England, Ireland, and Canada and the mutinous battlefields of the Indian countryside. The valence it acquired in association with rebellion and violence through the circulation of printed periodicals and newspapers across the world fundamentally defined its location in imperial culture.[6] Periodicals and newspapers from British India's metropolises like the *Delhi Gazette, Friend of India,* and the *Statesman,* were regularly syndicated across Great Britain, Australia, New Zealand, South Africa, and Canada. They made their way to the columns of the *Chicago Tribune* and the *New York Times* in the United States. These circuits of knowledge brought the empire to the ports and hinterlands in Britain just as they took Victorian ideas of race and gender into colonial contexts. Thinking through imperial culture takes Indian cannabis out from the preoccupations of the bureaucratic archive of British medicine, peopled by doctors and the observational practices of laboratory science, and resituates it in raced and gendered discourses of addiction, insurgency, and violence. This archive of empire captured cannabis not through scales of chemical composition, but through a constellation of associated meanings derived from military conquest, anticolonial rebellion, and ethnographic observation. Materialized as both spectacle and the everyday, both agentive and ubiquitous, Indian cannabis became a vivid presence available to Anglophone readers across the world.

One genre, the military dispatch, was particularly crucial to this process. Written by British soldiers or reporters posted across India during the rebellion of 1857–59, cannabis routinely preoccupied such supposedly authentic "eyewitness" accounts of violence and rebellion on the ground.[7] These dispatches were also translated into languages like French and Welsh, evidenced by the reportage in broadsheets like *Baner,* out of Denbigh in Wales. The dispatches drew on extant practices of everyday observational ethnography to construct Indian cannabis dually as a ubiquitous presence and a conduit to rebellion. Depending on whether the Indian subject was Muslim or Hindu, or on the contingencies of the violent encounter itself, cannabis could also mobilize contradictory responses. These perceptions of Indian cannabis persisted in the colonial record well after the rebellion, forming the fertile ground on which claims of cannabis-led lunacy could be made legible in the 1870s. The equation of Indian bhang with active rebellion by the writer of the missive to Belfast clearly indicates the need to historicize how Indian cannabis came to animate imperial culture, precisely when the English East India Company faced its most decisive crisis in colonial South Asia.

The crisis posed by the rebellion in northern India has a well-known metanarrative: colonial exploitation, widespread insurgency by diverse groups, and the ultimate seizure of the Indian territories away from the company into the formal ambit of the Crown and the British Parliament. Historians have studied the causes of the rebellion at length: the offensive cartridges greased with cow or pig lard; the political role of rumor, low pay, and forced overseas deployment of sepoys; higher taxes on agricultural land; the insult of the annexation of Oudh; the undying embers of the Anglo-Sikh war of 1849; and the delegitimization of Indian sovereignty through the Doctrine of Lapse.[8] The rebellion was thus a dispersed and disaggregated set of insurgent events that mutually reinforced one another and coconstituted, with radical democratic possibilities, a disruptive reckoning for empire. However, histories of cannabis, like histories of empire, are rarely written with disruption in the lead.[9] Reading for the disruptive potential of cannabis, otherwise subsumed under scholarship that focuses on the political will of the rebel, invites attention to its pivotal role in animating the rebellion and its interruptive presence in the way of imperial ambition.

The rebellion ossified multiple meanings of cannabis use into the body of the rebel, particularly through narratives of bhang drinking. If before the rebellion, Indian cannabis was a minor preoccupation of select British doctors and purveyors of tropical drugs, the rebellion dragged it outside networks of imperial science into the global archive of imperial politics. Here, bhang was used to explain the lack of Indian sovereignty and particularly Muslim violence to readers around the world, illuminating one element of what Sanjay Krishnan has called the institutionalization of the imperial global perspective.[10] To do so, the polyvalent habitations of cannabis in everyday socioreligious life in colonial India were flattened into a discourse of ubiquity. By not explicating the meanings behind cannabis use, empire centered it as an omnipresent substance that vitalized the specter of insurgency. Military dispatches written from battlefields and published across globally circulating periodicals and newsletters turned Indian cannabis into an archival object that was known through its vitiating power in the body of the rebel. However, the rebel was also an addict, in the broadest sense of the term. The addict, Susan Zieger has argued, is a figure whose trajectory tells us more about cultural configurations of race and sexuality than it does about the individual.[11] The invention of the addict in the nineteenth century, as one diseased of the will, failing morally in society, as well as earlier meanings of addiction as devotion or conviction, prefaced how the ubiquity of Indian cannabis was narrated. In the racialized and gendered figure of the Indian rebel that was an effect of an act of intoxication, ordinary ubiquity quickly led to extraordinary violence, prompting the question of how the habit of cannabis as moral failing constituted it as a catalyst of disruption and insurgency.

Ordinary Ubiquity

Studies of addiction have drawn on authorial articulations of experience in novels, dramas, and memoirs to show how its meanings have shifted from connotations of overpowering love and bondage of the self in devotion to God in early modern England to moral failure, resignation to bodily compulsion, and a debilitated mode of life in the nineteenth century.[12] In the colonial archive, populated more by European descriptive emplotments than authorial self-articulations, the experience of cannabis was cast as an outcome of the ubiquitous everyday presence of cannabis.[13] As Janet Brodie and Mark Redfield point out, since one can only be addicted to what is present, understanding modern institutions of technology, bureaucracy, and surveillance that make addicts and substances appear empirically present everywhere is key to contextualizing notions of habit.[14] Well before the intensification of colonial power through asylums, lock hospitals, and prisons in the 1870s, which followed the suppression of the Indian Rebellion, cannabis was depicted as a banal and routine presence since the early nineteenth century through ethnographic observations of colonial subjects. While these never quite reached the popular audiences that dispatches from the rebellion did, they nonetheless laid the groundwork for locating cannabis as a habit of leisure as well as devotion among Indians.

Missionary journals and smaller literary publications that depicted everyday Indian lifeworlds since the 1830s often captured cannabis through the presumptively keen ethnographic detail materialized by European writers. Domestic workers were the most immediate gateway into perceptions of Indian habits. A decade before the rebellion began, a three-column account titled "Indian Bhang" in *Chambers' Edinburgh Journal* narrated the author's frequent notice of "an old favourite servant as he sat over the orgies of the bhang."[15] The journal had recently carried reports on Egyptian hashish, prompting this commentary from India.[16] Peerun, the servant this writer was observing, carried his "bundle of bhang" everywhere and with fellow servants at midday, prepared a cupful for everyone. In a thornwood mortar and pestle, Peerun, would "pulverize the leaves" with water, strain it through muslin, and add sugar, ginger, and pepper to "make it palatable."[17] After consuming bhang with his friends, Peerun's "eyes became bloodshot, his speech thick, his mind confused," after which he slept for three hours. Yet, the writer noted, Peerun was not a debilitated addict but a "faithful and trustworthy servant." The key here was poverty. While Peerun was not impoverished under European employment, and could afford good food, he was better off than the "poor debauchee" who could become an addict through his own devices. Bhang "costs the Bengalee as much as our Souchong costs us," wrote this anonymous British observer, before noting that by proportion, the poor Indian nonetheless spent more on bhang than the Englishman did on black tea. Such British ethnographic accounts reproduced poverty as the fundamental marker of Indian life while relaying cannabis through comparison with other intoxicants like tea. While tea was widely cast as enervating for the Englishman, and cannabis stupefying to the Indian body, such contradictory but connective tissues nonetheless made bhang habits appear as everyday practice, as mundane and typical to India as poverty.

Ethnographies of religious sentiment and mass devotion similarly captured cannabis as a constituent of servility and superstition. By the 1850s a few scholarly publications had carried accounts of cannabis and Shaivism in India largely through analyses of ritual texts, not everyday worship. Besides that, W. B. O'Shaughnessy's short treatise on medicinal uses of cannabis, published in 1839, remained the only thorough point of reference for British officials in India.[18] All that changed when on April 19, 1856, months before the rebellion broke out, James Holms wrote from Calcutta recounting his observations of the Charak Pooja to the editor of the *Times*. He described the swinging festival as one enjoyed by "only the lowest class of the natives" in the country. Holms's letter, vividly recounting cannabis as an element of mass devotion for the first time, was syndicated across networks of the Anglophone press in every major newspaper in Britain, followed by publications in Canada and the United States.[19] Holms had traveled to the outskirts of Calcutta to witness the festival and returned aghast, his letter demanding that Parliament abolish hook-swinging immediately. Charak Pooja was a hook-swinging festival celebrating the deity Shiva in the last month of spring. The central attraction of Charak gatherings was a feat of the will—a performer swirled centrifugally from a pole while suspended on a cord hooked to the body. The hook passed through the top layer of muscle over the shoulder blades.[20] In the nineteenth century the practice of hook-swinging in multiple formats was widely common and debated among reformers, missionaries, and judges but had never been cast as a problem of cannabis.[21]

For Holms, on the other hand, who described this as a "tragic scene" and "degrading spectacle," cannabis was the glue that held it all together. The "crowds of Indians of every age," he reported, "were more or less excited" with bhang. The performer, a man with a "wild expression of countenance and glaring eyes," was also "infatuated" with bhang, "which he had consumed great quantities of during the three previous days to deaden the pain." In Holms's representation, this was "frightful," and in urgent need of abolition. "Men who undergo the swinging seldom survive it," he added without evidence, anecdotal or otherwise. Holms was not the first Englishman to describe the festivity. The Baptist missionary John Statham's less-known memoir *Indian Recollections* had described hook swingers as superstitious Hindus driven "by trouble or affliction" and the festival itself as one of two "most famous annual festivals of the Hindoos."[22] But the widespread international circulation of Holms's narrative catapulted colonial interest in the Charak Pooja into metropolitan consciousness.

Carefully negotiating custom and religion in India was critical to the maintenance of colonial order.[23] By 1853 British administrators in Bengal had mandated that magistrates report to superintendents of police all cases of Charak Pooja where instances of cruelty were recorded. More important, the colonial government had sought to make it a matter of consent. The 1853 order emphasized not the festivity or the consumption of bhang but those instances where hook-swinging "was enforced without the free consent of the parties submitting to it."[24] Such liberal notions of agency and consent, that otherwise structured debates on girlhood, marriage, and age in colonial India, became the mode through which the state cautiously approached the Charak Pooja. On the other hand, the celebrity of Holms's narrative at the cusp of the Indian Rebellion sensationally popularized bhang as the predilection of both a single individual and the attendant crowd, where cannabis mediated the former's superstitious extension toward death and the latter's excitement into devotional attachment.

In this mid-nineteenth century moment early modern English ideas of devotion, and the experience of being possessed with love for God, were thus recast in colonial conditions. The translation of cannabis habits through knowledge of other intoxicants, the curiosity for the everyday life of colonized subjects, and the narration of frightfulness at the uncivility of the colonized were symptoms of the raced and gendered collision of bodies under empire. Once cannabis was established ethnographically as a ubiquitous presence in the colony, multiple meanings of addictive experiences, filtered through racialized and gendered discourses, could be mobilized to explain Indian uses of bhang. Nothing illustrated this more than the figure of the Indian rebel.

Rebellious Bodies

The Indian rebel burst onto the imperial record wild with rage. On July 15, 1857, the second page of the *Manchester Guardian* greeted its reader with a sensational account, syndicated from Agra, of the ongoing rebellion against the British East India Company in its Indian territories.[25] It promised "a detailed account" of the "fearful massacre in Delhi" from the "pen of an eye-witness." According to this writer, Indian soldiers of the 3 Light Cavalry had arrived in Delhi from Meerut on the morning of May 11 "prepared to perpetuate the most awful crimes as they were fully armed and apparently wild with rage and excitement." Historians of the rebellion have dwelled on the mutiny in the Meerut barracks and the gradual outbreak of rebellious aspirations among other sepoys and diverse segments of colonial Indian society following this fateful march of the mutineers to Delhi.[26] Delhi was a turning point not simply because it housed the last reigning Mughal emperor whose formal position of imperial authority could potentially mobilize Indians against the company's military. It was critical also because the victory of the mutineers was followed by the public execution of British soldiers and officials who had managed to survive the battlefield outside Delhi. This specter of violence in the historic imperial capital quickly animated rumors of British downfall that spread across northern India's garrison towns like Aligarh and Lucknow.

Wild and spectacular violence was the nub of the reportage in the English press in Delhi, Agra, and abroad. The eyewitness report, for instance, noted both that the mutineers entered Delhi without resistance from the city police and when the locally stationed British men of the Fifty-Fourth Regiment fought back, their Indian soldiers deserted them and were later thanked by the mutinying troopers "for their forbearance." The troopers who had marched all night from Meerut were still in full uniform, wearing their medals. But underneath that demeanor, the wild rebel lurked. "The countenances of the troopers wore the expression of maniacs," the writer remarked. The one among them who stood out, "a mere youth, rushing about flourishing his sword," the writer further emphasized, was "displaying all the fury of a man under the influence of bhang."[27] Months before such reports proliferated among a global readership, bhang's association with irrational violence had briefly figured in the trial of Mangal Pandey, who claimed to have mutinied under its influence. Internal reports by officers in charge of the Thirty-Fourth Bengal Native Infantry, like Major General Hearsey, concluded that other soldiers did not stop "Mungul Pandy from behaving in a murderous manner" because "he had taken bhang to excess."[28] But once the rebellion and its simultaneous coverage spread, bhang performed the labor of tethering globally circulating discursive constructions of wild, armed, and enraged rebellious men rejecting colonial domination—the very foundations of imperial anxieties—to the material histories of everyday intoxication noted in earlier colonial ethnographies, thus bringing into view a fearless, irrational subject catalyzed by cannabis consumption.

In spectacular accounts of colonial conquest leading up to the rebellion, madness was often coded through the figure of an irrational Indian subject who didn't know when to give up. In 1839, years before the mutiny, when London's *Morning Post* carried a report on Man Singh's surrender of Jodhpur to the company's Twenty-Second Regiment, its metropolitan readers encountered both a defeated Indian king and a "mad old fool."[29] Man Singh, effectively the last dynast of Marwar before British conquest of the region, had reportedly seen the writing on the wall. Despite the armies being ready and gunpowder bags lined up for a confrontation on September 21, Singh surrendered the gate of Jodhpur fort. The company's regiments marched in and took possession of the fortress. But just as the victorious Captains Ludlow and Smith were "enjoying the beautiful view of the country and of the troops ascending the winding pathway," they were attacked by a lone old soldier. One captain dodged the bullet, and the other took some swipes from the attacker before overpowering and killing him. "Of course," wrote the correspondent, "he was mad, either with drink or bhang." The mad subaltern, never fully accepting his subjugation, thus kept the tame matter of the sovereign's surrender from being a closed chapter in the narrative of British dominion.

In fact, British dominion both before and after the Indian Rebellion was legitimated to metropolitan audiences through the figure of a sovereign incapacitated by bhang. Wajid Ali Shah, the last king of Oudh, was historically represented as either too weak or too distracted to maintain military sovereignty. In the days leading up to the swift annexation of Oudh by the company in 1856, Shah's reputation as a Muslim king unable to maintain peace between his Hindu and Muslim subjects capitalized on colonial strategies of using sectarianism to classify Indians and justify British rule as impartial and necessary. When, in 1855, reports of religious conflict emerged from Faizabad, the company's garrison at Lucknow was quick to respond. It was the threat of complete British annexation, the *Sheffield Daily Telegraph* reported, that kept Hindus and Muslims from sectarian violence.[30] Shah could not control Muslim "fanatics," the report declared, and in the deliberations over peacekeeping, was "in a continual state of stupefaction from opium or bhang," leaving his prime minister and "the English Resident and his assistants, as the real masters of the situation."[31] Three years later, when British troops were scrambling to retake territory lost to the rebels across northern India, one of the last holdouts was the revolutionary government in Bareilly, where the city's elite had selected Khan Bahadur Khan as its head.[32] Even the *Friend of India* acknowledged the provisional gains of his government in setting up a stable monetary and fiscal system in the city. British commentators from India begrudgingly hailed him, one writing to the *Times* praising his efforts to bridge religious divisions. "He has in the Mohamedan city of Bareilly," noted the writer, "forbidden the killing of cows and buried four amulets in each corner of the city with rites strictly Hindu to assure his followers of success." Further, it read, "the cowardly assassin [Khan] who never yet has headed troops in the field exhibits fertility of resources and power of combination beyond any of the leaders of the insurrection." Yet Khan's claim to sovereignty was already compromised, thus promising hope for the English counterinsurgency. Cannabis was his route to ignominy—"Khan is fast losing the little intellect and influence that bhang and opium had left him, and he's falling into second childhood." He might have been resourceful, but "it [was] beyond his power to resist the force which will be brought against his troops."[33] Whether before, during, or after the mutiny, cannabis was key to challenging the legitimacy of Indian sovereignty, providing succor to an imperial audience as proof of its fated decline.[34] Bhang thus became the alibi deployed to evacuate the insurgency of its political content.

During the rebellion, between 1857 and 1859, narratives of bhang consumption, especially by Muslims, animated nearly every theater of battle. Once the mutiny spread, many local newspapers in Britain attributed even the events preceding the battle in Delhi to the actions of Muslim soldiers, an "infuriated crew, thirsting for the blood of the infidel, and frenzied with bhang."[35] As mutiny dispatches became their own genre of reporting in the Anglophone press, rising numbers of eyewitness accounts poured in. Major Alexander Cobbe wrote to the *Hertford Mercury and Reformer* describing his battle in Delhi, where he witnessed rebels drinking bhang, who "consequently were more courageous than usual" and could charge the British forces fearlessly.[36] Each dramatic account added newer emphases on the role of intoxication. "By all accounts, they were perfectly mad from churrus or bhang and fought more boldly than they ever did before," read one report on a skirmish at Delhi.[37] A dispatch from the special correspondent of the *Times* in Bombay recounted how at Neemuch cantonment, a "fanatic Mahomedan of the 1st Bombay Lancers, maddened by bhang, appeared on the lines of his regiment and by his furious and inflammatory gestures and addresses, excited a considerable commotion" on August 10.[38] There was, the reporter noted, "only one madman at fault," who fired at Brigadier Macan's head but missed and was subdued quickly. *Lloyd's Illustrated Newspaper's* syndication of this report in London editorialized this as ominous evidence of the mutiny "defiling" the Bombay Presidency and spreading farther west.[39] To the east, in Barrackpore near Calcutta, newspapers continued reporting on instances of sepoys attacking adjutants under the influence of bhang.[40]

These dispatches from India were largely written by white soldiers in the British army. The *Observer*, in a special column titled "Race and Religion in India," wrote that dispatches "do not profess to give 'news' but the details they contain of the native character and manners throw some light on the causes of the insurrection."[41] Such dispatches were usually editorialized with comments on the military officer's record of service to legitimate to the reader their authority on both the mutiny and its causes. The dispatch by one Captain T, "eighteen years in the company's service and fifteen on the staff and civil employment," was quoted by the *Observer* at length. The captain declared in April 1858 that "no native mutineer or rebel has as yet given any reason for his conduct. The Mohammedans got up the plot to wrest the empire from us; the Wahabee Mussulman sectarians of Islam being the chief conspirators."[42] The Wahhabi movement in northern and central India had, since the 1840s, directly confronted the East India Company. Wahhabi leaders regularly attempted to gain the support of sepoys employed by European armies, causing British agencies to scramble for intelligence and proceed on charges of treason and sedition.[43] After the rebellion, in 1870, the colonial state introduced Section 124A, the clause against sedition, to the Indian Penal Code explicitly to curb the activities of Wahhabi groups.[44]

Organized Wahhabi opposition, cast by Britons as sectarian and scheming, combined with ideas of Asian primitivism and fatalism helped explain the origins of the mutiny. "Fatalism is the great mover in the disposition of the native. He runs mad, being naturally excited, adds bhang and other drugs to work up the system, and then says it is all fate that did it," wrote Captain T. Racialized as inherently weak and lacking masculine will, the Asian body was too susceptible to the lures of Wahhabi Islam's anti-British propaganda. While the Wahhabi movement "cleverly set the ball rolling," the captain went on, "the whole ran amuck as Asians only can do. It is an Asiatic disease like cholera, equally incurable and equally puzzling to sober Europeans."[45] To the lay reader, Captain T's record of "actively hunting out the rebels" and asking them their reasons "before hanging them" added an air of authority to this heady account of Islam, cannabis, and weak-willed fatalism. The phrase *running amuck* in the archive of imperial warfare has its own instructive transnational itinerary. Englishmen across Indian Ocean outposts since the late eighteenth century had used *amok*, derived from a Malay word meaning a furious charge at an enemy, to name a fixed cultural trait and an event of homicidal violence.[46] European medical officials and, later, psychiatrists, began counting and analyzing instances of *amok* in the early nineteenth century, some of the first of which were recorded among Malay Muslims, followed by Indigenous groups across Indian Ocean archipelagoes. *Running amok*, correspondingly, became a mutating phrase to capture culturally coded behaviors of irrational violence.[47] By the mid-nineteenth century the phrase was a shorthand descriptor for acts of violent rebellion that Europeans either could not comprehend or simply found lacking in strategy and rationality.

By July 1857 imperial Britons had encountered their most treacherous public enemy in the figure of Nana Sahib. The name was an adopted moniker of Dhondu Pant, a Maratha prince dispossessed of his inheritance by the East India Company. At Kanpur, his siege of the British army forced them to surrender. After guaranteeing safe passage to surrendered British residents in the town, he reportedly reneged and ordered their execution. The subsequent swirl of public vilification of Nana Sahib drew liberally on "Anglo-Indian rumor and self-promoting military dispatches."[48] The figure of Nana Sahib was used in transnational imperial culture, from playhouses to literary clubs, to gradually symbolize multiple forms of "native" excess such as treachery, rape, and bloodlust.[49] Nana Sahib escaped the British counterattack on Kanpur to flee north into the Himalayan kingdom of Nepal, adding layers of mystery to his subsequent representations. Cannabis was pivotal to the trajectory of such depictions, each indicating the prejudicial role of race and Blackness in Victorian popular consciousness.[50] For instance, the character of Jonathan Small in Arthur Conan Doyle's *Sign of Four* (1890), who exemplified the centrality of the Kanpur massacre to the genre of the mutiny novel, reminded the reader that the "black fiends" in British uniform were "drunk with opium and bang."[51] After Nana Sahib's escape, the *London Journal* carried a two-column excoriation, by one "Indian," of the British police for their lack of proper intelligence on his whereabouts. The author noted that Nana Sahib's widow, a "rather black creature," had failed to mourn according to custom, thus suggesting he was probably still alive.[52] When, in 1874, news of his capture at the hands of the Scindiahs emerged, it lit up the Anglophone press across the empire and the United States. However, disappointment quickly followed. Dr. Tressider, the civil surgeon at Kanpur during the siege, who had performed a surgery on Nana Sahib's foot, denounced the captive as an impostor.

But why would someone pretend to be arguably the most dreaded enemy in the British imperial imagination at the time? Cannabis. The correspondent of the *Times* in India, in a report later syndicated to the *Chicago Daily Tribune*, blamed the entire drama on "the effects of bhang." Noting that the prisoner's confession was made under the influence of bhang, "the native drug answering to rum or whisky in England, but with the effect of opium," the writer informed avid readers that he had once "fired every chamber of a six-chambered Colt" over a "man drunk with bhang, and could not wake him."[53] Tressider's testimony and the role of cannabis evidently saved British intelligence from embarrassment. For the *Times*, the impostor, whether or not he was the "real Nana," had taken the "convenient plea of bhang as a set-off against a crime," whereas for the *Saturday Review*, which blamed it on the Scindiahs trying to curry favor with the British Crown, the impostor effectively "relieved the British Government from a painful and embarrassing responsibility."[54] In other words, cannabis exemplified both the bloodlust of Nana Sahib and the fabrication of his impersonator, together rendering colonized bodies as wholly unreliable subjects.[55] Unreliability became the shared discursive ground on which racialized representations of irrationality, bloodthirst, and wildness could converge.

If in the early days of the mutiny, bhang animated the wildness of the rebels, then during the bloody counterinsurgency that followed, it also explained their continuing resolve. In November 1857, during the siege to take Delhi back, another slate of military dispatches recounted how the rebels were "losing what little organization and discipline they had left." But, one went on, "still their obstinate defence is wonderful and can only be attributed to bhang."[56] For other witnesses of the counterinsurgency, bhang vivified the gradual disarray of the rebel soldiers who were slowly losing the ground they gained a few months ago. One of the longest and most striking accounts to make its way across broadsheets, with a day-by-day breakdown of events, was written by a "young subaltern officer in the East India Company's service" employed in the attack on Lucknow. In a critical turning point in his narrative, first printed in London's *Daily News*, he was the sole officer alongside twenty Indian soldiers left in his quarters when a group of rebels attacked from a nearby mosque. The "wretched fighting from room to room, one corridor to another" spilled over from the quarters into the garden, after the officer and Indian soldiers "shot and bayonetted no less than eight in one small room," regrouped overnight, and took back the building. "The men," he wrote, gave him "very much the idea of being intoxicated with bhang, for they seemed to come on without any definite design, rushed madly about, apparently unconscious where they were going to."[57]

Military dispatches that recounted such disarray among the rebels, as the company's forces bore down on them, were unquestionably about colonial masculinity.[58] The facts of battle aside, the singular feature of such narratives was a contrast between a low-ranking white soldier, generally, fighting against odds in a landscape peopled by derelict buildings and unfathomable foes. In a letter to his father, written in the trenches outside Kanpur on November 26, 1857, A.C. of the Sixtieth Rifles was emotionally charged up. In his words, he was in a small mud fort with thirty men and "surrounded by 3000 of the 'beauties' all about."[59] Anyone who read this letter, printed in full in the morning news on January 23, 1858, might have been taken by the soldier's bravado. He wished the "beauties" would attack, from the other side of the bridge facing him, so he "could make a few of them [into] food for jackals." If there was scrimmage, he planned to stand at one end of the bridge and "walk [straight] into the n——s until a force comes down from the fort."[60] Explicit racial hatred and misogyny that translated the rebel as both Black and womanly to a global readership built on earlier racist characterizations of Blackness in the reports on Nana Sahib's wife, recalling what Alexander Weheliye has called the "nimble mutability of racial taxonomies."[61]

When the attack did take place, A.C. came to find that their spies were wrong and the number of rebels was closer to twenty-five thousand. "I never expected to get back to camp alive," he wrote, before adding, "I cannot think how we escaped." The next day they fought again, but "the sepoys in the adjacent ruins had done themselves up with bhang yesterday" so when "the brutes rushed at us with their swords, it was a dreadful sight to see the poor officers being cut up." But again, he wrote, "they were all around me but by the greatest mercy, I was not touched."[62] Miraculous escapes followed by gallant attacks, during which A.C. "blew the brains out" of a captured Indian spy, cast the white soldier's masculinity as an effect of the unbeatable odds represented by an Indian rebel intoxicated by cannabis. The rebel, vituperatively animalized as a "brute," was vitiated to irrational violence by cannabis while the hypermasculine violence of the white soldier shored up manhood in the service of empire as more rational.

The gendered body of the white soldier was also an orientation device for ordinary Britons to apprehend the scope of the empire they claimed and sought to retain. Military dispatches from India could take more than a month to reach England, and newspapers maintained regular contact with the families of soldiers posted in India. A *Morning Post* editorial in March 1858 argued that publishing such weekly or fortnightly letters to family members provided intelligence and news to lay Britons about their "great dependency of India."[63] Precisely due to such letters, Britain had become "acquainted with [its] power and the means of using it, [and] the dispositions, temper, and feelings of the Hindu and Mahomedan populations." Thus there was no reason to be so unprepared against mutiny in the future, argued the *Post*, before hailing Britain's use of artillery regiments as the way to cut the losses of infantrymen. By 1858 the counterinsurgency appeared to be succeeding, and British troops, under the leadership of Colin Campbell, appeared to be taking India back. Using "his overpowering artillery," the same editorial read, "Sir Colin Campbell will play on these refuse and sweepings of degraded Asiatic human nature, the mere quisquilia of human devilry excited by bhang and opium."[64] In the year since the mutiny had begun, cannabis had catalyzed a wide range of claims around civilizational superiority and become a vehicle for the nineteenth-century English public sphere's craving for military supremacy in the colonies. In animating several meanings of vitiation, like unreliability, fanaticism, the remedy of the weak-willed, and finally as the ultimate repository of Indian delinquency, cannabis came to serve as an extraordinary enemy in the imperial narrative of military conquest.

The narrative of Colin Campbell's military triumph at Lucknow, in March 1858, threw such associations into sharp relief. Campbell's biography, as the son of a poor Scottish carpenter who assumed his mother's surname; fought for the Crown in the War of 1812; and rose through service in British Guiana, Ireland, Punjab, Spain, Hong Kong, and Crimea, was well known. After decades spent repressing rebellions by enslaved and Indigenous peoples and building a reputation for cautious military strategy that prioritized reducing troop casualties in battle, he was a strategic choice for Prime Minister Lord Palmerston to complete the counterinsurgency operations in India. While imperial careering, long established as a means of negotiating class, masculinity, and status in the British Empire, decisively shaped Campbell's location, his caution was narrated as the necessary vehicle for establishing the peace under Victoria's rule.[65] The *Leeds Times* praised Campbell for trying to limit the mass executions of Indian rebels by white soldiers and civil officers after each battle, besides favorably noting his effort to work with Hindus against fanatical Muslims. At Jalalabad, the newspaper reported, "the Hindoos politely offered to assist him in killing all the Mahomedans" the day before he was attacked by "a party of Ghazees, intoxicated with bhang" who were seeking "only to fulfill a vow of self-immolation."[66]

Campbell's own account, written after he retired in England following the ultimate appointment of his imperial career, reinforced the same tropes through nearly two hundred illustrations and prose that closely resembled the blow-by-blow accounts of military dispatches. "Mahometans," he declared, "throughout were most cruel, ferocious, and bloodthirsty; those of the artillery and cavalry were the worst of the lot. . . . Excited with bhang, they galloped about like fiends, intent only on bloodshed and murder."[67] Contrasted against the "Hindu Sepoy," who was "true to his salt" and enabled the escape of British officers several times, Campbell's Muslim foes, always delirious with bhang, exemplified the politics of colonial difference and sectarian division that was used to legitimate the rebellion's final suppression. Defining cultural difference as sectarian division among Hindu, Muslim, and Sikh subjects was crucial to undo the perceived united front put up by rebels across Indian territories in the early days of the insurgency. Campbell's public persona as a judicious man from a humble background, who appealed to Britons across lines of social class and national origin, played the counterfoil to the disunity of the colonized.

In perhaps the most revealing account of Campbell's capture of Bareilly, reported in the *Times* weeks before he returned to England, his men were again attacked by "Ghazees, or fanatical Mussulmans, furious with bhang," who "like the Roman Decii devote their lives with solemn oaths to their country and faith."[68]

Like the famed plebeian family devoted to its soldiers and the republic, the description of Campbell's Muslim foes refracted early modern English ideas of addiction as devotion. Before addiction was cast as debility and abuse, Rebecca Lemon has argued for its multiple devotional valences as the ability to announce or utter one's commitment, vulnerability, hard work, and courage.[69] "Uttering loud cries," the report declared, "one hundred and thirty of these fanatics rushed out . . . with bodies bent and heads low, waving their tulwars with a circular motion in the air, they came on with astonishing rapidity." Incidentally, Campbell's forces had recently been joined by Sikh soldiers. Sikhs had been recruited by the company's military since the early nineteenth century for their presumed status as a martial race.[70] But when the "fanatical Muslims" attacked, "they were mistaken for the Sikhs" by English soldiers. Disarray and chaos ensued as white soldiers failed to distinguish friend from foe in the melee. "Fortunately, Sir Colin Campbell was close up. . . . His keen quick eye detected the case at once," following which he "closed the ranks" and led the bayonet charge that killed all 133 men.[71]

Campbell's tenure as commander in chief in India prefaced the tension between the required military recruitment of Indians and the expansion of the numbers of white British troops there. Unreliable Indian soldiers who could turn into rebels had produced several imperial anxieties, especially since the army was also the largest single employer in India. In Parliament George De Lacy Evans, the former British general, "denounced the ferocity and inhumanity of the sepoys who had been treated with the greatest kindness." The mutiny was, Evans argued, some kind of misadventure, "to be traced to the habit Indians had of taking bhang, when they were under excitement."[72] The mutineers, Evans pleaded after arguing for military expansion in India, should be "punished with the utmost severity" to reduce the odds of rebellion in the future.[73] After the initial wave of reprisals that included tying rebels to the mouths of cannons before they were fired, mutineers were incarcerated in penal colonies where they worked as convict labor alongside indentured workers.[74] Celebrations of such violence to recapture India, in the imperial public sphere, were also celebrations of an anticipated victory over bhang. The *Bombay Telegraph*'s editorial in July 1858 celebrating the English victory at Plassey a hundred years before went on to describe how England had "girded up her loins and prepared herself for the struggle" to retake India after the rebellion. The rebellious, it announced, "have been blown from guns, hanged, transported, and imprisoned," and the English were now "a thousand times more dominant race." Readers in Essex or Nottingham, who read a syndicated version of this editorial, may not have been familiar with the history of Plassey, but their investments in empire had been forged and reinforced through the stream of military dispatches that had continued to circulate. So, when the editorial went on to claim that "the prestige of our arms has everywhere been maintained and even bhang and fanaticism have recoiled before the British bayonet," it appealed to commonplace sentiments of racial supremacy.[75] The dominant white race, instead of losing, had "muzzled the rebels in the jungles like tigers in their den." Hence, it concluded, "the disappearance of something white will, we imagine, be their own winding-sheets."

Most mid-nineteenth-century Victorian Britons who devoured such narratives of spectacular cannabis-induced violence did not necessarily know much about the Indian colonies despite consuming Indian commodities like tea, cotton, jute, and indigo. For many in Britain and across the English-speaking colonies, such sensational and racist reports of the mutiny might have been the first vivid and literal description of the empire in India. A letter to the editor of the *Standard* by one Orion described common knowledge of India before mutiny dispatches thus: "So absolute was the ignorance or indifference on Indian subjects . . . that the majority of educated classes would have been at a loss to tell whether Aurungzebe was a Mussulman or a Hindoo." However, he went on, "the horrors of the rebellion had given a melancholy familiarity" with cities, kings, and the topography of India to all Britons. To Orion, it had also alerted the empire to the "arrogance and obstinacy" of British administrators in India whose "lust of annexation had caused the great rival sects [Hindus and Muslims] to merge their mutual animosities." Orion's long letter indexed the alarmed perceptions of the East India Company not just in England but across the British Empire. "Are we to punish only the miserable tools of this conspiracy, to slaughter the wretches whose crimes, hideous as they are, have been perhaps committed in the madness of fanaticism or the frenzy of bhang," Orion asked, "and to pass without censure or remark the misdeeds and negligence of those in authority, whether in Calcutta or Canning-Row?"[76] The question was indicative of a wider political shift against the East India Company. A year of fierce parliamentary debates on the colonization of India led to the Government of India Act in August 1858, which passed the colony formally from the East India Company over to the Crown and Parliament.[77]

For proponents of Britain's civilizing mission, the inclusion of India within a more formal state structure only increased the ambit of claims that could be made on behalf of the colony. Missionaries, for instance, had long considered the company's profits from the Opium Wars immoral, and the expansion of the colonial state in India drew intoxicants deeper into the ambit of missionary discourse. Even as the war in India was ending, a few miles south of Liverpool, Reverend A. O'Neale of Birmingham reminded his audience that the East India Company had, in fact, held a monopoly on the narcotics produced by Indian hemp. Drawing on Coleridge's experiments with laudanum, O'Neale liberally tried to relate cannabis and opium as equivalent narcotics. He associated their effects with Turkish "mischief" and Indian "desperation" before noting that the "good Bishop Wilson had said that the judgement of God would come down upon the English for their growth of opium in Bengal, and how fearfully that had been verified in the mutiny."[78] Similarly, at a meeting of missionaries in Bury, one Thomas Reynolds told the Reverends C. Elven and A. Tyler that "thousands of our fellow-subjects in India are oppressed" by the opium and bhang trade.[79] Bhang, he argued, had caused the "poor sepoys," many of whom were Muslims, to "throw themselves upon the British bayonets." Citing Coleridge as well, Reynolds attacked the violations of treaties effected by the opium trade and reminded his audience to sign a petition to Parliament asking for the prohibition of opium production. Missionary networks indexed the growing moral consciousness of temperance that reproduced Orientalist typologies to then bind up opium and cannabis as equivalent drugs. Instead of the state profiting from them, the argument went, it should work with missionaries to reduce the pervasive sway that drugs, in general, held in ordinary life in the colonies. The flat equivalence of cannabis with opium in British temperance politics after 1859 prefigured the panics of the late nineteenth century around cannabis and lunacy in India. Asylum officials routinely wrote in cannabis consumption as the likely cause of madness among Indians without proper investigation into the causes of mental health crises, vagrancy, or delinquency.[80] Anti-opium campaigners took up cudgels against Indian cannabis, further inflating the perceived addiction of the latter and leading to the lengthy inquiries of the Royal Commission on Opium and the Indian Hemp Drugs Commission in 1894. Testimonies to the commission revealed the excesses of temperance panics and asylum recording practices, but judicial commissions and laboratory knowledge were vastly limited in comparison to the ambit of popularity enjoyed by periodicals and newspapers that had established the place of cannabis as a conduit to rebellion among Indians.

Conclusion

Cannabis sativa produces an intoxicating resin that courses through its stalk, leaves, and flowers. In South Asian history, different social groups have harnessed the plant's intoxicating potency and used it in substances and commodities—ganja of multiple varieties from the flowering tops, bhang of multiple types from the leaves, and charas from the resin in the flower and stalk. Across the heterogeneous landscapes of South Asia, the terms *ganja* and *bhang* themselves are sometimes interchangeable, producing unstable but contextual forms of meaning. For instance, in male wrestling communities and Hindu ascetic culture in northern India, bhang is drunk as an anxiolytic to soothe the nerves and calm one's sense of desire.[81] In the Deccan, ganja-smoking and bhang-drinking was common in what Nile Green has called "barracks Islam," the everyday religious life of Muslim sepoys in military contingents of the Hyderabad princely state that were under British control especially after the rebellion.[82] In rural eastern Bengal, ganja consumption animated cosmological rituals of poor and low-caste communities that eschewed orthodoxies in both Hinduism and Islam for unitarian or millenarian cosmologies.[83] From unique godheads to ascetic monks and warrior-saints, South Asian practices of intoxication have thus animated diverse bodies that fluidly spanned multiple religious traditions and social movements.

Early nineteenth-century colonial records distilled this rich history fundamentally through a flattened framework of ubiquity. Few English scholars studied the religious cultures of meaning underlying Indian cannabis, despite devotion, intoxication, and divine possession being common themes in European religious thought. Instead, ethnographic accounts of labor and mass festivity cast cannabis as a drug of rife prevalence, perennially at hand to furnish wildness and irrational violence. While it is highly plausible that rebels regularly drank bhang, the continuous emplotment of cannabis as an extraordinary animating substance during the mutiny shows us the material effects of framing addiction as rebellion in the colony. It is not the phenomenology of the addictive experience but its use toward evacuating the political rationality of insurgency that constitutes Indian cannabis in the imperial archive. This does not mean that the sensory relation between the self and the intoxicant is absent. It is, in fact, the margin against which colonial power concentrated fluid meanings of addiction into the body of the Indian rebel. Ultimately, the missive republished in Belfast, in discursively casting bhang as the primer for extraordinary violence, illuminated material interventions that ideologically reinforced fantasies of racial supremacy in colonial India.

UTATHYA CHATTOPADHYAYA is assistant professor of history at the University of California, Santa Barbara. He teaches the social and cultural history of South Asia and British imperialism in global perspectives. His research explores how intoxicant substances inhabit histories of gender, labor, popular culture, and agrarian life.

Acknowledgments

I would like to thank Rebecca Lemon for reading several drafts and giving me thoughtful and critical feedback, and the anonymous reviewers for their suggestions and questions. Thanks also to Kate McDonald, Bishnupriya Ghosh, Antoinette Burton, Christine Peralta, and Sherene Seikaly for their extensive comments on previous drafts.

Notes

1   Hofmeyr, *Gandhi's Printing Press*, 13.
2   *Belfast News-Letter*, "A Hint." Emphasis added. This was merely ten years after Britain had suppressed the 1848 rebellion in Ireland and incarcerated Thomas Meagher in Australia.
3   On figures like Garcia De Orta and Thomas Bowrey, see Breen, *Age of Intoxication*, 98–104; da Costa, *Medicine*; and Mills, *Cannabis Britannica*, 18–32. On bhang use among warrior Sufis in Deccan courts, see Eaton, *Sufis of Bijapur*, 255–70.
4   Mills, *Madness Cannabis and Colonialism*.
5   Mills, *Cannabis Britannica*.
6   On periodicals and imperial culture, see Burton, *Burdens of History*, 97–126.
7   For responses to the mutiny by Indians in England, see Fisher, "Multiple Meanings of 1857."
8   Stokes, *Peasant Armed*; Bayly, *Indian Society*; Metcalf, *Aftermath of Revolt*; Anderson, *Indian Uprising*; Bates and Major, *Mutiny at the Margins*; Roy, *Politics of a Popular Uprising*; Wagner, *Great Fear*; Fuerst, *Indian Muslim Minorities*; Wagner, *Skull of Alam Bheg*.
9   Burton, *Trouble with Empire*.
10   Krishnan, *Reading the Global*.
11   Zieger, *Inventing the Addict*.
12   Lemon, *Addiction and Devotion*.
13   On critiques of experience as a framework for understanding addiction, see Alexander and Roberts, *High Culture*; and Brodie and Redfield, *High Anxieties*.
14   Brodie and Redfield, *High Anxieties*, 5–6.
15   *Chambers' Edinburgh Journal*, "Indian Bhang."
16   On the demedicalization of Egyptian hashish in France in the same period, see Guba, *Taming Cannabis*, 150–86.
17   Guba, *Taming Cannabis*, 63.
18   O'Shaughnessy, *On the Preparations of Indian Hemp*.
19   "Swinging Festivals of India" appeared in Lancashire's *Preston Chronicle*, the *Belfast News-Letter*, Reading's *Berkshire Chronicle*, Yorkshire's *Leeds Times*, Bangor's *North Wales Chronicle*, and the Scottish *Paisley Herald and Renfrewshire Advertiser* on June 14, 1856. Devon's *Trewman's Exeter Flying Post* carried it the next week.
20   Yule and Burnell, *Hobson-Jobson*, 220.
21   Dirks, "Policing of Tradition"; Banerjee, "City of Dreadful Night"; Oddie, *Popular Religion*; Brown, "Abject to Object."
22   Statham, *Indian Recollections*, 118. Notably, Statham had recorded bhang consumption as a constitutive part of widow femicide in India. For an earlier account, via Richard Blechynden, see Robb, "Children, Emotion, Identity, and Empire," 185–86.
23   Sturman, *Governance of Social Life*; Dirks, "Policing of Tradition."
24   Beaufort, *Digest of the Criminal Law*, 765.
25   *Manchester Guardian*, "Delhi."
26   Palmer, *Mutiny Outbreak*; Mukherjee, *Awadh in Revolt*.
27   *Manchester Guardian*, "Delhi." The same report was carried by publications like the *North Wales Chronicle*, the *Leicestershire Mercury*, the *York Herald*, and the *Birmingham Gazette* and by the *John O'Groat Journal*, published in Wick, Scotland.
28   Pandey attacked his superiors in Barrackpore on March 29, 1857, and was executed on April 8. See Hearsey to Secretary, Government of India, April 9, 1857, in Chick, *Annals*, 66.
29   *Morning Post*, "East Indies."

30   *Sheffield Daily Telegraph*, "Anticipated Outbreak at Oude."

31   This report circulated widely outside London, from Yorkshire to Dorset, where the *Sherborne Mercury* carried it on October 30, 1855.

32   Usmani, "A Note"; Hussain, "Bareilly in 1857."

33   Syndications of this letter appeared in multiple newspapers. See *Examiner*, "Rebels at Bareilly."

34   By the 1890s fictionalized accounts of Tipu Sultan's losses in 1799 also featured bhang-intoxicated failures. See Henty, *Tiger of Mysore*, 148.

35   Small newspapers like the *Cheltenham Looker-On* and the *Bucks Herald* of Aylesbury carried this report on July 18, 1857.

36   *Hertford Mercury and Reformer*, "Letters from Delhi."

37   *Hereford Times*, "Action on the 14th before Delhi." This report ran the next day in *Reynolds' Newspaper* in London.

38   *Daily News*, "The Indian Mutinies." This report ran in the *Bath Chronicle and Weekly Gazette* on October 1, 1857.

39   *Lloyd's Illustrated Newspaper*, "Second Mutiny at Neemuch."

40   *Exeter and Plymouth Gazette*, "Indian Revolt."

41   *Observer*, "Race and Religion in India."

42   *Observer*, "Race and Religion in India."

43   Khan, "Wahabis in the 1857 Revolt." The term *Wahhabi* also homogenized others, like Sufi Muslims, who were part of the rebellion.

44   On afterlives of imperial anxieties around Wahhabis, see Stephens, "Phantom Wahhabi." For earlier iterations of paranoia about Islam, see Mallampalli, *Muslim Conspiracy*.

45   *Observer*, "Race and Religion in India."

46   Krishnan, *Reading the Global*, 78–93.

47   Spores, *Running Amok*; McCollom, *History on Its Side*.

48   Wallace, "Nana Sahib," 592.

49   Frith, *Rebel or Revolutionary?*; Wagner, *Vengeance against England*.

50   On the mutiny novel as the transition of India from a site of adventure to a site of domesticity, see Lakshmi, "Mutiny Novel."

51   Glazzard, *Case of Sherlock Holmes*, 128.

52   Indian, "Nana Sahib."

53   *Chicago Daily Tribune*, "Effects of Bhang."

54   *New York Times*, "Capture of Nana Sahib"; *Saturday Review*, "Nana Sahib."

55   Unreliability was a common theme. Before his execution at Barrackpore, Mangal Pandey had claimed to have been under the influence of bhang and thus unaware of his actions that later instigated the rebellion. See Wagner, *Great Fear*, 87.

56   *Leeds Times*, "Fall of Delhi."

57   *Daily News*, "Leaguer of Lucknow."

58   Sinha, *Colonial Masculinity*; Streets, *Martial Races*.

59   The letter was published across two columns in many newspapers after London's *Morning Post* and the *Norfolk Chronicle* carried it on January 23, 1858. See *Norfolk Chronicle*, "Entrenched Camp Guard, Cawnpore."

60   The N-word, a common racial epithet outside the United States, was variably used by white soldiers to describe Indians. For the definitive argument on the term's usage, see Pryor, "Etymology of the N-Word."

61   Weheliye, *Habeas Viscus*, 67. On a later controversy around Blackness and imperial democracy, see Burton, "Tongues Untied."

62   *Norfolk Chronicle*, "Entrenched Camp Guard, Cawnpore."

63   *Morning Post*, "London."

64   *Morning Post*, "London."

65   On imperial careering, see Lambert and Lester, *Colonial Lives*.

66   *Leeds Times*, "India: Another Great Victory."

67   Campbell, *Narrative of the Indian Revolt*, 52, 80.

68   The report from the *Times* was syndicated across the world. See *Dundee Courier*, "Battle of Bareilly"; and *Illustrated Times*, "Attack on Bareilly."

69   Lemon, *Addiction and Devotion*, 7–10.

70   After the defeat in the Anglo-Sikh wars, many Sikhs joined the imperial military for employment. See Anderson, "Transportation of Narain Sing."

71   *Illustrated Times*, "Attack on Bareilly."

72   *Examiner*, "Imperial Parliament."

73   *Leeds Times*, "India." Here the reporter also glossed Evans's comments by adding that bhang was "a spirit more maddening than any known in Europe."

74   Carter and Bates, "Empire and Locality"; Wagner, *Skull of Alam Bheg*; Anderson, "Convicts and Coolies." Vasily Vereshchagin, the famous Russian realist painter, reproduced this moment in his 1884 work *The Suppression of the Indian Revolt by the English*.

75   *Essex Standard*, "Present State of India." The *Nottinghamshire Guardian* had published the editorial the day before.

76   Orion, "Indian Affairs."

77   Bender, *1857 Indian Uprising*; Robb, "On the Rebellion of 1857." On the subsequent reproduction of Englishness through mutiny touring, see Goswami, "'Englishness.'"

78   *Cheshire Observer*, "Lecture on the Opium Traffic."

79   *Bury and Norwich Post*, "Traffic in Opium."

80   Mills, *Cannabis Britannica*, 84–92.

81   Alter, *Wrestler's Body*, 154–57. Alter uses *hashish*
     to refer to bhang.
82   Green, *Islam and the Army*.
83   Chattopadhyaya, *Naogaon and the World*.

Works Cited

Alexander, Anna, and Mark Roberts. *High Culture:
     Reflections on Addiction and Modernity*. Albany:
     State University of New York Press, 2003.
Alter, Joseph. *The Wrestler's Body: Identity and
     Ideology in North India*. Berkeley: University of
     California Press, 1992.
Anderson, Clare. "Convicts and Coolies: Rethinking
     Indentured Labour in the Nineteenth
     Century." *Slavery and Abolition* 30, no. 1
     (2009): 93–109.
Anderson, Clare. *The Indian Uprising of 1857–1858:
     Prisons, Prisoners, and Rebellion*. London:
     Anthem, 2007.
Anderson, Clare. "The Transportation of Narain
     Sing: Punishment, Honor, and Identity from
     the Anglo-Sikh Wars to the Great Revolt."
     Modern Asian Studies 44, no. 5 (2010): 1115–45.
Banerjee, Sumanta. "City of Dreadful Night: Crime
     and Punishment in Colonial Calcutta."
     Economic and Political Weekly 38, no. 21 (2003):
     2045–55.
Bates, Crispin, and Andrea Major, eds. *Mutiny at the
     Margins*. 7 vols. New Delhi: Sage, 2013–17.
Bayly, C. A. *Indian Society and the Making of the
     British Empire*. Cambridge: Cambridge
     University Press, 1988.
Beaufort, F. L. *A Digest of the Criminal Law of the
     Presidency of Fort William and Guide to All
     Criminal Authorities Therein II*. Calcutta,
     1859.
Belfast News-Letter. "A Hint." February 20, 1858.
Bender, Jill. *The 1857 Indian Uprising and the British
     Empire*. Cambridge: Cambridge University
     Press, 2016.
Breen, Benjamin. *Age of Intoxication: Origins of the
     Global Drug Trade*. Philadelphia: University of
     Pennsylvania Press, 2019.
Brodie, Janet, and Mark Redfield, eds. *High
     Anxieties: Cultural Studies in Addiction*.
     Berkeley: University of California Press, 2002.
Brown, Rebecca. "Abject to Object: Colonialism
     Preserved through the Image of Muharram."
     RES: Anthropology and Aesthetics 43 (2003):
     203–17.
Burton, Antoinette. *Burdens of History: British
     Feminists, Indian Women, and Imperial Culture,
     1865–1915*. Chapel Hill: University of North
     Carolina Press, 1994.
Burton, Antoinette. "Tongues Untied: Lord
     Salisbury's 'Black Man' and the Boundaries of
     Imperial Democracy." *Comparative Studies in
     Society and History* 42, no. 3 (2000): 632–61.

Burton, Antoinette. *The Trouble with Empire:
     Challenges to Modern British Imperialism*.
     Oxford: Oxford University Press, 2015.
Bury and Norwich Post. "The Traffic in Opium."
     March 4, 1859.
Campbell, Colin. *Narrative of the Indian Revolt: From
     Its Outbreak to the Capture of Lucknow*. London,
     1858.
Carter, Marina, and Crispin Bates. "Empire and
     Locality: A Global Dimension to the 1857
     Indian Uprising." *Journal of Global History* 5,
     no. 1 (2010): 51–73.
Chambers' Edinburgh Journal. "Indian Bhang."
     January 27, 1849, 62–63.
Chattopadhyaya, Utathya. "Naogaon and the World:
     Intoxication, Commoditisation, and
     Imperialism in South Asia and the Indian
     Ocean, 1840–1940." PhD diss., University of
     Illinois, 2018.
Cheshire Observer. "Lecture on the Opium Traffic."
     February 5, 1859.
Chicago Daily Tribune. "The Effects of Bhang."
     December 14, 1874.
Chick, Noah Alfred. *Annals of the Indian Rebellion*.
     Calcutta, 1859.
da Costa, Palmira Fontes, ed. *Medicine, Trade, and
     Empire: Garcia de Orta's "Colloquies on the
     Simples and Drugs of India" (1563) in Context*.
     New York: Routledge, 2016.
Daily News. "The Indian Mutinies." October 1, 1857.
Daily News. "The Leaguer of Lucknow: Havelock's
     Last March." January 16, 1858.
Dirks, Nicholas. "The Policing of Tradition:
     Colonialism and Anthropology in Southern
     India." *Comparative Studies in Society and
     History* 39, no. 1 (1997): 182–212.
Dundee Courier. "The Battle of Bareilly: Desperate
     Attack by Fanatical Mussulmans." July 7,
     1858.
Eaton, Richard. *The Sufis of Bijapur, 1300–1700:
     Social Roles of Sufis in Medieval India*.
     Princeton, NJ: Princeton University Press,
     1978.
Essex Standard. "The Present State of India." August
     6, 1858.
Examiner. "Imperial Parliament." August 15, 1857.
Examiner. "The Rebels at Bareilly." June 5, 1858.
Exeter and Plymouth Gazette. "The Indian Revolt:
     Origin and History of the Bengal Mutiny."
     September 5, 1857.
Fisher, Michael. "Multiple Meanings of 1857 for
     Indians in Britain." *Economic and Political
     Weekly* 42, no. 19 (2007): 1703–9.
Frith, Nicola. "Rebel or Revolutionary? Representing
     Nana Sahib and the Bibighar Massacre in
     English- and French-Language Texts and
     Images." *Interventions: International Journal of
     Postcolonial Studies* 12, no. 3 (2010): 368–82.

Fuerst, Ilyse. *Indian Muslim Minorities and the 1857 Rebellion: Religion, Rebels, and Jihad*. London: Tauris, 2017.

Glazzard, Andrew. *The Case of Sherlock Holmes: Secrets and Lies in Conan Doyle's Detective Fiction*. Edinburgh: Edinburgh University Press, 2018.

Goswami, Manu. "'Englishness' on the Imperial Circuit: Mutiny Tours in Colonial South Asia." *Journal of Historical Sociology* 9, no. 1 (1996): 54–84.

Green, Nile. *Islam and the Army in Colonial India: Sepoy Religion and the Service of Empire*. Cambridge: Cambridge University Press, 2009.

Guba, David A., Jr. *Taming Cannabis: Drugs and Empire in Nineteenth-Century France*. Montreal: McGill-Queen's University Press, 2020.

Henty, George Alfred. *The Tiger of Mysore*. London, 1896.

Hereford Times. "The Action on the 14th before Delhi." September 19, 1857.

Hertford Mercury and Reformer. "Letters from Delhi." September 5, 1857.

Hofmeyr, Isabel. *Gandhi's Printing Press: Experiments in Slow Reading*. Cambridge, MA: Harvard University Press, 2013.

Hussain, Iqbal. "Bareilly in 1857." *Proceedings of the Indian History Congress* 65 (2004): 692–708.

Illustrated Times. "The Attack on Bareilly." August 14, 1858.

Indian. "Nana Sahib." *London Journal*, July 5, 1862.

Khan, Iqtidar Alam. "The Wahabis in the 1857 Revolt: A Brief Appraisal of Their Role." *Social Scientist* 41, nos. 5–6 (2013): 15–23.

Krishnan, Sanjay. *Reading the Global: Troubling Perspectives on Britain's Empire in Asia*. New York: Columbia University Press, 2007.

Lakshmi, Aishwarya. "The Mutiny Novel: Creating the Domestic Body of Empire." *Economic and Political Weekly* 42, no. 19 (2007): 1746–53.

Lambert, David, and Alan Lester. *Colonial Lives across the British Empire: Imperial Careering in the Long Nineteenth Century*. Cambridge: Cambridge University Press, 2006.

Leeds Times. "The Fall of Delhi." November 21, 1857.

Leeds Times. "India." August 15, 1857.

Leeds Times. "India: Another Great Victory." June 19, 1858.

Lemon, Rebecca. *Addiction and Devotion in Early Modern England*. Philadelphia: University of Pennsylvania Press, 2018.

Lloyd's Illustrated Newspaper. "Second Mutiny at Neemuch." October 4, 1857.

Mallampalli, Chandra. *A Muslim Conspiracy in British India? Politics and Paranoia in the Early Nineteenth-Century Deccan*. Cambridge: Cambridge University Press, 2017.

Manchester Guardian. "Delhi." July 15, 1857.

McCollom, Joanie. "History on Its Side: Narratives of 'Malaysia' and Beyond." PhD diss., University of California, Santa Cruz, 2010.

Metcalf, Thomas. *The Aftermath of Revolt: India, 1857–1890*. Princeton, NJ: Princeton University Press, 1964.

Mills, James. *Cannabis Britannica: Empire, Trade, and Prohibition, 1800–1928*. Oxford: Oxford University Press, 2003.

Mills, James. *Madness Cannabis and Colonialism: The Native-Only Lunatic Asylums of British India*. Basingstoke: Macmillan, 2000.

Morning Post. "East Indies." December 11, 1839.

Morning Post. "London." March 22, 1858.

Mukherjee, Rudrangshu. *Awadh in Revolt, 1857–1858: A Study of Popular Resistance*. Delhi: Oxford University Press, 1982.

New York Times. "Capture of Nana Sahib." October 31, 1874.

Norfolk Chronicle. "Entrenched Camp Guard, Cawnpore." January 23, 1858.

Observer. "Race and Religion in India." April 4, 1858.

Oddie, Geoffrey. *Popular Religion, Elites, and Reforms: Hook-Swinging and Its Prohibition in Colonial India*. New Delhi: Manohar, 1995.

Orion. "Indian Affairs." *Standard*, September 19, 1857.

O'Shaughnessy, W. B. *On the Preparations of Indian Hemp or Gunjah*. Calcutta, 1839.

Palmer, J. A. B. *The Mutiny Outbreak at Meerut in 1857*. Cambridge: Cambridge University Press, 1966.

Pryor, Elizabeth Stordeur. "The Etymology of the N-Word: Resistance, Language, and the Politics of Freedom in the Antebellum North." *Journal of the Early Republic* 36, no. 2 (2016): 203–45.

Robb, Peter. "Children, Emotion, Identity, and Empire: Views from the Blechyndens' Calcutta Diaries." *Modern Asian Studies* 40, no. 1 (2006): 175–201.

Robb, Peter. "On the Rebellion of 1857: A Brief History of an Idea." *Economic and Political Weekly* 42, no. 19 (2007): 1696–1702.

Roy, Tapti. *The Politics of a Popular Uprising: Bundelkhand in 1857*. Oxford: Oxford University Press, 1994.

Saturday Review. "Nana Sahib." October 31, 1874.

Sheffield Daily Telegraph. "The Anticipated Outbreak at Oude." October 22, 1855.

Sinha, Mrinalini. *Colonial Masculinity: The "Manly Englishman" and the "Effeminate Bengali" in the Late Nineteenth Century*. Manchester: Manchester University Press, 1995.

Spores, John. *Running Amok: An Historical Inquiry*. Athens: Ohio University, Center for International Studies, 1988.

Statham, John. *Indian Recollections*. London, 1832.

Stephens, Julia. "The Phantom Wahhabi: Liberalism and the Muslim Fanatic in Mid-Victorian India." *Modern Asian Studies* 47, no. 1 (2013): 22–52.

Stokes, Eric. *The Peasant Armed: The Indian Revolt of 1857.* Oxford: Clarendon, 1986.

Streets, Heather. *Martial Races: The Military, Race, and Masculinity in British Imperial Culture, 1857–1914.* Manchester: Manchester University Press, 2004.

Sturman, Rachel. *The Governance of Social Life in Colonial India: Liberalism, Religious Law, and Women's Rights.* Cambridge: Cambridge University Press, 2012.

Usmani, M. S. "A Note on the Provisional Revolutionary Government of Rohilkhand." *Proceedings of the Indian History Congress* 43 (1982): 618–24.

Wagner, Kim. *The Great Fear of 1857: Rumours, Conspiracies, and the Making of the Indian Uprising.* Oxford: Lang, 2010.

Wagner, Kim. *The Skull of Alam Bheg: The Life and Death of a Rebel of 1857.* Oxford: Oxford University Press, 2018.

Wagner, Kim. "Vengeance against England: Hermann Goedsche and the Indian Uprising." In *Global Perspectives.* Vol. 3 of *Mutiny at the Margins: New Perspectives on the Indian Uprising of 1857,* edited by Marina Carter and Crispin Bates, 150–69. Delhi: Sage, 2013.

Wallace, Brian. "Nana Sahib in British Culture and Memory." *Historical Journal* 58, no. 2 (2015): 589–613.

Weheliye, Alexander. *Habeas Viscus: Racializing Assemblages, Biopolitics, and Black Feminist Theories of the Human.* Durham, NC: Duke University Press, 2014.

Yule, Henry, and A. C. Burnell. *Hobson-Jobson: A Glossary of Colloquial Anglo-Indian Words and Phrases and of Kindred Terms, Etymological, Historical, Geographical, and Discursive.* London: Murray, 1903.

Zieger, Susan. *Inventing the Addict: Drugs, Race, and Sexuality in Nineteenth-Century British and American Literature.* Amherst: University of Massachusetts Press, 2008.

Opium and Logistical Nightmares

SUSAN ZIEGER

Abstract   This essay argues that opium's pivotal role in nineteenth-century political economy and aesthetics constructed addiction as a relationship between labor and capital that has persisted throughout the twentieth and into the twenty-first century. Nineteenth-century discourses on opium addiction frame it as a crisis of sovereignty for individuals and masses in ways that veil its relationships to labor, collectivity, and community. Yet addiction arises within broad systems as much as it does within individuals: in this exemplary case, of labor, empire, opium, and logistics. This essay rereads nineteenth-century discourses of opium addiction through "the logistical sublime," in which all manufacturing and distribution processes go smoothly, and "the logistical nightmare," in which they descend into chaos. It reframes opium addiction as a logistical technique that secured and maintained the preeminence of British, and later, Chinese and US imperial capital.

Keywords   opium, addiction, nineteenth century

Without opium, there would have been no [British] empire," wrote the historian Carl Trocki.[1] Grown in India by coerced peasant labor, smuggled to Canton harbor on clipper ships, and distributed overland to low-wage peasant workers, opium became so valuable in the early decades of the nineteenth century that it could be used as cash, especially when the collapse of the Spanish empire in Latin America created a worldwide shortage of silver. The steady flow of high-quality opium from India to Canton secured the British domination of trade with China, while financing the East India Company's rule of India. In the aftermath of British losses in North America, this triumph of manufacturing and distribution secured the financial grounds of the empire. Its great significance to British global power explains why the government underwrote merchants' losses when the Chinese confiscated their cargo; and why it dispatched warships to force the Chinese market to remain open, starting the first Opium War in 1839. (A second Opium War, from 1856–1860, repeated the point.) As a mover of goods and troops, as a substitute for cash, as the security of territory and trade routes, and thus as the empire's foundation, opium—a habit-forming substance—is one of a handful of world-changing commodities of the nineteenth century.

ENGLISH LANGUAGE NOTES

60:1, April 2022 DOI 10.1215/00138282-9560254
© 2022 Regents of the University of Colorado

But my claim in this essay is even bigger: I suggest that opium's pivotal role in nineteenth-century political economy and aesthetics coalesced a relationship between labor and capital that has persisted throughout the twentieth and into the twenty-first century. This relationship went by several names and settled in the early twentieth century as *addiction.* The general understanding of addiction as the desire and need to use a substance as a result of having used it in the past obscures its sites of emergence within historical economic conditions. Nineteenth-century discourses on opium addiction frame it as a crisis of sovereignty for individuals and masses in ways that veil its relationships to labor, collectivity, and community. Yet addiction is never solely about individuals; it is the outcome of relations between broader systems—in this case, of labor, empire, and opium. An unlikely but eminently useful heuristic for revealing these relations is logistics. This article reframes opium addiction as a logistical technique that secured and maintained the preeminence of British, and later, Chinese and US imperial capital. Thinking about addiction through logistics brushes against the grain of assumptions about will, agency, and culture. It opens up the topic to new interpretations attentive to aesthetics, politics, and economics.

Logistics is the art and science of moving goods, people, and information to maximize profit. A textbook formula describes "the seven rights" of supply-chain management that form the logistical ideal: to deliver the right product to the right place at the right time to the right customer in the right condition at the right price and in the right quantity.[2] The formula suggests precision, coordination, calculation, measurement. A self-evident rationality, it valorizes order, convergence, closure, and arrival. Only by getting all the factors right and completing the delivery does logistics optimize the journey of the goods, people, or information, and thereby succeed in maximizing profit for the firm. In the nineteenth century a genre of general-interest periodical literature I call "the manufacturing narrative" described the orderly sourcing, production, and distribution of goods, reflecting the logistical ideal. Literary and visual texts in this popular genre, which were themselves widely distributed and consumed throughout the British empire, made logistical procedures central to economic prosperity—perhaps most of all in relation to the opium trade, which brought wealth to British firms throughout the first half of the century.

Recognizing the popular genre of the manufacturing narrative, with its descriptions of logistical relations, helps highlight a key yet overlooked feature of logistics: even as it is a branch of scientific management, it is also an art. Its rationalizing and technoscientific aspects are in tension with its less-measurable aesthetic, affective, and sensual dimensions. As an instrument of the dismal science, logistics at first glance seems too dry to inspire aesthetic feeling, but it does. In this essay I will discuss two of the most important aesthetic dimensions of logistics at stake in understanding its complex relations to opium, and to addiction. The first is the sublime, an eighteenth-century aesthetic category describing an encounter with a marvel of nature so large it exceeds the imagination and can only be apprehended by reason. As theorized by Edmund Burke and Immanuel Kant, the sublime could take the shape of both awe and terror. At the turn of the nineteenth century, writers began to use the term to refer to manufactured structures and activities, such as the large new docks of London and Liverpool and the global trade they facilitated. Tamara Plakins Thornton calls this "the capitalist sublime," but I identify it more specifically as "the logistical sublime": what is astonishing and marvelous is not the abstraction of capitalism but its developing technique, logistics.[3] It is not the docks themselves or the financing that built them but the mind-boggling complexity of goods from all over the world arriving at this single point and resolving the chaos of global imperial trade into specific delights for metropolitan consumers.

The pleasing and even sublime organizational potential of the London docks is thrown into relief by their imagined opposites: the shipwreck and the lost cargo and lives; or the spoilage, theft, graft, and other mishaps whereby the goods do not reach their destination and the seven rights remain unmet. Such misery goes in twenty-first-century parlance by the colloquial phrase "logistical nightmare"—the second of my two aesthetic categories. It is the unresolved chaos of unfamiliar materials from unknown lands, goods that have not reached their destination and thus have not fulfilled their destiny but remain jumbled and discomposed in incoherent transit. Because logistics' core values are precision, coordination, and calculation, the logistical nightmare is that which cannot be measured, counted, articulated, and organized. Either the nightmare is rationalized, its awe and terror tamed by reason and thus transformed into sublime order, or it becomes an endless hell. My thesis is that the foundational, late Romantic expression of opium addiction, Thomas De Quincey's *Confessions of an English Opium-Eater* (1821), describes a logistical nightmare that undoes the precise organization of the manufacturing narrative, placing the logistical sublime beyond reach.

In De Quincey's text, the horror of opium addiction, as a logistical nightmare, is embedded in imperial and racialized aesthetics. It connected the surreal terror of a disordered, unproductive imagination, in which nothing arrives at the right place or time, to the suffering of Southeast Asian masses, in passages that evoke the misery of life on the lower rungs of capital. De Quincey gestured toward but could not fully describe the range of possibilities and limits on human agency and affect that opium production and consumption generated. A second discourse, which crossed both Anglo and Chinese contexts, accentuated opium's resemblance to poison, a strategy that, like De Quincey's, foreclosed a realistic description of collective or community opium addiction as contoured by the demands of capital. This article is an attempt, necessarily partial, that opens an imaginative space in which to read addiction in the human context of logistics. Here addiction might be an eminently rational, emotionally complex way of coping with the true nightmare, that is, the apparently sublimely organized logistical world of capital flows. My conclusion uses the nineteenth-century case study to think about the opioid crisis and its redefinition of addiction in relation to pain.

The Logistical Sublime

The logistical sublime grows from the manufacturing narrative, a genre describing the orderly production and distribution of goods and running through middlebrow journals, penny magazines, publications aimed at workingmen, pamphlets, and books. Best exemplified by George Dodd's popular sketches of factory procedures in the *Penny Magazine* and *Household Words* in the 1830s, such as "A Day at the Hat Factory," and "A Day at the Cigar Factory," the genre presented a pleasingly simple picture of industrial life, in which raw materials are transported to London, transformed into commodities, and redistributed to consumers. For example, the assembly of a beaver hat passes through the sequenced phases of washing the animal's fur, drying it in one room, carding it in another, "bowing" or thinning it in a third, "felting" or pressing it into wool, and so on.[4] Charles Babbage's *On the Economy of Machinery and Manufactures* (1832), like Dodd's work, published by the populist editor Charles Knight, foregrounds the logistical aspect of manufacturing, explaining the time it takes to learn industrial skills, the shelf life of the goods and durability of machinery, the location of factories, the measurement of efficiency, and the general streamlining of operations; Andrew Ure's *Philosophy of Manufactures* (1835) took up similar issues. Ure's magisterial *Dictionary of Arts, Manufactures, and Mines* (1839) sought to document all the processes whereby natural substances were transformed into saleable commodities. It took 1,334 pages to explain them all, from "abb-wool" to zinc: such was the sublime scale of logistical assembly. Reflecting the Victorian era's penchant for monumental, march-of-mind projects, these and similar works aimed to explain all things built, fabricated, crafted, and extracted to middle- and working-class readers.[5] Such sketches avoided mention of the glitches, delays, and failures that attend every scene of production. They normalized capital's material transformations by maintaining silence about workers' welfare, wages, and political subjectivities. Though their ostensible topic was manufacturing, they also created a tacit, generalized sense of assembly as something that began outside the factory walls, in the sourcing and harvesting of materials, and also ended beyond them, in the shape of finished products transported to wholesalers and retailers. This expanded scene of transformation—beavers into hats—is that of the logistical sublime.

The logistical sublime emerges when the manufacturing narrative, combined with ekphrastic descriptions or visual culture, imagines assembly on a grand scale. Writing about the sublime, both Edmund Burke and Immanuel Kant emphasized the way awe can tip over into fear or even terror when one is confronted with monumental scale from a position of safety.[6] By the nineteenth century the sublime also applied to colossal technological marvels such as the Erie Canal or the first transcontinental railroad. These have been proposed as examples of "the American technological sublime," but the phenomenon also appeared in places such as London—for example, London's West India Docks—and, I contend, in Bengal.[7] One of the century's best examples was the tremendously popular set of six prints by Walter S. Sherwill, a lieutenant colonel in Bengal, of the Sudder opium factory in Patna circa 1851. Sherwill shows the manufacturing process in his prints *The Examining Hall*, illustrating where the harvested plant is sorted and labeled; *The Mixing Room*, where it is transformed into paste; *The Balling Room*, where the paste is shaped into cakes; *The Drying Room*, where the cakes are rotated and punctured to prevent fermentation; *The Stacking Room*, where they are prepared for packaging; and, lastly, *The Opium Fleet*, which transports the opium to China.[8] I wrote that sentence largely in the passive voice to reflect the images' erasure of the laborers who perform those productive activities. Though they are present, Sherwill's workers are dwarfed

Figure 1. Walter S. Sherwill, *The Stacking Room*, in *Illustrations* (1851).

by the monumental architecture of the rooms, rendered through single-point perspective. Each of the rooms vanishes in the distance; the stacking room (fig. 1) also features a long vertical axis of high shelves reached by ladders, and tiny figures of boys traversing them.

As Hope Childers describes them, the prints' streamlined quality creates a triumphal imperial perspective, appealing to the metropolitan readers of the *Graphic*, visitors to the Great Exhibition, where they were shown, and the numerous viewers and readers who encountered them in reprints throughout the rest of the century.[9] What makes these images sublime is the towering space, seemingly infinite regression, and inhuman scale; what makes them logistical is their representation of a smooth, technoscientific process of flow extending beyond the factory to distribution: the product's transportation by the fleet. In Sherwill's prints, the logistical sublime creates a sense of awe at the imperial might that commands such vast production and distribution. This power both orders the cathedral-like space of the factory and connects it to the global system of transport on the open sea. Amitav Ghosh's historical novel *Sea of Poppies* (2008), intervening in this imperial imaginary, presents the weighing room through the eyes of his peasant protagonist, Deeti: "The space in front of her was so vast that her head began to spin. . . . The ceiling soared so high above the beaten floor that the air inside was cool, almost wintry."[10] I will return to this seemingly infinite architecture of assembly in the next section.

The opium fleet depicted in Sherwill's final print (fig. 2) moves the precision, order, and speed of the monumental factory interior outward to the sea. Called into

Figure 2. Walter S. Sherwill, *The Opium Fleet*, in *Illustrations* (1851).

existence to service the opium trade, the clipper ship coalesced the ideology of efficiency and speed in the service of British imperial power. The surge in investment
in Indian-grown opium generated demand for vessels faster than the old "country
ships" of the eighteenth century, which carried mixed cargoes of opium, textiles,
guns, and ammunition along routes from India to Southeast Asia, trading them
for spices, tin, and silver in the Strait of Malacca.[11] The clippers featured streamlined hulls, more sails, and small cargo spaces for their dedicated commodity.
They made nonstop journeys up to three times a year, including monsoon season,
maintaining a steady flow of opium to China and silver back to India. Consistent
and nimble, they also navigated a complex system of bribery to deliver their illegal
goods. A clipper arriving in Lintin discharged opium to floating hulks, then proceeded with its legitimate cargo to Whampoa; the Chinese buyer would pay customs officials, then retrieve and remove the opium balls from their chests, packing
them in bags and placing them in armed small boats with crews of fifty to seventy.[12]
The small boats, known as "centipedes" or "scrambling dragons," would beach the
opium at spots hidden along the coast.[13] The clippers themselves were also armed
and manned with crews skilled in fighting to protect their expensive cargoes from
pirates. Logistics is also a military science. Pivoting at any moment from cargo ship
to fighting ship, the clipper embodies the key logistical priority of security. In both
modes, the ships demonstrate a precise choreography in their drive toward delivery.
The clippers' principal historian, Basil Lubbock, romanticized their agility and efficacy as part of "the glorious profession of seafaring": the merchant adventurer risk-

ing capital for a thousandfold return, the sailor running contraband on an uncharted coast, the shipmaster's outwitting of Chinese pirates and custom officials.[14] Fast, specialized, securitized, armed, and, above all, fortune-making, clippers represented a logistical aesthetic.

Thus the logistical sublime is an aesthetic that valorizes capital's ability to affect a kind of magic—the massive transformation of poppies into opium, its transport across the sea, and its consumption by an entirely different people—without acknowledging the human labor that made it happen.

The Nightmare of Logistics

The logistical sublime is one aesthetic strategy for fetishizing opium's world-building economic power. De Quincey's *Confessions* represented another. As Benjamin Breen details in this issue, though De Quincey did not pioneer the drug addiction memoir, his *Confessions* cast a long shadow over the literature of intoxicated and addicted experience, far into the twentieth century, and far from Britain.[15] The most influential and memorable passages of his literary memoir were his opium dreams, hallucinatory visions that may have resulted from his high dosage and prolonged use. One of them was inspired by his listening to Samuel Taylor Coleridge describe Giovanni Battista Piranesi's *Carceri d'Invenzione* (*Imaginary Prisons*), a set of sixteen prints published in 1750 that depict gloomy monumental interiors. As De Quincey describes them, they are "vast Gothic halls, on the floor of which stood all sorts of engines and machinery, wheels, cables, pulleys, levers, catapults, &c. &c., expressive of enormous power put forth and resistance overcome."[16] The description evokes a factory as enormous as Sherwill's images of Sudder. Instead of the plethora of automated machinery De Quincey sees, however, we might see the figures of the laborers, who perform the work of cables, pulleys, and levers by running and climbing throughout the scenes. Both De Quincey and Sherwill emphasize the complex processes that harness energy to break down natural materials and transform them into commodities. An oneiric fragment, De Quincey's factory is not rational, orderly, or productive. Piranesi himself appears as a laborer within it, multiplied on ascending stairs that terminate abruptly and begin again, "until the unfinished stairs and Piranesi both are lost in the upper gloom of the hall. With the same power of endless growth and self-reproduction did my architecture proceed in dreams" (*C*, 71). Canonical criticism of De Quincey, such as M. H. Abrams's *Milk of Paradise* (1934) and Alethea Hayter's *Opium and the Romantic Imagination* (1968), interprets this and similar passages along psychological and psychoanalytic lines, but its evident resemblance to a factory and its emphasis on labor also suggest a relationship to political economy. Like Sherwill's rooms at the opium factory in Patna, De Quincey's are vertical images of continuous labor, a never-ending effort. The eternal quality of this growth reflects the requirements that capital circulate to generate profit, that the assembly of products never ceases, and that logistics never stop moving goods. De Quincey's haunted architecture appears as a surreal satire of the logistical sublime: the monumental space and complex processual machinery is present, but nothing is ever actually assembled, completed, and delivered.

De Quincey's emphasis on power, growth, resistance, and self-reproduction in those passages indicates the *Confessions'* interest in human labor, also seen in the text's motif of a desire for rest. At first De Quincey felt that opium represented "a sabbath of repose; a resting from human labours," "a tranquility . . . resulting from mighty and equal antagonisms; infinite activities, infinite repose" (*C*, 49). As in the Piranesian factory, the relentlessness of capital generates a compensatory human longing for rest. Opium seems to supply the balm that soothes the stresses of modern life, with its round-the-clock undertakings. Yet, because its doses are dictated by the rhythms of industrial labor, it either becomes a mechanical, habitual adjunct to labor or deepens repose into lethargy, inculcating a corrosive stasis. The opium addict wishes to be productive but lacks the power even to try: "He lies under the weight of incubus and nightmare; he lies in sight of all that he would fain perform. . . . He curses the spells which chain him down from motion" (*C*, 67). The passage limns the Romantic fascination with nightmare; the artist Henri Fuseli depicted it similarly, as a demon sitting on the dreamer's chest. Kinesis was the sense of normative bodily movement as autonomous, enacting the individual's will; the opposing condition of lethargic motionlessness thus acquired new and deviant connotations.[17] Freedom of personal movement and progress were together pitted against terror, personal stasis, and ruin. Burgeoning movements for mass education, temperance, and reform aligned the individual worker's potential for energetic labor and wealth accumulation with the former. The early nineteenth-century model of industrial political subjectivity aligned with the perpetual motion of assembly, logistics, and productivity, culminating in the sublime aesthetics of completion and delivery. Its opposite was an off-kilter nightmare, where work never ends, nothing ever arrives at its destination, and one cannot join meaningfully in the choreographed order. Like Piranesi's incomplete stairs, nothing connects. The nightmare develops in opposition to industrial organization, symbolized by the orderly assembly of logistics. Both were durable Romantic forms.

De Quincey's opium nightmares are conventionally discussed as repressed returns of imperial and racial anxiety or guilt, such as in John Barrell's *Infection of Thomas De Quincey* (1991); here I want to evoke the specifically logistical character of that formation. "The sea appeared paved with innumerable faces . . . imploring, wrathful, despairing, surg[ing] upwards by thousands, by myriads, by generations, by centuries": here we might see an image of the incredible human power that builds and rebuilds the world (*C*, 72). Walter Benjamin identified it as the barbarism of coerced labor and suffering that underwrites every architectural testament to civilization.[18] "Paved" with faces, De Quincey's sea becomes a smooth, depthless surface of maritime logistics and globalizing trade routes built from human material. The scale of human suffering induces awe and horror—not unlike the sublime. Yet when De Quincey grounds this total human power in South Asia, he resorts to racist tropes to make the individual faces cohere in their vast extent across time and space. The territory, he writes, is "the part of the earth most swarming with human life; the great *officina gentium*. Man is a weed in those regions" (*C*, 73). In this convoluted concept of a "workshop of peoples," he erases the labor of biological reproduction by transposing it to a manufacturing setting and literalizing the reproduction of labor.

De Quincey, as Marcus Boon notes, conceived of political economy as a mechanism.[19] The endlessness of the human labor of mass production and logistics staggers his imagination, but Chinese racial difference bears his affective repulsion. "I could sooner live with lunatics, or brute animals" (C, 73). In this way, the violent reordering judgment of racist reason intervenes to rescue the narrator and his compliant readers from identifying with the oppressed mass. The nightmare of addiction is the white English writer's imagined forced intimacy with the foreign workers who have supplied him with his drug.

De Quincey's *Confessions* thus mobilizes the opium nightmare as a complex response to industrial modernity. The logistics of assembly is so vast, so abstract, so timeless, so unauthored, and so essentially uncontrolled that it acquires a monumental aura of inevitable doom.[20] Significantly, De Quincey's sea of faces is not merely the first and obvious sense of a "logistical nightmare" as a simple reversal or failure in which the goods go awry, the ship sinks, the stairs never reach the next floor, and the opium-addled worker never rises from their bed. It is also the horror that results when all operates according to plan, and the goods are assembled and distributed to their destinations. Completion, delivery, and fulfillment are themselves the horror, because their centuries of exploitation have caused untold human suffering horrific to behold. Seeing the supply chain ruins the high. De Quincey imagines both "the logistical nightmare" and the nightmare of logistics; the lack of fulfillment; and its completion.[21] His racism arrives to rescue him from exposure to this rebarbative vision. But he leaves readers with a sense of the labor involved in the assembly and distribution of consumer delights—and the circularity of this economy, as English workers take a drug harvested by Indian ones, to relieve the pains of their own labor and hasten repose.

Poison

De Quincey's *Confessions* was influential because it was a slightly scandalous, counterhegemonic text that dressed an indulgence in the sensual and the ephemeral in erudite language and manners. But the dominant discourse, drawn from temperance and teetotal movements and, increasingly, medical writings, also formed in relation to logistics as the expanded scene of manufacturing. And it, too, had difficulty fully imagining and sympathizing with opium use as a means of resting from labor or relieving its pains. To illustrate this discourse requires a return to China—specifically, to Humen, a small town on the southern coast.

The enormous scale of the Patna opium factory, the speed and constancy of the clippers' delivery, and the wealth they accrued to the Raj formed a powerful ideological node for English readers and consumers of visual culture. Consider, then, the spectacular disruption to that triumphal imperial narrative that occurred on June 1, 1839, in Humen, when Lin Zexu, imperial commissioner of the Qing dynasty, destroyed over a thousand tons or 3 million pounds of opium, confiscated from British smugglers. Lin's act established China's hard line against the trade. Julia Lovell calls it "one of the most celebrated moments in nineteenth-century Chinese history."[22] Lin became a national hero, staunchly defending his people against Britain's drug-pushing traders; in the enduring legacy of this status, a statue in New York

City's Chinatown honors him as a pioneer in the war against drugs.[23] Lin reckoned that had he burned all the opium, it might have been collected and resold; therefore he thoroughly decomposed it. It took three weeks for workers to crush the opium balls with their feet in a shallow area, other workers to stir it into a froth, cover it with lime and salt so it could ferment, and then empty it into the river.[24] The opium's destruction undoes both the manufacturing narrative and the logistical ideology driving it: the goods are not merely spoiled but systematically unmade; they do not miss their destination by happenstance but by deliberate calculation. Taking care to annihilate the opium, Lin opposed logistics' ability to pivot, or capital's ability to extract value by reassembling a commodity even from dregs and ashes. In a poem Lin composed for the occasion, he bade the Spirit of the Sea—"you who wash away all stains and cleans all impurities"—to warn sea creatures to keep away from the pollution of the dumped opium.[25] Invoking values on the margins of capital—divine intervention, environmental concern, and care for the Chinese people—Lin's confiscation and destruction of the opium diametrically opposed the logistical techniques at the heart of British imperial power.

By attacking distribution, Lin amplified and consolidated an enduring idea in British and Chinese culture: that opium is a substance both poisonous and irresistible to humans; if it is made available, they will automatically consume it. His famous letter to Queen Victoria, begging her to exert her sovereignty to check the trade, articulated the point. In it, Lin excoriated the English traders, "a depraved and barbarous people . . . [who] seduce and lead astray the simple folk." "How can it be borne," he asks, "that the living souls who dwell within these seas, should be left willfully to take a deadly poison!"[26] The poison metaphor helped conceptualize opium's use as abject addiction, in which mere exposure subjugates the user, an idea that took hold in nineteenth-century English political discourse. The idea clearly borrowed from the temperance and teetotal movements, which often warned that the first sip of alcohol could suddenly and completely "enslave" its consumer. And it was strikingly similar to the theory, formulated into policy in the slaveholding states of the United States, that slaves could not be given alcohol because they could not consume it without becoming addicted to it. Operating on similar elitist assumptions, not unlike the trope of Indian rebels stoking their irrationality with cannabis, documented by Utathya Chattopadhyaya in this issue, Lin's term *simple folk* encodes the resentment of elites observing masses taking up their erstwhile fashionable pastime.[27] The poison metaphor thus evacuates agency and forecloses a deep or granular subjectivity on the part of the addictive substance's users. On its back, the Society for the Suppression of the Opium Trade rose to prominence in the 1870s to protest the trade's inculcation of addiction among Chinese peasants—a practice implicating the British government after it assumed control of India from the East India Company following the Indian Rebellion of 1857.[28] Creating mass addiction violated the alibi of British imperialism, the bringing of enlightenment to ostensibly savage races. Opposition to the opium trade left that racism intact. When Lin imagined that Chinese peasants exposed to opium inevitably became addicted to it, falling into inhuman desuetude, he was exerting his elite privilege; when English readers did so, they were expressing racism. Both these defects prevented them from imaginatively engaging with addiction as a collective, socially and economically contextualized human experience—as well as one born from imperial and capital domination.

Neither Chinese nor English circulators of the "poison" metaphor could imagine with any degree of realism the uses that opium fulfilled. Recent scholarship, attempting to recuperate the historical agency of Chinese peasants, has suggested instead that their consumption of opium was a matter of "narcotic culture," as Frank Dikötter, Lars Laamann, and Zhou Xun conclude: "Opium smokers . . . were perfectly able to determine the desired level of consumption. They could moderate their use for personal and social reasons and even cease taking it altogether without help."[29] Similarly, Joyce A. Madancy conjures moderate use and easily managed withdrawal symptoms hiding in the historical record and obscured by missionaries' moralistic and political agendas. Perhaps, she suggests, "abstinence and withdrawal simply were not that difficult, either because the drug was not as addictive as supposed or because most Chinese were moderate users."[30] Virginia Berridge, in a foundational piece of revisionist scholarship, demonstrated that the fabled opium dens of Arthur Conan Doyle and other late Victorian popular writers, where Chinese workers in Britain supposedly smoked themselves into human detritus, were in actuality simple lodgings where they lived together.[31] These assessments are refreshing alternatives to the racism and paternalism of both the nineteenth-century poison model and De Quincey's counteraesthetic. They more richly conjure opium use as a real human activity, layered with agency, affect, and community.

Building on this work, we can reimagine opium addiction as a reasonable option for mitigating the pains and sufferings of labor. While laborers used drugs as palliatives before the modern imperial era on opium, tea, and other cash-crop plantations, management encouraged their use "as a cheap means of keeping people working longer and perhaps harder than they otherwise might have."[32] As Curtis Marez writes, "In contexts in which little else was available, the drug killed the pain of difficult daily labor, served as a prophylactic against certain diseases, and reduced malarial and other fevers."[33] Under the constraint of exploitation, opium use nonetheless was an exercise of agency and an attempt to maintain and restore health. Even the anti-opium lobby discourse, correctly reframed as speaking from a position of cultural elitism and blindness, recognized the problem of opium dependency by workers in India. In 1893 Bishop Thoburn testified before the Royal Commission on Opium that "coolies have told me that if they carried, for instance, 80 lbs., an opium pill would give them abnormal strength—sufficient to enable them to carry 120 lbs."[34] Though the commission sought to investigate the deleterious effect of opium on Chinese consumers, Thoburn was speaking about the Indians who performed the intensive labor of harvesting and manufacturing opium. He also testified to the large share of the peasants' wages that went to opium, simply to allow them to continue working. As Nitin Varma documents, a similar strategy took place on tea plantations in Assam, where government and capital colluded to create addiction among peasants as a method of labor coercion.[35] Opium use, along with debt peonage, indenture, and restrictions on subsistence farming, formed a network of techniques for extracting the excess labor required by cash crops. Peasants chose to produce opium for the government, but these choices were highly constrained.[36]

And what accounts for the rise in opium use among Chinese workers in the second half of the century, when a surge in domestic production lowered the price? Madancy calls it "one of the most intriguing mysteries of the late Qing era. . . . We may never fully understand why the Chinese consumed the drug in ever-increasing quantities."[37] But perhaps the acceleration of trade through enhanced logistics had something to do with it—both when Lin wrote his letter and as the century wore on and China expanded its own domestic and foreign production. Opium had to be harvested by hand in volumes daily measured by the ounce. In the case of Chinese immigrants working opium farms in Southeast Asia, relief from backbreaking labor came in smoking cheap preparations and dross. In the Indian factories, surveillance and security had attempted to keep workers from consuming the product; in the Chinese-run plantations, such leakage was systematized in a system of debt peonage. The plantations "depended on most of [the coolies] never getting out of debt, and on a significant proportion of them being permanently trapped by opium in the cycle of labor, indebtedness, addiction, and ultimately death."[38] The trade in these indentured migrant workers made the wealth of the elite Chinese diaspora and the port city enclaves, Singapore, Hong Kong, Penang, and Macao.[39] I am interpreting this context as one in which accelerated, and importantly, continuous logistical distribution created a whiplash effect, both forward, to increase supply, and backward, to expand production. People had to consume more opium to produce more of it, precisely because they never saw the enhanced profits their labor generated. The interpretive challenge here is to see laboring addicts neither merely as determined by their circumstance nor as utterly rational and putatively "free" subjects but as caught somewhere in the middle. Moreover, despite such workers' global circulation—the technique could be seen from Japan to Peru—such nuance must not reinscribe the coolie figure's "particular plasticity" within a liberal capitalist modernity transitioning from the slavery of colonial mercantilism to a new mode of international trade.[40]

The imagination of their labor was not emphasized in nineteenth-century English or Chinese discourse, because even when it ventured inside factories, it remained entranced by the abstracting force of the manufacturing narrative and the logistical sublime. In 1891, when W. S. Caine published *Picturesque India: A Guidebook for Travelers*, the manufacturing narrative was still in full force: "The raw opium arrives from the district where it is grown. . . . Every pot is carefully tested for quality. . . . The raw opium is then cast into big vats." Laborers do not appear in these sentences. Moreover, in an echo of De Quincey's imagery of a sea paved with suffering faces, Caine describes the large volume the vats hold as "sufficient to destroy the whole population of India."[41] The genocidal impulse lurking in that figuration of sublime scale conceals another: the systematic subjugation of the population through the production and distribution process itself. Opium was among the most important commodities of the nineteenth century, not only because it established British imperial power and multiplied its wealth but because it made addictive drug use into a logistical technique, designed to secure and reliably position laborers, manage their labor, and increase their productivity.[42] Via opium, logistics penetrated the body, installing itself within a worker's physiology; its infrastructure includes not just the clipper ships, the chests, and the dried opium balls, but the nerves and muscles of the men and women who harvested and prepared it. Contra De Quincey, it was not a nightmare of disorder, but a putatively rational technique of workers integrating themselves into an oppressive system of production, debt, and indenture. The supply chain fosters opium use, both by peasant workers and by elites, who are better resourced to cope with its ravages. Its subaltern users attempt to rehumanize themselves within inhuman regimes. Like all agency, that of procuring and using an addictive drug is a series of decisions constrained by context; it is both logical and self-defeating.

I have been suggesting that one way to move beyond the conceptual frames that organized thinking about opium addiction—individual choice, poison, undue influence, exploitation, and so on—is to acknowledge its radical duality. Opium addiction was a rational strategy for coping with the pressures of globalizing modernity: unceasing labor, geographic displacement, crushing debt. These pressures arose from the logistical demands of capital for smooth, continuous production and flowing distribution—aspects of exploitation. As Mark W. Driscoll has argued, "The logistical complexity of Anglo-American narcotrafficking to China was unprecedented."[43] Addiction, so often depicted in late nineteenth-century British culture as unnatural and dehumanizing, may actually have been a way to remain a person in the face of powerful, deforming forces that moved massive quantities of goods around the world with unprecedented precision, continuity, and speed. A well-educated white man of privilege such as De Quincey could express addictive struggle in ways rewarded by literary establishments and canons of culture but inaccessible to illiterate Chinese peasant workers. Thus my suggestion arises from an analysis of incommensurate sources: De Quincey's detailed literary nightmares on the one hand, and the largely secondhand or abstracted reports of lives of subaltern workers on the other. Yet there is a place for such imaginative engagement, especially as it brushes against the grain of addiction discourse's signature paradoxical demand: that only the individual can speak with authority about their addiction and yet cannot be trusted to report it accurately. On a topic with such a vexed relationship to documentary truth, an engagement with the aesthetic—always contextualized within its political economy—represents an alternative historical approach.

Conclusion

I have used the lever of logistics to begin to pry apart the operations of capital, to understand how addiction might operate within and apart from the standard rhetoric of valorized self-sovereignty that obscures relations between capital and labor.[44] The generic rules of writing in realistic detail about addiction place narrative pressure on individual will, creating suspense, sentiment, and other affects through the question of whether or not the addict will overcome their problem. Except in nonfiction texts grounded in political economy, or anthropological texts about ritual uses, far less is ever said about addiction among laboring communities, where agency is more complexly distributed. Yet it is not difficult to see how addiction continues to operate as a logistical substance to facilitate labor, because that is one of several facets of the recent opioid crisis in the United States.

Beginning in the early 2000s, the traffic in heroin from Mexico to the United States underwent a startling logistical modernization. Family farmers in the isolated region of Nayarit began growing poppies, processing heroin, and distributing it in US cities.[45] In the fabled cartel structure of the 1970s and 1980s, and in the smaller Mexican organizations that sprang up in its wake, every intermediary took a cut of the profits and adulterated the drug. The Nayarit family organizations' vertical integration allowed them to run the operation all the way "from flower to arm," delivering heroin of hitherto unseen purity into the veins of addicts, who accordingly began to overdose in alarming numbers.[46] The market for heroin across the US heartland had been primed by the legal prescription of OxyContin by Purdue and other large pharmaceutical corporations for chronic pain management. The Nayarit distributors exhibited logistical prowess, using codes to navigate directly to buyers on the streets of US cities with small balloons of black tar heroin stuffed in their cheeks. As salaried workers who did not themselves use the product, they worked long days, eschewed violence, and reinvested their money in their *ranchos* back in Xalisco. This high-volume, wide-distribution operation dropped the price, making heroin an affordable substitute for those who could not obtain prescription OxyContin.

Who were the legions of Americans consuming these opioids? The crisis had begun when Purdue, Pfizer, and other pharmaceutical companies began to aggressively market narcotics for the ongoing management of pain. Opioid users included professional and skilled workers, such as lawyers and nurses, as well as semiskilled ones, such as prison guards, prostitutes, painters, and construction workers. Especially as the United States has continued to shift from a manufacturing to a service economy, widespread opioid addiction has not occurred exclusively among manual laborers toiling in fields and factories. Rather, work-related pain has included chronic ailments such as back pain from sitting, headaches, and the stress of affective labor, any of which could trigger the prescription of Schedule II opiates or a short walk to the corner to pick up a balloon of heroin. The situation has arisen through global capital's destruction of living wages, public spaces, institutions, and social rituals, the basis of thriving communities in the period after World War II until the effects of neoliberal financial policies began to be felt in the 1980s. As Anne Case and Angus Deaton have documented, it is coextensive with the rise in disability compensation, the mental-health crisis, ill health related to the obesity epidemic, and joblessness following the financial crisis. Opioid addiction relieves "pain," where that term no longer connotes acute specific suffering in a body part but a generalized malaise, an entire network of physical, emotional, and spiritual injury and ill health.[47] It is beyond the scope of this conclusion to detail the crucial differences between the lives of Indian laborers at the Sudder factory, Southeast Asian workers on a Chinese-run opium plantation in Singapore, and US workers in the twenty-first century. But this conclusion only draws attention to the broad similarities of opiate use among these groups in their attempts to live within logistical regimes that streamlined the flow of wealth away from them.[48]

What literary genres are capable of describing addiction as the human cost of the nightmare of logistics? Perhaps they do not currently exist; but when they emerge, they will not model themselves after De Quincey's *Confessions*, a highly individualized, self-aggrandizing drama of self-sovereignty that invoked the spectacle of Southeast Asian workers' suffering only to denigrate it from a racist perspective and heighten the pathos of his own struggle. Nor will they rehash the tired nineteenth-century patriarchal laments about opiates as "poison" that people have no choice but to take. Perhaps they will find a way to redefine the common understanding of addiction as something more specific than "the desire and need to use a substance as a result of having used it in the past." It is possible that literary models, traditionally bound by individualism, reach the limits of their expressivity when they encounter both the sublime and the nightmarish passages, through the labor of our logistical lives.

SUSAN ZIEGER specializes in nineteenth-century British and related literatures and cultures, with an emphasis on the novel, ephemera, and other mass-media forms. She is author of *Inventing the Addict: Drugs, Race, and Sexuality in Nineteenth-Century British and American Literature* (2008) and *The Mediated Mind: Affect, Ephemera, and Consumerism in the Nineteenth Century* (2018) and is doing research for her next book, tentatively titled *Logistical Life*, a cultural history of the rise of logistics and its relationship to modern consumption from 1750 to the present. With Nicole Starosielski and Matt Hockenberry, she is editing the forthcoming volume *Assembly Codes: The Logistics of Media*.

Notes

1   Trocki, *Opium, Empire, and the Global Political Economy*, 59.
2   Swamidass, *Encyclopedia of Production*, 371.
3   Thornton, "Capitalist Aesthetics," 172.
4   Dodd, *Day at the Factories*, 137–60.
5   Ure, *Philosophy of Manufactures*; Ure, *Dictionary of Arts, Manufactures, and Mines*.
6   Burke, *Philosophical Inquiry*, 187; Kant, *Critique of Judgment*.
7   See Nye, *American Technological Sublime*. On the London and Liverpool docks, see Thornton, "Capitalist Aesthetics."
8   Sherwill, *Illustrations*, n.p.
9   Childers, "Spectacles of Labor," 172–73.
10 Ghosh, *Sea of Poppies*, 91.
11 Trocki, *Opium, Empire*, 49–50.
12 Morse, *International Relations*, 179; Greenberg, *British Trade*, 121.
13 Jay, *High Society*, 144.
14 Lubbock, *Opium Clippers*, 1–2.
15 Zieger, *Inventing the Addict*, 33–60.
16 De Quincey, *Confessions*, 70 (hereafter cited as C).
17 Cervenak, *Wandering*, 5.
18 In his words, "there is no document of civilization which is not at the same time a document of barbarism" (Benjamin, "Theses on the Philosophy of History," 200).
19 Boon, *Road of Excess*, 39.
20 Toscano, "Lineaments of the Logistical State," n.p.
21 For a theoretical discussion of this dynamic of the logistical nightmare and the nightmare that is functioning logistics, see Rossiter, *Software, Infrastructure, Labor*, 138.
22 Lovell, *Opium War*, 69.
23 Chen, "Chinatown's Fujianese Get a Statue," n.p.
24 Platt, *Imperial Twilight*, 380–81.
25 Waley, *Opium War*, 55–56.
26 *Chinese Repository*, "Remarks," 4.
27 Zheng, *Social Life of Opium in China*, 99.
28 Berridge, *Opium and the People*, 176.
29 Dikötter, Laamann, and Xun, *Narcotic Culture*, 56.
30 Madancy, *Troublesome Legacy*, 21.
31 Berridge, *Opium and the People*, 195–205.
32 Jankowiak and Bradburd, *Drugs, Labor, and Colonial Expansion*, 21.

33 Marez, *Drug Wars*, 49.
34 Royal Commission on Opium, *Final Report*, 16.
35 Varma, *Coolies of Capitalism*, 38.
36 See Bauer, *Peasant Production of Opium*, 7.
37 Madancy, *Troublesome Legacy*, 80.
38 Trocki, "Drugs, Taxes, and Chinese Capitalism."
39 Arrighi, *Adam Smith in Beijing*, 337.
40 Lowe, *Intimacies of Four Continents*, 27.
41 Caine, *Picturesque India*, 324.
42 Neilson and Bamyeh, "Drugs in Motion," 6.
43 Driscoll, *Whites Are Enemies of Heaven*, 6.
44 On the operations of capital, see Mezzadra and Neilson, *Politics of Operations*.
45 This discussion is indebted to Quinones, *Dreamland*.
46 Quinones, *Dreamland*, 122.
47 Case and Deaton, *Deaths of Despair*.
48 For a different comparison between the groups, see Haiven, *Revenge Capitalism*, 119–40.

Works Cited

Arrighi, Giovanni. *Adam Smith in Beijing: Lineages of the Twenty-First Century*. London: Verso, 2007.

Babbage, Charles. *On the Economy of Machinery and Manufacture*. London, 1832.

Bauer, Rolf. *The Peasant Production of Opium in Nineteenth-Century India*. Leiden: Brill, 2019.

Benjamin, Walter. "Theses on the Philosophy of History." In *Illuminations*, edited by Hannah Arendt, translated by Harry Zohn, 196–209. New York: Mariner, 2019.

Berridge, Virginia. *Opium and the People: Opiate Use and Drug Control Policy in Nineteenth and Early Twentieth Century England*. London: Free Association Books, 1981.

Boon, Marcus. *The Road of Excess: A History of Writers on Drugs*. Cambridge, MA: Harvard University Press, 2002.

Burke, Edmund. *A Philosophical Inquiry into the Origin of Our Ideas of the Beautiful and the Sublime*. In *Burke's Writings and Speeches: Volume the First*. London, 1887.

Caine, W. S. *Picturesque India: A Guidebook for Travelers*. London, 1891.

Case, Anne, and Angus Deaton. *Deaths of Despair and the Future of Capitalism*. Princeton, NJ: Princeton University Press, 2020.

Cervenak, Sarah. *Wandering: Philosophical Performances of Racial and Sexual Freedom*. Durham, NC: Duke University Press, 2014.

Chen, David W. "Chinatown's Fujianese Get a Statue." *New York Times*, November 20, 1997.

Childers, Hope Marie. "Spectacles of Labor: Artists and Workers in the Patna Opium Factory in the 1850s." *Nineteenth-Century Contexts* 39, no. 3 (2017): 167–91.

Chinese Repository. "Remarks on the Present Crisis in the Opium Traffic." May 1839, 1–37.

De Quincey, Thomas. *Confessions of an English Opium-Eater*, edited by Grevel Lindop. Oxford: Oxford University Press, 1985.

Dikötter, Frank, Lars Laamann, and Zhou Xun. *Narcotic Culture: A History of Drugs in China*. London: Hurst, 2004.

Dodd, George. *A Day at the Factories, or, The Manufacturing Industries of Great Britain Described*. Series 1. London, 1843.

Driscoll, Mark W. *The Whites Are Enemies of Heaven: Climate Caucasianism and Asian Ecological Protection*. Durham, NC: Duke University Press, 2020.

Ghosh, Amitav. *Sea of Poppies*. New York: Picador, 2008.

Greenberg, Michael. *British Trade and the Opening of China, 1800–1842*. Cambridge: Cambridge University Press, 1969.

Haiven, Max. *Revenge Capitalism: The Ghosts of Empire, the Demons of Capital, and the Settling of Unpayable Debts*. London: Pluto, 2020.

Jankowiak, William, and Daniel Bradburd, eds. *Drugs, Labor, and Colonial Expansion*. Tucson: University of Arizona Press, 2003.

Jay, Mike. *High Society: The Central Role of Mind-Altering Drugs in History, Science, and Culture*. Rochester, VT: Park Street, 2010.

Kant, Immanuel. *Critique of Judgment*. 1790. www.gutenberg.org/ebooks/48433.

Lovell, Julia. *The Opium War: Drugs, Dreams, and the Making of Modern China*. New York: Overlook, 2011.

Lowe, Lisa. *The Intimacies of Four Continents*. Durham, NC: Duke University Press, 2015.

Lubbock, Basil. *The Opium Clippers*. Glasgow: Brown, Son and Ferguson, 1933.

Madancy, Joyce A. *The Troublesome Legacy of Commissioner Lin: The Opium Trade and Opium Suppression in Fujian Province, 1820s to 1920s*. Cambridge, MA: Harvard University Asia Center, 2003.

Marez, Curtis. *Drug Wars: The Political Economy of Narcotics*. Minneapolis: University of Minnesota Press, 2004.

Mezzadra, Sandro, and Brett Neilson. *The Politics of Operations: Excavating Contemporary Capitalism*. Durham, NC: Duke University Press, 2019.

Morse, Hosea. *The International Relations of the Chinese Empire*. Taipei: Ch'eng Wen, 1910.

Neilson, Brett, and Mohammed Bamyeh. "Drugs in Motion: Toward a Materialist Tracking of Global Mobilities." *Cultural Critique*, no. 71 (2009): 1–12.

Nye, David E. *The American Technological Sublime*. Cambridge, MA: MIT Press, 1994.

Platt, Stephen. *Imperial Twilight: The Opium War and the End of China's Last Golden Age.* New York: Knopf, 2018.

Quinones, Sam. *Dreamland: The True Story of America's Opioid Crisis.* London: Bloomsbury, 2015.

Rossiter, Ned. *Software, Infrastructure, Labor: A Media Theory of Logistical Nightmares.* London: Routledge, 2016.

Royal Commission on Opium. *Final Report.* Vol. 2. London, 1894.

Sherwill, Walter S. *Illustrations of the Mode of Preparing Opium Intended for the Chinese Market.* London, 1851.

Swamidass, Paul M., ed. *Encyclopedia of Production and Manufacturing Management.* Boston: Springer, 2000.

Thornton, Tamara Plakins. "Capitalist Aesthetics: Americans Look at the London and Liverpool Docks." In *Capitalism Takes Command*, edited by Michael Zakim and Gary J. Kornblith, 169–98. Chicago: University of Chicago Press, 2012.

Toscano, Alberto. "Lineaments of the Logistical State." *Viewpoint Magazine*, September 28, 2014.

Trocki, Carl. "Drugs, Taxes, and Chinese Capitalism in Southeast Asia." In *Drug Regimes: China, Britain, and Japan, 1839–1952*, edited by Timothy Brook and Bob Tadashi Wakabayashi, 79–104. Berkeley: University of California Press, 2000.

Trocki, Carl. *Opium, Empire, and the Global Political Economy: A Study of the Asian Opium Trade.* New York: Routledge, 1999.

Ure, Andrew. *A Dictionary of the Arts, Manufactures, and Mines.* London, 1839.

Ure, Andrew. *Philosophy of Manufactures.* London, 1835.

Varma, Nitin. *Coolies of Capitalism: Assam Tea and the Making of Coolie Labour.* Berlin: de Gruyter Oldenbourg, 2017.

Waley, Arthur. *The Opium War through Chinese Eyes.* 1958; repr., New York: Routledge, 2000.

Zheng, Yangwen. *The Social Life of Opium in China.* Cambridge: Cambridge University Press, 2005.

Zieger, Susan. *Inventing the Addict: Drugs, Race, and Sexuality in Nineteenth-Century British and American Writing.* Amherst: University of Massachusetts Press, 2008.

All Aboard

Reading, Writing, and Drinking with Ernest Hemingway

ELLEN LANSKY

Abstract   This essay situates Ernest Hemingway's iconic "Hills Like White Elephants" as a short story about drinking. From this perspective, Hemingway's story enables readers to experience a personal and deeply felt emotional engagement with the characters, the scene, and the situation. Moreover, his technique enlists readers as "drinking buddies" and provides an entrée into the culture of alcohol. Despite the macho image that Hemingway himself helped construct and deploy, his work invites women into the scene and, indeed, centralizes a key figure often overlooked in the history of modern American fiction criticism: the drinking woman.
Keywords   Ernest Hemingway, gender, alcohol

> Some things punch you in the face and you fly through the
> air and land somewhere completely different. You walk on
> from there.
> —Miranda July, "Doing Nothing Isn't Enough"

Two Unfinished Beers: The Drinking White Woman
in "Hills Like White Elephants"

In the fall quarter of 1989, after a long, hot summer full of drinking and its discontents, I taught Ernest Hemingway's "Hills Like White Elephants," for the first time, in sections of freshman composition at a Minneapolis south suburban community college. At the end of an afternoon section, a young male student came up to me after class and said, "I just had a conversation exactly like this." I looked at him and nodded and said something like, "I know exactly what you mean." He seemed to appreciate my reply, though I felt at the time as if I had just revealed more of my personal life than was appropriate for a professional. I wish I had said, "It's funny how another writer can tell the story of your life."

I had not meant to teach this story in that way. I had not meant to teach a story that felt so personal to me, nor had I meant to tell that young man, or any other student or any other person at all, that it felt that way to me. The story and my connection to it and to Hemingway were already confounding to me, as a bisexual lesbian (a fairly common category in late 1980s uptown Minneapolis). I had been hired at the last minute and was handed a preordered rhetoric and a reader. I was following the sample syllabus's suggestion that I teach patterns of composition, starting with narration and description. I had read most of Hemingway's novels and some of his stories, but I hadn't read "Hills Like White Elephants" before. I figured I knew enough about Hemingway and was just teaching a Hemingway story as an example of description (or lack thereof)—not as the story of my life, more or less. That classroom scene was one of many in which the teacher learns more from the students than the students learn from the teacher.

In the fall quarter of 1990 my situation had changed: I was sober and teaching at a different suburban community college. Once again the textbook I used for one of the courses I was assigned included Hemingway's "Hills Like White Elephants," and I felt better able to teach it with a bit more grounding this time, emotionally and academically. I used it as a model in the text section called "finding patterns." First, I read "Hills" aloud to the class, and then we looked for repetitions, starting with the number two. After counting eight appearances of the number two in a three-page story, everybody agreed that the repetition of *two* must be significant. Somebody pointed out that "two's company; three's a crowd" was part of the conflict or the source of disagreement in the story. After that, we counted the number of drinks and agreed that two big beers and a shot of Anis del Toro (two for the man) was a lot of alcohol to consume in the space of forty minutes—when they'd catch a train. In a reflection, a student focused on the word *hot* and wrote that the combination of the bickering, the drinks, and the weather made for a conflict and a problem that was, literally and metaphorically, hot.

Of course, the classroom discussions included the "hot topic" of abortion, but teaching "Hills" as a story about drinking and bickering was meant, at least in part, to avoid the discussion getting derailed by a clamorous debate about abortion. In the process of preparing my class notes, I came across Doris Lanier's article "The Bittersweet Taste of Absinthe in Hemingway's 'Hills Like White Elephants,'" an essay that shifts the critical focus from abortion or the various signifying functions of the bead curtain or the train tracks or the river or the landscape's fecundity or aridity to the presence of alcohol. Lanier's article on absinthe gave me an avenue through which to study the story's other alcoholic drink: beer.

Many readers and critics have read "Hills Like White Elephants" as a story about abortion, but few beyond Lanier, Velma Kale and her students, and my students and I have read "Hills Like White Elephants" as a story about drinking. One reason why many readers do not register much response to the alcoholic drinking in this story is that the characters are drinking beer. Although the Volstead Act "classified as alcoholic all beverages containing more than one-half of 1 percent alcohol by volume," which includes beer, readers have largely not remarked on the presence of beer as an alcoholic beverage in this story.[1] Apparently, for some readers, beer is insignificant in this story, or less significant than the details of the setting or the literal and metaphoric aspects of abortion. Nevertheless, beer drinking has specific signifying functions as well as specific effects on the drinkers. As several beers appear on the table and disappear into the bodies of the characters, the

characters become less and less articulate, more and more disembodied and ethereal, and ultimately silent. Moreover, my analysis of Hemingway's story focuses on
a figure that is central, if largely unremarked in the classic and contemporary criticism, to the American modern fiction canon: a woman (usually white) under the
influence of alcohol.

The effects of alcohol complicate Hemingway's story from beginning to end.
First, he sets it in a train terminal in summertime Spain. Although they are sitting
in the shade, the temperature and atmosphere of the scene are both "very hot."[2]
They order beer and absinthe and bicker about white elephants. When the second
round of beers appears on the table, they agree that the beer is "nice and cool" ("Hills,"
212). The beer seems to take the heat off the situation, literally and metaphorically.
As the story unfolds and the drinks arrive, the table undergoes a metamorphosis.
It becomes an operating table—evocative of the image Eliot uses in the opening
stanza of "The Love Song of J. Alfred Prufrock." At this operating table, the American man and the girl have two big beers and shots of absinthe and discuss the
vicissitudes of what the man calls a "perfectly simple operation." As the two wait
for the train and have their discussion, the alcohol they drink takes on the quality
of "pre-op" anesthesia—a dose of medicine to calm their nerves before a surgi-
cal procedure.

Then Hemingway presents a scene that simultaneously reveals certain bodily
operations (such as drinking beer and absinthe) and suppresses others. No one
vomits, urinates, sweats, or even complains—beyond remarking that "it's pretty
hot" ("Hills," 211). It seems unlikely and unrealistic that an articulating subject in
a body—a human being—could sit outside on a hot Spanish afternoon drinking
beer and absinthe, bickering, pregnant, and indecisive and not register some kind
of acute corporeal discomfort. But that's the rub right there. Hemingway has constructed for "the girl" a body that begins to disappear as it metabolizes alcohol. Sitting at that table in the shade in that hot situation, drinking beer and absinthe, she
becomes a talking spirit, an ethereal voice: a fume.

Indeed, in "Hills" Hemingway's technique is to compress the scene to mostly
dialogue: spoken words with little description or even attribution. The story opens
with a brief expository description of the setting. The reader does not know what the
characters are wearing or what color their hair might be or if they are wearing glasses
or a beard or earrings or a necklace or rings. Instead of deploying embodied characters as he does, for example, in *The Sun Also Rises*—in which the reader knows that
Brett Ashley "wore a slipover jersey sweater and a tweed skirt, and her hair was
brushed back like a boy's. . . . She was built with curves like the hull of a racing
yacht,"[3] what Hemingway offers in "Hills Like White Elephants" is almost entirely
voices only. The descriptions of the characters are limited to "the American" and
"the girl," and after they've been served their drinks at the operating table, the dialogue proceeds with quotation marks and indentations to mark shifts in speakers.
Few and then no speech tags distinguish the speakers. The disappearing details
and speech tags suggest that once they start drinking, their bodies and their embodi-
ment, by which I mean that their sense of themselves in bodies that might be
responding to, say, heat or the effects of alcohol or the discomforts of early preg-
nancy, disappear.

The story's close reveals how the girl's "perfectly simple" responses to the man's questions results in an acutely heart-wrenching silence. After they have had several rounds of drinks and several rounds of argumentative exchanges about the "awfully simple operation," their discussion takes on the flailing quality of a boxing match in which each fighter is too punch-drunk to connect and finish off their opponent ("Hills," 212). Finally, the girl says to the man, "'Would you please please please please please please please stop talking?'" ("Hills," 214). Saying *please* seven times in a row is quite a feat of articulation for someone who is irritated, hot, pregnant, and drunk. This feat finally exhausts both the girl and the man. Weakly, he tries to protest that he does not "want [her] to . . . [he doesn't] care anything about it" ("Hills," 214). She replies, "'I'll scream,'" but at this point it is clear to both characters and the reader that she hasn't the breath for it ("Hills," 214). The man gets up from the table, at which the perfectly simple operation is not going very well, and moves their bags. On his way back to the table, he stops in the barroom. He drinks another Anis and "looked at the people" ("Hills," 214). Here, one might pause to consider "the people" in the barroom. In the story's present tense, the scenes of public drinking in the culture of alcohol were shifting from a mostly male homosocial saloon culture to a more "mixed" drinking environment. In her 1979 essay "Ladies Entrance: Women and Bars," Mary Jo Lupton notes that in the United States, ironically, "it was not until after Prohibition went into effect that 'respectable' women began frequenting bars. With the coming of the speakeasy, it grew common for women, particularly city women, to see bars as a source of social contact."[4] A train-station bar in a terminal between Barcelona and Madrid is far from an American urban speakeasy, and the fact that the American and the girl are sitting outside the barroom suggests that the barroom itself is likely to be a male enclave. In the barroom, the American notices that these people, probably men, are "all waiting reasonably for the train" ("Hills," 214). In a story that eschews details and modifiers, the appearance of "reasonably" calls attention to itself. Outside the barroom waits the most unreasonable creature in the world: a hot, irritated, pregnant drinking woman. When the American returns to the (operating) table, he asks her, in "post-op" tones, "'Do you feel better?'" She smiles and says to him, "I feel fine" ("Hills," 214).

In "Hills Like White Elephants," the word *fine* functions much like the repetition of *please* earlier. Beyond polite discourse, *fine* is a terminal signifier that shuts down further inquiry. She says she feels fine, but how can she—given the emotional and physiological circumstances? Nevertheless, *fine* is her last word, Hemingway's final word. Despite the desire of readers and Hemingway critics such as Paul Rankin, who notes that "a summation of majority opinion might produce something like this: "Hemingway's unnamed American protagonist dominates the meeker, weaker-sexed Jig . . . until broken, she submits to his will and consents to aborting the child" or Kale's students' sense that the man has prevailed because "the more she drinks, the less she fights," it is also possible that there is simply nothing more to say.[5] The story is over, but the conflict is not resolved. On the table are two unfinished beers.

Drinking and Reading with Hemingway

My connection to Hemingway did not begin with "Hills Like White Elephants." In fact, it began with a conflict of interpretation. When I was in the ninth grade at

Indian Creek Junior High School in Overland Park, Kansas, I had to read *The Old Man and the Sea* and give a report on it to my teacher, Mrs. Nitschke. Mrs. Nitschke was related to Ray Nitschke, the legendary football player, and though she wasn't as physically imposing as Ray, she was as formidable as an NFL middle linebacker. Mrs. Nitschke did not like my attitude, and I feared and loathed her.

I approached her to give her my report a few minutes before class or during a break. It was a rush, anyway, as I recall. She asked me a few technical questions to make sure I had read the book, and then she asked what I thought *The Old Man and the Sea* was about, what it meant.

I said, "Fishing."

She said, with exasperation, "Anything else?"

She wanted me to say that the theme was Man versus Nature or that the fish symbolized something or other, I knew, but I felt embarrassed to say that to somebody who was peremptory at her best and, in that moment, already seemed to find me annoying.

I said, "Nope. Fishing."

She frowned at me and gave me a not very good grade on my report.

Now, many, many years later, Hemingway's grandson says much the same thing that I did. In a heretofore unpublished story in the *New Yorker*, titled "Pursuit as Happiness," Hemingway writes about fishing and writing and drinking. I love this story because I love most of Hemingway's work, even when he gets a bit grandiose and "meta." I also love that Hemingway was doing autofiction way back when. In addition, I love what Hemingway's grandson, Sean, says to Deborah Treisman about the story and its title: "I think it is a very apt title for this unpublished story, because it is not just about catching and losing a large marlin—in the same way that *The Old Man and the Sea* is not just about catching and losing a large marlin to sharks. It is about the joy of fishing and the happiness that it brings."[6]

After reading what Sean Hemingway says about *Old Man* and "Pursuit as Happiness," I recalled again that classroom scene with Mrs. Nitschke and realized I was right, or at least I felt vindicated. *Old Man* is not only or just simply about Man versus Nature or some great symbolic thing that is embarrassing to say to an English teacher who is impatient and sometimes mean. It is also a story about fishing and, it seemed to me then and now, pursuit and disappointment.

After my disappointing ninth-grade English class with Mrs. Nitschke, I began to take reading and drinking seriously in the spring quarter of 1977 at Shawnee Mission South High School. I was a sophomore, and I enrolled in Mr. Allen's Ethnic Literature minicourse because he was my softball coach, and I figured he would take it easy on me. I was wrong about that, but my experience with Mr. Allen turned out to be much bigger and better than I had anticipated.

While I was reading about rage and oppression in books such as *Invisible Man* and *Native Son* and *A Raisin in the Sun*, I was also learning how to procure and drink alcohol. This was a major project in Kansas—a dry state with complicated liquor regulations and much denial about rage and oppression. The next year, in junior American lit, the world of literature seemed to open up for me even more when I read F. Scott Fitzgerald's *The Great Gatsby*. I loved that book. Nick and Daisy and Tom, and especially Gatsby and his entourage, seemed like people I knew in Overland

Park—a meretricious, nearly all-white suburb of Kansas City that was rather like West Egg, Long Island. White people driving around in big cars, getting drunk at parties in ostentatious houses: that was my summertime scene.

In college, the link between literature and drinking deepened, and my connection to Hemingway strengthened. In the first summer I lived away from home, after my sophomore year, I worked in a bar at night and on my brother's recommendation read Hemingway's novels by day. When I went to France the following spring semester, I already knew how to make and drink Pernod cocktails while sitting on the terrace of a café. I just followed Hemingway's directions in *The Sun Also Rises* and *A Moveable Feast*.

Later, while I was an MA student in Binghamton, New York, in 1985, I met up with Hemingway again in Mary Lynn Broe's Feminist Theory seminar. The first two required texts were *The Sun Also Rises* and Djuna Barnes's *Nightwood*. I gave a presentation on *The Sun Also Rises*, and my job was to discuss the classic midcentury Hemingway critical essays that provided a "masculinist" framework for reading *The Sun Also Rises*, including Mark Spilka, Leslie Fiedler, Jackson Benson, and Philip Young. As a class we'd just read Sandra Gilbert's 1983 essay "Soldier's Heart: Literary Men, Literary Women, and the Great War" as well as essays by Annette Kolodny and Adrienne Rich to give ourselves a feminist framework for reading Hemingway's novel. In addition, Linda Wagner was already contributing to feminist readings of Hemingway with *Hemingway: Five Decades of Criticism*, and Susan Beegel's work on Hemingway would be appearing shortly in the *Hemingway Review*. On that day in the spring of 1985, our seminar did a close reading of the first chapter of *Sun* and counted the appearance of the word *girl* or *lady* as a strategy to infantilize, disempower, and diminish women. We observed that Hemingway made Brett Ashley a more powerful or palatable girl/woman by giving her a man's name and "her hair brushed back like a boy's"—in addition to sexual prowess and an ability to drink alcohol and watch bullfights with the "chaps."[7] Almost everybody in the class, including the lone student who was a man, hated *Sun*, but I still liked it, and I read it probably three more times after that class, and I put it on my booklist in my doctoral program at the University of Minnesota. Brett and Jake seemed like people I knew.

I had the same sort of relationship with other books by or about alcoholics or drug addicts: I adored *The Basketball Diaries*; I read Jay McInerney's *Bright Lights, Big City* in one sitting. I loved Madame Bovary for her single-minded attention to her compulsions, her addiction to her desire (for what?); and I held Raymond Carver's short stories (particularly "What We Talk About When We Talk About Love") in highest esteem. Unsurprisingly, my first published short story was about a twelve-year-old girl getting drunk for the first time at a family reunion. That story practically wrote itself.

When my career as an active teenage alcoholic ended at the age of twenty-nine, I began to look at my environment: the people I knew, the books I liked, and the way I wrote and read and thought. While I was sorting all of this out, I also had to figure out what I wanted to say about these books that I had admired, read, and loved as a teenager and still admired, read, and loved (albeit from a different perspective) as an adult. I wanted to figure out why these books were so influential—not only for me but for other people I knew and people whose criticism I had read. I wanted to figure out why readers like myself would read books like *The Sun Also Rises* and stories like "Hills Like White Elephants" and respond so viscerally.

After many starts and shifts, I began to see that what I liked—on the simplest level of "identification," I suppose, about "Hills," for example, or *The Sun Also Rises,* or the novels of Scott and Zelda Fitzgerald, or Dorothy Parker's "Big Blonde," or Djuna Barnes's *Nightwood,* or Jane Bowles's *Two Serious Ladies* and Paul Bowles's *The Sheltering Sky*—was that at or near the center of each text was a woman drinking alcohol. Here, it seemed to me, was my starting point. People had been working on alcoholism in the lives and texts of white American modern authors, but except for of a pair of articles that focused on the alcoholism of women in *Nightwood,* the white woman drinking alcohol had been largely overlooked as a significant figure in American modern fiction. New ways of reading these canonical texts are possible when one centralizes this figure. For example, in *The Sun Also Rises,* Brett Ashley's transformation and her overall presence in the novel is more interesting than that of Jake Barnes; Jig is more interesting and more central to "Hills Like White Elephants" than the mansplaining American white man is. I saw myself in that landscape; I was on my way. My doctoral dissertation, "Something for the Lady: Women Alcoholics and their Partners in American Modern Fiction," turned out to be much more work and, overall, a much more satisfying project than I had anticipated. I wrote my dissertation, and my dissertation wrote me.

As a coda, in the spring of 2021, I was watching the Ken Burns documentary *Hemingway* on PBS. Edna O'Brien looks directly at the camera and makes this claim: "I think many women feel and indeed broadcast the idea that Hemingway hated women and wrote adversely always about them. This isn't true."[8] While I would suggest, with the utmost respect and deference to Edna O'Brien, that many men, and many of them influential critics and professors, felt and indeed broadcast the idea that Hemingway hated women, her statement confirms my long-held thesis that Hemingway makes room for women in his fiction.

Hemingway's Drinking Buddy Reader

My process and progress from ninth grade until now taught me something else about reading, writing, and drinking with Hemingway: I was meant to notice that drinking woman in Hemingway's fiction and to want to be like her. In fact, Hemingway conscripted me as a drinking buddy the second I opened *The Sun Also Rises.*

A problem of interpretation that alcoholic authors and their texts present to readers is that alcoholism resists distinctions between "fiction" and "life." Frequently, to an alcoholic, life *is* a fiction. Alcoholics often begin with a factual event and bring imagination and invention to bear on it to produce a cohesive, powerful narrative. In the alcoholic's case, they hope the fictional narrative will provide compelling explanations, excuses, or reasons for insane behavior. The alcoholic's partner—drinking buddy, spouse, lover, friend, associate—corroborates the narrative because they need to believe in the verisimilitude of the alcoholic's fiction to preserve their own sanity—paradoxical as that may sound.

Writers such as Hemingway lived lives that were sometimes indistinguishable from the fiction they wrote. Trying to separate lives from fictions is frequently futile, especially when the authors themselves may not concern themselves with maintaining a boundary or aesthetic distance between life and fiction. For example, it is well documented that in 1925 Hemingway went to Pamplona and got drunk day and night for a week, and he danced with the natives and ran with the bulls. Right after the fiesta, he began writing *The Sun Also Rises*. There is not much distance between the "real life" events and people and the fictional events and characters. In fact, although Hemingway wrote to Maxwell Perkins that "it is going to be a swell novel with no autobiography and no complaints," many Hemingway biographers and readers have shown that the novel does contain autobiography.[9] James Mellow elaborates:

> With a few noticeable exceptions, he began with the real names: Nino de la Palma, Hemingway himself, Loeb, Duff, Pat Guthrie, Bill Smith, Don Stewart. Even Hadley made an appearance in the novel to be. . . . Hemingway—"Hem" in the first draft—eventually became the narrator, Jake Barnes; Bill Smith and Don Stewart merged to become . . . Bill Gorton. . . . Pat Guthrie became Mike Campbell. And Duff, after a stint as Duff Anthony, settled into the novel as Lady Brett.[10]

Both the fictional characters and their real-life counterparts enact the same kinds of scenes in the same places.

Jackson Benson's assertion that "the burden on the professional reader of Hemingway's work to maintain a sense of separateness and otherness is particularly demanding. We succeed or fail as critics of his work not just in pointing to his failures in distance but in maintaining our own" is a useful reminder.[11] However, maintaining this distance can be a challenge because Hemingway wants readers to participate in his drinking enterprise. Hemingway enlists his readers as drinking partners through pronoun shifts and other rhetorical strategies. He needs participant readers to validate his own drinking projects, and readers often find validation for their own drinking inscribed in his novels and stories.

To illustrate, Hemingway uses pronoun shifts to construct the reader as a drinking buddy, someone who will drink right along with him and assure him that his drinking is fine. For example, by using pronoun shifts from Jake's first-person *I* to the second-person *you*, Hemingway not only acknowledges the reader's presence but also makes room for the reader as a character—the "you" that Jake addresses in the novel. For example, in chapter 2 Jake comments on Robert Cohn's preoccupation with W. H. Hudson's "The Purple Land," and he makes a significant address to the reader: "'You understand me, he made some reservations, but on the whole the book was sound to him.'"[12] Later Jake makes the same move on the reader in his description of Pernod cocktails: "Pernod is greenish imitation absinthe. When you add water, it turns milky. It tastes like licorice and it has a good uplift, but it drops you just as far."[13] Although one might argue that Hemingway's use of *you* is an impersonal *you*—the equivalent of the third-person singular *one*, certain dynamics still enable a reader to consider herself the "you" that Jake addresses—especially if the reader wants to be part of the novel's public drinking crowd. Jake explains what happens when you drink Pernod, and you can follow his instructions. You can go to Pamplona and run with the bulls; you can go to the Closerie des Lilas and the Select and other cafés in Paris. These spots have become real-life tourist traps due in large part to the success of Hemingway's fiction. Hemingway does not want aesthetic distance; Hemingway wants you to participate in his novel. He wants you to have a drink. For the drinking-buddy reader of *The Sun Also Rises*, verisimilitude becomes virtual reality.

Readers have been more than willing to pierce or obliterate these traditional boundaries between reader and text and fiction and life. Hemingway novels have been received as *romans à clef*—a mode of fiction that invites readers to make connections between people, places, and things in fiction and real life. The drinking characters model behavior that readers can replicate: they can get drunk in the same way that the characters and their authors do. Through such resources as "A Moveable Feast! Self-Guided Hemingway Tour, Paris," readers can go to cafés in Paris and Spain and Berlin and drink right along with the authors and characters. Readers who cannot literally go to Europe can imagine themselves going to those cafés while they read and drink. In *A Moveable Feast*, Hemingway explains how this process works: "I was writing about up in Michigan and since it was a wild, cold, blowing day it was that sort of day in the story. . . . In the story the boys were drinking and this made me thirsty and I ordered a rum St. James. This tasted wonderful on the cold day and I kept on writing."[14] This kind of combined literal and imaginary activity makes the conventional boundary between fiction and life seem not only restrictive but also unnecessary.

Furthermore, Hemingway's novels publicize drinking and authorize their readers to participate in the drinking culture. Beyond offering the reader a vicarious experience, Hemingway enables his readers to participate in the culture of drinking that he represents in his fiction. Readers can drink along with the author and the characters and reenact the scenarios that the author describes; they can "live the novels." *The Sun Also Rises* in particular became a culturally iconic narrative that authorized drinking for its readers when it first appeared in Prohibition America. In *Exile's Return*, Malcolm Cowley reports that *The Sun Also Rises* "was a good novel and became a craze—young men tried to get as imperturbably drunk as the hero, young women of good families took a succession of lovers in the same heartbroken fashion as the heroine, they all talked like Hemingway characters and the name was fixed."[15] The key for both Hemingway drinking characters was that this public drinking required control. The "problem" drinkers in his novels are the ones who publicize their drunkenness; they are out of control. Jake, for example, is not a problem drinker because he gets "imperturbably drunk." In public, he appears to be in control of his drinking, and this is the behavior that readers are encouraged to emulate or enable. Consequently, when Jake Barnes observes "We're none of us sober," his first-person plural subject easily encompasses all the characters in *The Sun Also Rises*, the author, and his readers as well.[16]

In addition, *The Sun Also Rises* demonstrates that novels can be agents and products of alcoholism and the catastrophic melodrama that often attends it. The novels are informed by the catastrophic melodrama in the authors' life, and they serve as "conduct books" for their readers. For example, in *After the Lost Generation* John Aldridge recalls trying to conduct his life according to Hemingway's novels. Acknowledging Hemingway's influence on the next generation of writers, he writes,

"I remember hikes we took in the country when we carried along with us the big loaf of hard bread, the wedge of sour cheese, and the dry red wine of those magnificent moments at Caporetto, the Swiss ski lodge, and the fishing stream in Spain. I remember nights of drinking in front of an open fire when everybody sooner or later began talking like Nick Adams and trying to seduce somebody else's girl with the practiced indifference of Harry Morgan. I remember too the nice girls who came to those parties and drank too much and tried to live up to Brett's frantic example, and how some of them were never quite the same afterward."[17] Unfortunately, as those "nice girls" found out, readers who live the novels often find themselves telling the same story of sadness, frustration, and despair. Not everybody who drinks alcohol and tries to emulate Hemingway or Brett Ashley turns into an alcoholic. However, those of us who are already predisposed to addiction and who do take the conduct books seriously and situate ourselves as Hemingway's drinking buddies and become alcoholics frequently find ourselves producing our own similar stories of alcoholic melodrama and catastrophe.

Hemingway's Invitation to Possibilities

In the summer of 2020, as I was reading Hemingway's short story "Pursuit as Happiness," one element that caught my eye was his attention to the details of the Floridita's daquiris. Here Hemingway's pursuit of the happiness in fishing and writing expands to include the pursuit of the perfect drink—the one that will lift you or move you but won't get you too drunk, won't get you in trouble, won't leave you wanting another one and one more and, what the hell, might as well just keep going until you throw up or pass out or just wake up and it's the next day and it's time to go fishing—that drink. This pursuit finds its origins in "Hills Like White Elephants," in which the two characters are traveling around Europe in pursuit of happiness, involved in "looking at things and trying new drinks" ("Hills," 212). The shift to fishing comes later in Hemingway's oeuvre, but the impulse is the same.

I used to think that Hemingway was an old man when he died, but now I think differently. He was not quite sixty-two years old. He wasn't even old enough for Social Security. He was a little bit older than I am now. Even on my worst days, I don't feel old or worn out or half dead, but he did. There he was, with his toe on the trigger, probably thinking to himself, "there's nothing wrong with me. I feel fine."

Finally, it is possible to read "Hills Like White Elephants" as a kind of opening or an invitation to possibilities. There are the characters at the station, waiting for the express from Barcelona to Madrid. The station is not exactly a crossroads and not a terminus either. Instead the station offers the two people a moment to collect their thoughts and consider their options—none of which seems particularly promising for the young woman in the story. You can keep going and know what is going to happen, or you can do something that is different, and your life will surprise you in ways you never really considered. The divergence, or the point of departure, that happened between Hemingway and me has gone something like this: Hemingway and I had the same problem with liquor. Mine was removed by a power greater than myself; his was removed when he blew his head off eight days after I was born. When Hemingway and I were at the equivalent of the station waiting for the express from Barcelona to Madrid, he and I boarded different trains.

ELLEN LANSKY is an English instructor at Inver Hills Community College in Inver Grove Heights, Minnesota. She teaches composition, literature, and creative writing. Her essays have appeared in the *Carson McCullers Society Newsletter, Dionysos: The Literature and Addiction Triquarterly, Literature and Medicine,* and several anthologies. Most recently, her essay "Trashed: Women under the Influence of Alcohol in Wright's *Native Son*" appeared in *Southern Comforts: Drinking and the U.S. South,* edited by Conor Picken and Matthew Dischinger (2020).

Acknowledgments

Thanks to Lisa DuRose and Ross K. Tangedal for their careful attention to this essay. Parts of this essay first appeared in *Dionysos* and *The Languages of Addiction,* edited by Jane Lilienfeld and Jeffrey Oxford (1999). Thanks to Roger Forseth, Marty Roth, and Jane Lilienfeld for their helpful editorial comments and support in those publications.

Notes

1 Foner and Garraty, *Reader's Companion to American History.*
2 Hemingway, "Hills Like White Elephants," 211 (hereafter cited as "Hills").
3 Hemingway, *The Sun Also Rises,* 22.
4 Lupton, "Ladies Entrance," 578.
5 Rankin, "Hemingway's 'Hills Like White Elephants,'" 234; Kale and Raskauskas, "Hemingway's 'Hills.'"
6 Treisman, "Ernest Hemingway's Grandson."
7 Hemingway, *The Sun Also Rises,* 22.
8 Burns and Novick, *Hemingway.*
9 Mellow, *Hemingway,* 303.
10 Mellow, *Hemingway,* 304.
11 Benson, *Ernest Hemingway,* 156.
12 Hemingway, *The Sun Also Rises,* 9.
13 Hemingway, *The Sun Also Rises,* 15.
14 Hemingway, *Moveable Feast,* 5.
15 Cowley, *Exile's Return,* 3.
16 Hemingway, *The Sun Also Rises,* 143.
17 Aldridge, *After the Lost Generation,* 24–25.

Works Cited

Aldridge, John. *After the Lost Generation.* New York: New York Books for Libraries Press, 1971.

Benson, Jackson. "Ernest Hemingway: The Life as Fiction and the Fiction as Life." In *Hemingway: Essays of Reassessment,* edited by Frank Scafella, 155–68. New York: Oxford University Press, 1991.

Burns, Ken, and Lynn Novick, dirs. *Hemingway: A Writer (1899–1929).* PBS, 2021.

Cowley, Malcolm. *Exile's Return.* New York: Viking, 1964.

Foner, Eric, and John Arthur Garraty, eds. "Volstead Act." In *The Reader's Companion to American History.* Boston: Houghton Mifflin, 2014. ihcproxy.mnpals.net/login?url=https://search .credoreference.com/content/entry/rcah /volstead_act/0?institutionId=4458.

Hemingway, Ernest. "Hills Like White Elephants." In *The Complete Short Stories of Ernest Hemingway,* 211–14. New York: Scribners, 1987.

Hemingway, Ernest. *A Moveable Feast.* New York: Scribners, 1964.

Hemingway, Ernest. *The Sun Also Rises.* New York: Scribners, 1970.

Kale, Verna, and Jessica Raskauskas. "Ernest Hemingway's 'Hills Like White Elephants.'" *Explicator* 79, nos. 1–2 (2021): 69–73.

Lanier, Doris. "The Bittersweet Taste of Absinthe in Hemingway's 'Hills Like White Elephants.'" *Studies in Short Fiction* 26, no. 3 (1989): 279–88.

Lupton, Mary Jo. "Ladies Entrance: Women and Bars." *Feminist Studies* 5, no. 3 (1979): 571–88.

Mellow, James. *Hemingway: A Life without Consequences.* Boston: Houghton Mifflin, 1992.

Rankin, Paul. "Hemingway's 'Hills Like White Elephants.'" *Explicator* 63, no. 4 (2010): 234–37.

Treisman, Deborah. "Ernest Hemingway's Grandson on an Unpublished Story from the Author's Archive." *New Yorker,* June 1, 2020. www.newyorker.com/books/this -week-in-fiction/ernest-hemingway-06 -08-20.

Serving His Lord
Ishiguro and Devotional Addiction

ANTHONY CUNNINGHAM

Abstract   This essay considers devotional addiction in Kazuo Ishiguro's *The Remains of the Day*. The novel tells the story of Mr. Stevens, a constant English butler in a rapidly changing world. Having spent his best years in service to Lord Darlington, he must adjust to an American employer, someone untethered to the traditions that have ruled life at Darlington Hall. Told in the form of a travel journal, covering a span of six days in 1956, the journey is an inner one at heart, an extended bout of self-reflection, with Mr. Stevens thinking about his calling as he has never done before. In the end, how clearly he sees himself and his vocation remains an open question, but careful consideration of his story can illuminate vital details about dedication—*addiction* in the sense of steadfast devotion. Specifically, the novel explores how Mr. Stevens is *embodied* by his vocation, having *become what he does* in a world where professional butlers revere their station and its duties. Unlike external addictions, like drugs or alcohol, devotional addictions cultivate and ultimately *constitute* a self in ways resistant to changing course at will. In the case of Stevens, the self gathers around a calling that can only be jettisoned at the risk of *implosion*.

Keywords   Kazuo Ishiguro, vocation, devotional addiction

> A butler of any quality must be seen to inhabit his role,
> utterly and fully; he cannot be seen casting it aside one
> moment simply to don it again the next as though it were
> nothing more than a pantomime costume.
> —Kazuo Ishiguro, *The Remains of the Day*

Kazuo Ishiguro's *The Remains of the Day* tells the story of a constant English butler in a rapidly changing world. Having spent his best years in service to Lord Darlington, Mr. Stevens must adjust to an American employer who could hardly be more different than his former lord. The days of noble gentlemen running England from the likes of Darlington Hall are waning, and butlers are fast becoming artifacts from a bygone era. The novel takes the form of a travel journal, covering a span of six days in 1956, as Mr. Stevens drives to the West Country, ostensibly to solve

ENGLISH LANGUAGE NOTES

60:1, April 2022 DOI 10.1215/00138282-9560276
© 2022 Regents of the University of Colorado

a "faulty staff plan" by hiring a former housekeeper, Miss Kenton.[1] At heart the journey is an inner one, an extended bout of self-reflection, with Mr. Stevens thinking about his calling as he has never done before. Ultimately, the question of just how clearly he sees himself and his vocation remains an open one, but careful consideration of his story can illuminate vital details about dedication, or if one prefers, *addiction* in the sense of steadfast devotion.

Disparate factors inform the journey. Mr. Stevens has reached an age given to looking back on life. More road lies behind than before him, so reflection bends his mind from things achieved to the regret of things lost, from his profession to personal affairs of love that might have been but were not. Moreover, the changes in his world shake his confidence, not only with respect to his role in an altered Darlington Hall but also regarding his understanding of the relationships between his role, his duty, and his life.

At the beginning of his motor trip, Mr. Stevens experiences no small anxiety about his departure and the journey ahead. With Darlington Hall receding and new horizons approaching, he gives voice to his worries. "But then eventually the surroundings grew unrecognizable and I knew I had gone beyond all previous boundaries. . . . The feeling swept over me that I had truly left Darlington Hall behind, and I must confess I did feel a slight sense of alarm—a sense aggravated by the feeling that I was perhaps not on the correct road at all, but speeding off in totally the wrong direction into a wilderness" (R, 23). These words might as well describe his inner journey. Mr. Stevens has spent his life reflecting carefully and constantly on *how* to be a butler, not *whether* to be one. Indeed, given the realities of his station and its duties, the latter question isn't one Stevens could seriously entertain before coming to the crossroads of his inner journey.[2] Though he doesn't realize it when he sets out, his trip will eventually lead him beyond the practical *how* to the more complicated *whether*. His journey is nothing short of an existential one.

By *existential* I mean an understanding of *who Stevens is*, his very identity. Like most human beings, his form and function are intimately connected. If people devote themselves to practically anything for long enough, they tend to be psychologically shaped by their efforts. Essentially, we become what we do in key respects. Of course, such effects vary in kind and by degree. With Mr. Stevens, his criteria for professional excellence guarantee an airtight connection between form and function. He firmly believes a great butler must have "dignity" and must also serve a "distinguished household," with the former criterion requiring absolute dedication to the profession.

> And let me now posit this: "dignity" has to do crucially with a butler's ability not to abandon the professional being he inhabits. Lesser butlers will abandon their professional being for the private one at the least provocation. For such persons, being a butler is like playing some pantomime role; a small push, a slight stumble, and the façade will drop off to reveal the actor underneath. The great butlers are great by virtue of their ability to inhabit their professional role and inhabit it to the utmost; they will not be shaken out by external event, however surprising, alarming or vexing. They wear their professionalism as a

> decent gentleman will wear his suit: he will not let ruffians or circumstances tear it off him in the public gaze; he will discard it when, and only when, he wills to do so, and this will invariably be when he is entirely alone. It is, as I say, a matter of "dignity." (*R*, 42)

For Mr. Stevens, his profession must be a form of *being* for a true butler, not just a matter of doing a job. As he insists, butlers should "inhabit their professional role and inhabit it to the utmost." Thus anything less than being a butler *through and through* is a professional shortfall in his book. He believes some people, like "Continentals" and "Celts," are not psychologically suited since they lack the required "emotional restraint" (*R*, 43). He clearly believes he has the right stuff, even if he is reluctant to say so out loud.

We aren't told how Mr. Stevens came to his profession, but there can be little mystery to a young man of his ilk following his father into the profession in the early twentieth century. Indeed, for anyone born into his class in his day, the idea of freely choosing to become *whatever* he might like would make little more sense than deciding to become a lord. Effectively, Stevens was born to his station, just like Lord Darlington. Furthermore, given his high-minded conception of the role of a distinguished household, the attractions of the profession are deep and abundant. If the fate of civilization rests in the hands of gentlemen like Lord Darlington, aristocrats responsible for the "progress of humanity," then his dedication to his lord might indirectly make a difference in world affairs (*R*, 114). For Mr. Stevens, his faithful service qualifies as truly noble work, the kind that serves important men doing great things. For someone of his social class, this sense of high-minded duty would surely feel like heady stuff, akin to being a right-hand man to the gods, the great and mighty who hold the fate of humankind in their hands.

Someone looking for "balance" between this work and a "personal life" with Mr. Stevens must look elsewhere. While an attraction to Miss Kenton tests his professional constancy, his staunch refusal to give in to temptation confirms his steadfast dedication. Miss Kenton arrives at Darlington Hall as housekeeper in 1922, and her relationship with Mr. Stevens gets off to a rocky start after he reprimands her for addressing his father as "William," even though she is accustomed to using the "Christian" names of underservants. When she takes umbrage at his correction, he chides her for missing details that should be "self-evident" and "obvious," cutting remarks from Mr. Stevens, for whom noticing everything in a household is crucial (*R*, 54). Feeling unfairly maligned, Miss Kenton makes it her business to impress on Mr. Stevens that his father is no longer as capable as he takes him to be, and his stubborn resistance in the face of her compelling evidence frustrates her. Then suddenly William Stevens takes ill, and Miss Kenton not only lets her festering resentment go but rises to the occasion by seeing to him so Mr. Stevens can attend to the smooth running of Lord Darlington's 1923 conference. When he recollects this difficult evening, Mr. Stevens marks it as the moment he "came of age as a butler," proof beyond any doubt that he would not be "shaken out by external event, however surprising, alarming or vexing" (*R*, 70). Thereafter his relationship with Miss Kenton warms considerably.

The pair take to conducting nightly cocoa meetings to review the doings of the day and to consider what might need doing the next. Mr. Stevens characterizes these sessions as "overwhelmingly professional in tone," but he obviously enjoys her company (R, 147). Just as surely, he considers celibacy a professional necessity, at least for the likes of him, a butler serving such a distinguished household. When he first interviews Kenton for the position, he emphasizes how "liaisons" between staff members are a "serious threat to the order in a house" (R, 51). His father married and had children, but then again, William Stevens never rose to his son's heights in the profession. Presumably, Mr. Stevens considers marriage incompatible with his higher station.

Nonetheless, the two eventually grow familiar enough for Miss Kenton to tease him good-naturedly about his supposed aversion to "pretty girls" on the staff, an exchange he indulges and acknowledges as fit for their ears only ("You must understand we would never have carried on in such a vein within the hearing of staff members") (R, 156). But when Miss Kenton ups the intimacy ante by entering his "pantry," his private refuge, backing him into a corner to pry a book from his hands, a "sentimental love story," Mr. Stevens can no longer avoid the distinct sense "that things between Miss Kenton and myself had reached—no doubt after a gradual process of many months—an inappropriate footing" (R, 169). Alarmed, he resolves to put things right, and he soon does so by ending the cocoa meetings after a tired Miss Kenton begs for mercy one evening as he discusses the fine details of an upcoming event. Her numerous pleas to reinstate the meetings fall on deaf ears, and her reluctant gravitation away from Darlington Hall reaches its conclusion with her acceptance of a marriage proposal and eventual departure in 1936.

Twenty years later Mr. Stevens arrives in Weymouth, long after the dust of his lord's tarnished reputation has settled, and by this point there can be no doubt that he hopes Mrs. Benn (the former Miss Kenton) will return to Darlington Hall, and not purely to solve his staff plan, as he claimed at the start of his journey. Having reexamined their years of service together, he now realizes how his decision to discontinue their cocoa meetings rendered "whole dreams forever irredeemable," an extraordinary admission (R, 179). When they meet for tea, he pays her a different kind of attention: that of an admirer.

> She had, naturally, aged somewhat, but to my eyes at least, she seemed to have done so very gracefully. Her figure remained slim, her posture as upright as ever. She had maintained, too, her old way of holding her head in a manner that verged on the defiant. Of course, with the bleak light falling on her face, I could hardly help but notice the lines that had appeared here and there. But by and large the Miss Kenton I saw before me looked surprisingly similar to the person who had inhabited my memory over these years. That is to say, it was, on the whole, extremely pleasing to see her again. (R, 232)

However, his hopes for a reunion are soon dashed when she informs him that with a grandchild on the way, she will not be returning to service. After mentioning that she left all those years ago as something of a "ruse" to annoy him, and that she only gradually came to love her husband over time ("You spend so much time with some-one, you find you get used to him"), she makes a weighty confession (*R*, 239). "That doesn't mean to say, of course, there aren't occasions now and then—extremely desolate occasions—when you think to yourself: 'what a terrible mistake I've made with my life.' And you get to thinking about a different life, a *better* life you might have had. For instance, I get to thinking about a life I may have had with you, Mr Stevens" (*R*, 238). Mr. Stevens understands her, as evidenced by his own confession that "at that moment, my heart was breaking," but he says nothing about his feelings (*R*, 238). Instead, he escorts her to a bus stop and bids her a sad good-bye, knowing they will likely never meet again, wishing her well and saying, "'You really mustn't let any more foolish ideas come between yourself and the happiness you deserve'" (*R*, 239). True to form, Mr. Stevens maintains his professional "dignity" in the sense of not being "shaken out" by this "external event" so far as outward appearances are concerned. The constant butler carries on resolutely, as always. But the revelation that Miss Kenton's confession moves him so deeply testifies to how much she truly meant to him, even if he didn't realize it during their time together. And if he resolutely *banished* such thoughts and feelings in his years of faithful service to his lord, it was all in a hard day's work.

I suspect that few contemporary readers will be moved to raise a full-throated cheer for Mr. Stevens and his resolute choice of profession over love in *The Remains of the Day*. For one thing, some may insist that he fails *on his own terms* by ignoring abundant signs that Lord Darlington's well-intentioned sympathy for Germany crossed a line into unwitting complicity with the Nazis. In other words, though he sought to work for the good of humanity, Mr. Stevens effectively ended up serving bad ends by serving his misguided lord. In fact, Mr. Stevens seems to come around to this conclusion during his journey, even if he resists it. Early in the novel, he defends Darlington as a "truly good man at heart, a gentleman through and through," someone "I am today proud to have given my best years of service to" (*R*, 61). Moreover, he defends his loyalty to Lord Darlington as "intelligently bestowed."

> I refer to that strand of opinion in the profession which suggested that any butler with serious aspirations should make it his business to be forever reappraising his employer—scrutinizing that latter's motives, analysing the implications of his views. . . . For it is, in practice, simply not possible to adopt such a critical attitude towards an employer and at the same time provide good service. . . . If a butler is to be of any worth to anything or anybody in life, there must surely come a time when he ceases his searching, a time when he must say to himself: "This employer embodies all that I find noble and admirable. I will hereafter devote myself to serving him." This is loyalty *intelligently* bestowed. What is there "undignified" in this? (*R*, 200)

However, by the end of the trip, after he has revisited key events like Darlington's order to fire two Jewish maids, his involvement with "Sir Oswald Mosley's 'blackshirts' organization," and his lord's secret meeting with the German ambassador at Darlington Hall, the highest praise Mr. Stevens can muster for his lord is "Lord

Darlington wasn't a bad man. He wasn't a bad man at all" (*R*, 243). And in the next breath, as he considers how he trusted in his lordship, he asks a damning question: "Really—one has to ask oneself—what dignity is there in that?" (*R*, 243).

Given the reality that as his lord goes, so goes Mr. Stevens, his lordship's fall from grace would seem to doom his professional devotion, at least so far as the cause of serving humanity is concerned. Furthermore, if Mr. Stevens engaged in willful ignorance and self-deception to convince himself that his loyalty to Darlington was "intelligently bestowed" beyond any sensible expiration point for it, then his error would seemingly be compounded, an instance of propping up a sinking ship with implausible fibs. Indeed, if he somehow established his lordship's wisdom and goodness as unassailable givens, akin to axioms for a geometrical proof, while turning a blind eye to any serious possibility of a life with Miss Kenton, his fate would seem like a *rigged* choice rather than a matter of straightforward misjudgment. Viewed in this light, Mr. Stevens may seem like a junkie, someone determined to get his professional fix in whatever way he can, whether he must lie to others or himself. And like some junkies, even those accustomed to fooling the world and themselves, perhaps Mr. Stevens ultimately experiences a moment of existential clarity when he confronts the unpalatable idea that he failed on both fronts with respect to the two essential criteria for being a great butler—working for a morally distinguished household and embodying dignity.

Aside from this *procedural* problem with Mr. Stevens's fidelity, a case of devotion failing on its own internal terms irrespective of the object of devotion, some readers may think that he makes a poor choice by forsaking romantic love in favor of his profession, either because love should always conquer all, or because love should at least prevail in this instance over the specific choice for his profession. The former proffers a general claim about love, that it matters more than *any* profession, while the latter takes the weaker position that love is simply more important than being a great butler. Both claims involve a calculus of worth, and their measurements don't rely purely on a felt sense of what matters. They take the position that Mr. Stevens could firmly believe that nothing is more important than serving his lord, yet he could be wrong, not only because he gets his lord wrong but because love is simply more important than anything he might accomplish with and for his lord, even if Darlington hadn't gone astray with the Nazis.

A key idea with a long history and distinguished pedigree in the history of Western philosophy looms here, one involving the notion of "the good," as in what matters or what is valuable. The perspective in question holds that *objective* value—what's truly good—isn't purely a matter of sheer valuing in the sense of an individual simply believing that something matters or someone wanting something. On this view, human *wisdom* consists in knowing what sorts of things are genuinely *worth* wanting; the wanting itself never settles whether something is valuable. Wise practical agents are said to be capable of stepping outside their yearnings to consider whether they are fitting objects of desire, and if they conclude that they aren't, they must put them aside, hard as it may be to do so.

This perspective on the nature of value mirrors a common conception of empirical truth, where human beings strive to track the objective truth about the external world. For instance, astrophysicists strive to discern the nature of celestial phenomena. They do so knowing that these phenomena may remain elusive. Nature may refuse to give up its secrets, not just now, but forever. Nonetheless, whether anyone ever comes to know what they are, black holes are something, and that something is not a matter of opinion. Scientists do not *make* black holes one thing rather than another by believing whatever they believe about them, no more than someone's opinion about my having fifty cents in my pocket settles the issue of what I have. I have it or I don't, and someone gets the answer correct only if the inquirer tracks the truth about my money. On this view of objective truth and value, our thoughts and desires never decisively settle the questions of what is true or good. Instead, things are just so, and things matter in such ways that we must track their independent truth and value, with the possibility of our beliefs being mistaken despite our best efforts to track the truth or the good.

If this philosophical perspective on the nature of value is the proper way to think about what matters, then the perils of an addiction in the sense of any psychologically compelling calling should be clear. If a calling misses the mark with respect to the good, whether by skewing sound judgment or by overriding its proper authority, it comes between a person and the pursuit of what matters. In this vein, an interchange between Stevens and Mr. Cardinal, Lord Darlington's godson, may seem like a prime example of sound judgment being corrupted in this fashion. Cardinal appears on the evening when the British prime minister, the foreign secretary, and the German ambassador are conducting the sensitive meeting arranged by Lord Darlington. His appearance is unexpected but no accident. As a columnist specializing in international affairs, he has a keen interest in what he sees as a nefarious meeting, and, told by Darlington to make himself scarce for the night, Cardinal expresses his frustrations to Stevens.

> His lordship has worked wonders to bring this meeting about, and he believes—faithfully believes—he's doing something good and honourable. . . . His lordship has probably been the single most useful pawn Herr Hitler has had in this country for his propaganda tricks. All the better because he's sincere and honourable and doesn't recognize the true nature of what he's doing. . . . His lordship has been crucially instrumental in establishing links between Berlin and over sixty of the most influential citizens of this country. . . . Herr Ribbentrop's been able virtually to bypass our foreign office altogether. . . . At this very moment, his lordship is discussing the idea of His Majesty himself visiting Herr Hitler. (*R*, 221, 224, 225)

Confronted with these charges, Stevens professes an unwavering faith in his lord. "'I'm sorry, sir, but I cannot see that his lordship is doing anything other than that which is highest and noblest. He is doing what he can, after all, to ensure that peace will continue to prevail in Europe'" (*R*, 225). One might insist that Mr. Stevens is merely attesting to his lordship's good *motives* when he defends him against Cardinal's criticisms, but his words—"I cannot see that his lordship is doing anything other than that which is highest and noblest"—suggest more, at least if taken at face value. People with benign intentions can unwittingly do bad things, but if

Mr. Stevens considers it something along the lines of a given that whatever Lord Darlington does must be good, as if his deeds might be good *by definition*, then his unwavering confidence looks more like blind loyalty, not loyalty "intelligently bestowed." This sort of possible confirmation bias, where one finds the evidence one wishes and ignores any contrary evidence, carries the potential to distort practical judgment in fundamental ways. And if his professional calling somehow condemns him to such a fate, one where his lord can do no wrong and Miss Kenton can never stand a real chance, then perhaps Mr. Stevens is the equivalent of a junkie who only has eyes for his all-consuming fix. In this case, maybe he is a victim of professional addiction, and his story a cautionary tale.

It's worth noting that Mr. Stevens experiences personal doubts and regrets about his choices at the end of his journey, though he oscillates between indicting his dignity and entertaining the idea that his fidelity had value regardless of his lord's mistakes:

> The hard reality is, surely, that for the likes of you and I, there is little choice other than to leave our fate, ultimately, in the hands of those great gentlemen at the hub of this world to employ our services. What is the point in worrying oneself too much about what one could or could not have done to control the course one's life took? Surely it is enough that the likes of you and I at least try to make our small contribution count for something true and worthy. And if some of us are prepared to sacrifice much in life in order to pursue such aspirations, surely that is in itself, whatever the outcome, cause for pride and contentment. (*R*, 244)

The novel ends on an ambiguous note, with Mr. Stevens observing people conversing amiably on a pier:

> As I watch them now, they are laughing merrily. It is curious how people can build such warmth among themselves so swiftly. It is possible these particular persons are simply united by the anticipation of the evening ahead. But, then, I rather fancy it has more to do with this skill of bantering. Listening to them now, I can hear them exchanging one bantering remark after another. It is, I would suppose, the way people like to proceed. . . . Perhaps it is indeed time I began to look at this whole matter of bantering more enthusiastically. After all, when one thinks about it, it is not such a foolish thing to indulge in—particularly if it is the case that in bantering lies the key to human warmth. (*R*, 245)

Thus he resolves to take up the practice of "banter" with renewed enthusiasm, a practice favored by his new employer, but one that makes Mr. Stevens nervous, since "one is given very little time to assess its various possible repercussions before one is called to give voice to it, and one gravely risks uttering all manner of unsuitable things" (*R*, 131). Is this final resolution simply more of the same, a matter of Mr. Stevens clinging to his professional calling, or is it an epiphany, a case of coming to a new appreciation of the importance of human warmth? The answer isn't clear, but on the philosophical perspective of objective value, nothing much hangs on the answer, since any given calling derives its legitimacy from the accuracy of its bead on the good. Callings that miss the mark on the objective good, no matter how compelling they may feel, sound a false and regrettable note.

Ultimately, any philosophical perspective on the nature of value can only be as good as it is true, and this influential conception of objective value mischaracterizes human lives and their callings. To explain why it misses the mark, it might help to imagine a different life for Mr. Stevens, just to be sure that a servant's life doesn't somehow inordinately color our judgment. After all, a butler's life probably holds little allure for most people reading these words, so let us suppose that young Stevens had the opportunity to pursue music seriously. Picture him as the son of a renowned musician, and say he set his sights from an early age on being a concert pianist. Excellence in such a demanding field is a ruthless master. Sacrifices must be made. You can depend on anyone with this goal not having the "luxury" of a "normal" life in the sense of casually dabbling in things. If this person enjoys a wealth of disparate interests, he will need to prepare many a no to devote himself adequately to music. Mastering the piano isn't something people can accomplish in their "spare" time. And the longer he pursues the piano seriously, as he must to be any good, the deeper his identification with it will be. At some point, asking him to step away from music to consider a different life will be a matter of asking him not simply to *do* something else but to *be* someone else.

Obviously, people can change their course in life. Such alterations are often imposed and unwelcome. Thus, as she ages, the opera singer can no longer hit the high notes, and the aging baseball player can't hit a big fastball. Nothing lasts forever, even prodigious talent. When the changes aren't imposed involuntarily by way of sheer disruption or disintegration, something important likely changes on the inside. Perhaps the pianist wakes up one day in midlife and suddenly realizes he's thoroughly unhappy. He's lost his musical calling somewhere along the way. Or perhaps he realizes that he never truly loved the piano in the first place. Maybe he merely wanted to make his father happy by following in his footsteps, something he never realized, until one day he did. Callings needn't last forever, and sometimes they can even be a precarious house of cards.

Note that no matter how resilient callings may be, there is no such thing as a "god's-eye view" where they are concerned. Observers might sensibly insist that the concert pianist's life of *endless* piano could never possibly suit them. No, it would simply be too much of one thing; they would miss out on too many other good things. Fair enough. But we should tread carefully with such judgments if we mean them as anything beyond a simple acknowledgment of how one life inevitably closes doors on others or how this person's calling can leave another cold. When it comes to answering a call from one love or another, human beings do not track some form of the "good" independent of the yearnings they discover and cultivate along the way. The fact is that Mr. Stevens answered a call to service that carried no warrant or necessity beyond the fact that it spoke deeply to him, not simply as someone born into a social station but as someone with the right stuff to perform the weighty duties of his station at the highest levels.

This isn't to imply that evaluative judgments of different possible lives have no sensible place in a human life. For instance, if your child wishes to do nothing but play an arcade game like Donkey Kong, you would reasonably worry, even if your child fairly professed to be more content than you.[3] Forsaking all human experiences, relationships, and activities for the sake of playing such a game would seem like a poor choice to most people, even if they could offer no indisputable proof of the soundness of their opinion. Nonetheless, if we believe that we can step back and offer an authoritative evaluation of any given calling, be it music or being a butler, we edge down a perilous path of wishful thinking, a philosophical sleight of hand where we manufacture an imprimatur for a life that doesn't rightly warrant one. Perhaps human beings relish the psychological comfort of *believing* that one life is "objectively" better than another. Indeed, without such confidence, many people might feel terribly lost, vexed and anxious that their lives might be capricious endeavors, devoid of any true meaning and value because they do not hew to some true and unerring good. However, even if this might be psychologically true about human beings, it wouldn't prove a thing about "objective" values.

If you should be tempted to believe in the idea that lives must be moored to anything like objective values to have any true or deep meaning and value, I invite you to engage in a brief thought experiment. Imagine you dearly love a child, and say you know beyond any doubt that this love is objectively valuable, that it is ordained in the stars or written into the metaphysical fabric of the universe. Leave aside *how* you know it. Let's just say you do—end of story. Thus your love unerringly tracks the indisputable truth about what matters; were you not to love this child, you'd be making an undeniable mistake because your child matters objectively, just as two and two make four, or water is two parts hydrogen and one part oxygen. Now I ask you to imagine the same child and the same love but subtract the objective value. Say you come to know there is no such thing. Once again, leave aside how you know it. You just do. At this point, I ask you: What would the difference between these two lives and loves be? Would you love the child more with the assurance of objective value, or would you love the child less without it? And if the difference wouldn't be a matter of one love being more and the other less, precisely how would the two loves be qualitatively different? Provided you love the child, I don't believe they would be, and this observation bears on Mr. Stevens and his vocation.

While we can't lay bare the psychological roots of his calling, we can safely say that it wasn't predicated on wild fancy. Mr. Stevens is no Don Quixote, detached from reality as he tilts away at windmills. Stevens was born into a social class that defined his range of professional possibilities. Given these constraints, he dedicated himself to his allotted station and its duties. Moreover, he had good reason to believe that Lord Darlington was one of those fine English gentlemen entrusted with the "progress of humanity." True, Lord Darlington ended up serving Nazi ambitions, but he didn't set out to do so. Like many people, he did bad things from benign motives. However, we—and Mr. Stevens—could easily imagine a different outcome. Suppose Darlington helped ease the burdensome Treaty of Versailles in ways that headed Hitler's rise off at the pass. If his efforts were successful in preventing World War II, we'd never know it, since we'd never know what would have transpired without them, but in this case, Mr. Stevens's trust in his lordship's wisdom and good intentions would have paid off. Nothing about his fidelity to his lord destined Mr. Stevens to the fate of serving a Nazi appeaser.

We do well to bear in mind that not every deep calling has a happy ending. Indeed, many do not. The child I love so dearly may go on to lead a miserable existence, sending my life off the rails. The concert stage may not prove to be all it was cracked up to be to the young pianist. And a distinguished household may do more harm than good, effectively undermining the best intentions of a dedicated butler. Even after things go awry, the attachments and commitments manifested by deep vocations are not given to being flipped off at will like a switch. A parent, a concert pianist, and a butler like Stevens are *embodied* by these vocations. In a meaningful sense, *they become what they do*. If things go badly, observers may be apt to think of such vocations as "addictions" in a pejorative sense, immoderate and compulsive attachments that do their victims harm. When the addiction is to an external entity, like drugs or alcohol, we can point to deleterious effects on physical and psychological health, and we can sensibly paint the addiction as a dangerous adversary, one prone to destroying a life. Without a doubt, some addictions are unhealthy ones. However, with the addictions of parents, pianists, and constant butlers like Stevens, the potential threat to the self comes in the form of an *implosion*, not some destructive blow from the outside. The self inevitably takes its psychological shape around its deepest loves, where they are callings we cannot create or choose purely at will, and jettisoning the loves to save the self cannot help but fundamentally alter the self. Without indulging in any hyperbole, we can say that these people eventually *become their loves*; take their loves away and you're left with someone else as the self *disintegrates*. In other words, the self crumbles from within from the loss of the loves that constitute it.

In some cases you may be tempted to think, "So be it. Crumble. Be someone else. For your own good or the good of others." However, we should be wary of easy depictions of a self that do not square with the facts of our empirical psychology. Philosophical depictions of values and choices that are detached from the realities of our psychology and circumstances are no better than fantasies, and when they encourage false narratives of human life and character, they are pernicious ones. The reality is that we never straightforwardly choose our loves, even if we can choose to lean into them or to turn away. Tell the beleaguered parent to forget her wayward, self-destructive child. Tell the abused altar boy to walk away from his beloved church and never look back. Tell the long-suffering writer to put down the painful pen and take up golf or knitting instead. Or tell a devoted butler like Stevens to give up his profession for a chance at love with Miss Kenton. If your advice is predicated on anything along the lines of the idea that we possess the power to refashion ourselves at will, akin to reshaping modeling clay as we please, then such thinking is wishful thinking, just as fanciful as thinking that "the good" is somehow inscribed in the fabric of the universe in some way that we must track, much like we track the truth about the natural world. Navigating from one self to a new one is never a matter of simply *deciding*, which isn't to deny that human beings sometimes actively cultivate a new self, and sometimes they turn their backs on deep attachments and commitments to do so. But when this happens, it's never the result of simply deciding at will to be someone else. We are not unencumbered selves in the sense of being free from psychological attachments and commitments that largely make us who we are at our core.

An adequate appreciation of a true calling requires judicious perspective on how a dedicated self sees the world. Thus, for someone like Mr. Stevens, the lines between blind loyalty and loyalty "intelligently bestowed" can be vague and blurry. One doesn't need to hold that "love is blind" to accept the fact that deep attachments inevitably color one's vision. When Mr. Stevens contemplates Lord Darlington's doings, he does so with a generous benefit of the doubt, the kind that comes with the territory of striving to think the best of people and pursuits we hold dear. Mr. Stevens can no more turn off such generosity than he can sprout wings to fly. This benefit of the doubt is no less than what it means to be partial where our loves are concerned. There are times where impartiality is in order. Justice wears her blindfold and holds her scales so she can restore moral order to the universe without unfairly favoring one party over another. But herein we see an essential difference between love and justice. Impartial love is scarcely love at all. Arguably, Mr. Stevens gave his lord too great a benefit of the doubt, for too long, but had he refused Lord Darlington any such benefit, all talk of "loyalty" would be misplaced, and while loyalty itself can always be misplaced, any calling devoid of loyalty is akin to a bird without wings. Such a bird can't fly. Had Mr. Stevens been prepared to abandon his lord at the first signs of trouble, he wouldn't have been Mr. Stevens. His professional station and its duties compelled him to stick by his lord—not unconditionally, but with a full and weighty measure of charity.

For some people, the idea of a life bereft of any true calling, whether it be a butler's vocation or any other, may seem a form of psychological emancipation from being beholden to anyone or anything. Indeed, such a life may seem gloriously free—*free from* any addiction. Without a doubt, deep attachments and commitments operate as practical constraints on a life, closing off some paths in favor of others. However, these psychological constraints also give shape and substance to a human life, infusing it with its abiding sense of meaning and value. This isn't to say that all addictions necessarily end well. Like most things, they come with no guarantee, as we see in the case of Mr. Stevens. Nonetheless, even if such loves are never sufficient conditions for living well, they are necessary conditions, or something close to it.

Like so many readers, I find *The Remains of the Day* a poignant tale, rich and perceptive as a depiction of a man trying to understand himself as he reflects on the clarion call of his life's work. He heeded the call steadfastly, but this isn't to say that he fully understood its terms and implications at the time, and in this regard, he is no different than most people. To borrow from Søren Kierkegaard, life must be lived going forward, but understood looking backward. As he motors along to the West Country, Mr. Stevens does some hard work to know himself, and arguably, he understands himself better by the end of his journey. Nonetheless, to my mind, he cuts a lonely and forlorn figure as he sits on a pier, watching strangers socialize and contemplating what to make of the remains of his days as he makes ready to return to Darlington Hall. He seems a less contented man, but of course, greater self-knowledge can sometimes have this effect on people.

Ultimately, I appreciate Mr. Stevens's devotion, and I can easily imagine a different ending for him, one where he has a hand in serving the "progress of humanity" by playing a part in helping Lord Darlington avert World War II. However, even with this happy ending, one that Mr. Stevens might well imagine for himself, I would still feel for him because he would miss out on "human warmth." I understand that in this scenario, missing out on love would simply be the price of one life closing the door on another, something that comes with virtually any calling. After all, many a parent or caregiver must live with occasional thoughts of "what might have been," with professional ambitions pushed aside for the sake of attending to loved ones.

In the end, I can't help but lament that Stevens lived in a time and place where the outcome of any choice between his lord and love was all but certain from the start. My lamentation doesn't hinge on any assumption of one life being objectively "best" for Mr. Stevens. Undeniably, his calling shaped his vision of his best possible life, and that vision closely tracked the perceived duties of his social station. Given his world, one where class strictly defined the sorts of professions that a man like Stevens might ever consider, love never stood much of a chance, not for a constant butler like him. The walls of his unfailing dedication were simply too high and robust for love to breach them. Nevertheless, I wish that he might have experienced more of the "human warmth" he so obviously longs for at the end of the novel.

Then again, to be fair, a different path with Miss Kenton wouldn't necessarily have turned out well. Love, even fabled "true love forever," needn't last, and it can sometimes undo people as it weaves an unwitting path of destruction. Love, like any calling, comes with no guarantee. Yet, despite this uncertainty, I can't help but linger on how Mr. Stevens admits the high price of love lost when he acknowledges how his decision to end his cocoa meetings rendered "whole dreams forever irredeemable." Even a most dedicated butler like Mr. Stevens can experience fleeting moments of doubt along the way. I can readily imagine them, some gnawing sense of something missing from life. And because I feel for Mr. Stevens, I like to imagine a different scenario, where human warmth somehow finds a crack in the formidable walls of his professional calling. Had love found such an opening, Mr. Stevens might have experienced a change of heart with respect to his sense of what matters. Such things can happen, a pivot from one calling to another, even if this kind of *metanoia* usually seems a mystery to observers. Understandably, any such change is apt to look like a Damascene conversion, the shedding of one self for another, and well it should, for the change is always an existential one, a seismic shift in identity. Wish as I might for Mr. Stevens, I also realize that I look on a different world, one without his station and its duties, and this difference makes all the difference.

ANTHONY CUNNINGHAM teaches in the Department of Philosophy at St. John's University. His philosophical publications include *The Heart of What Matters: The Role for Literature in Moral Philosophy* (2001), *Modern Honor: A Philosophical Defense* (2013), and essays and reviews in the *American Philosophical Quarterly*, the *Dalhousie Review*, *Dialogue*, *Ethics*, the *Journal of Value Inquiry*, *Mind*, *Philosophy and Phenomenological Research*, and other journals.

Notes

1   Ishiguro, *The Remains of the Day*, 5 (hereafter cited as *R*).
2   My phrasing here nods to F. H. Bradley's essay "My Station and Its Duties," in which he outlines a social conception of the self and its ethical responsibilities (*Ethical Studies*, essay 5).
3   The documentary *The King of Kong: A Fistful of Quarters* (dir. Seth Gordon, 2007) offers a fascinating look at an obsession with Donkey Kong, a video arcade game. The film follows Steve Wiebe as he attempts to break Billy Mitchell's high score in the game.

Works Cited

Bradley, F. H. *Ethical Studies*. London, 1876.
Ishiguro, Kazuo. *The Remains of the Day*. New York: Knopf, 1989.

Approaching Addiction
A Brief History

STEVE SUSSMAN AND ERIKA WRIGHT

Abstract   This essay seeks to illuminate the shifting definitions of addiction over time by providing a brief, anecdotal history of addiction as well as a review of how it has been conceptualized by the American Psychiatric Association's *DSM* classification system. While all addictions have in common the attempt to experience an appetitive effect (satiety), preoccupation, loss of control, and negative or undesired consequences, including physical danger, social complaints, or inability to carry on one's life roles, the meaning of addiction has not always been consistent. By approaching addiction from the historical/anecdotal and the official/medical perspectives, this essay provides a framework for working toward a common understanding of this complex phenomenon.
Keywords   addiction, *DSM*, dependence

Approaching Addiction

In the 1980s the American Psychiatric Association (APA) convened an international group of addiction experts to revise the section on "substance-related disorders" in the *Diagnostic and Statistical Manual (DSM)*.[1] While they agreed to define this "syndrome" as "compulsive, uncontrolled, drug-seeking behavior," they could not come to consensus on "what label should be used": should they use the word *addiction*, or should they use *dependence* to describe the contents of this category? In the end, *dependence* was viewed as "more neutral" and won by a single vote, as some feared that the term *addiction* was too "pejorative and would lead to alienation of patients."[2] The *DSM-III-R* refers, therefore, to "drug dependence." This term ultimately caused confusion for educators, as "physical dependence," which is a "normal physiological response," is different from "addiction," which is a "drug-seeking behavior."[3] Eventually, the *DSM-V*, the series' most current version, revised the title of the overall section to be "Substance-Related and Addictive Disorders" and included subcategories on "substance-use disorder" and "non-substance use disorder."

The debate over whether *addiction* is an appropriate label or not speaks to the ongoing desire and challenge associated with defining this common and complex concept. Words matter. But while it is true that "we all know how to use the term [*addiction*],"[4] it is equally true that we have struggled to determine what it is and how best to manage it, as the various reactions, attitudes, and policies around addiction have evolved over time, marking a range of behaviors, things, and people as weak-willed, immoral, diseased, or neurodiverse.[5] Clinicians and researchers generally understand addiction as a pathological preoccupation with and loss of control over substance use, as well as other behaviors related to dysregulated activation of the neurobiological motivation-reward system.[6] But it is also more (and less) than that, depending on geographic location, sociocultural context, and health care policies and politics.

By providing some context for understanding the modern struggles to define what, by all accounts, is a familiar concept, we might learn how best to address social and medical ramifications of addiction. The following discussion provides an overview of some of the ways *addiction* has been defined and concludes with a survey of the *DSM* to highlight both the evolving concept of addiction and a commitment to securing a stable, if capacious, definition.

Toward a Definition of Addiction

Current views of addiction, both medical and political, imagine it as an individual and social problem to be solved—a disease to be cured—yet its history pushes against this single narrative trajectory. The earliest uses of the term in ancient Rome, in fact, contrast with the medical uses by modern researchers. The word *addict* has its origin in contract law, but these legal meanings are overwritten by its devotional invocations, which are then also overwritten by medical uses.[7] Originally, *addiction* generally referred to "giving over" or being "highly devoted" to a person or activity,[8] or engaging in a behavior habitually,[9] which could have positive or negative implications. *Addicere* (also see *addico, addixi,* or *addictus*), the Latin verb from which *addiction* derives, means "to give or bind, or even to enslave, a person to one thing or another."[10] With the growing variety of substances and behaviors that have been categorized by researchers and practitioners as addiction, it is important to acknowledge the complex history and varied cultural attitudes that surround addiction, challenging a simple definition while also calling for a shared understanding of what it is and what it may become.

Often framed as a phenomenon that involves overpowering urges, the term itself is increasingly associated with disease,[11] as conceptualizations of addiction, which date back to the end of the eighteenth century, pertain to a malfunction of the central nervous system in some way.[12] Indeed, contemporary scientific research has turned to the brain and to biology, with recent studies establishing addiction's neurobiological underpinnings,[13] sometimes associating addiction with "brain disease."[14]

While addiction has long been considered a problem of substance use, whether it is configured in terms of abuse or misuse, its relationship to survival has also shaped how we understand it. Evolutionary biologists, ethologists, psychiatrists, motivation psychologists, and neuroscientists have described addiction in terms of "appetitive needs"—that is, "a natural desire to satisfy bodily needs" that is universal among human beings. In fact, these "needs" may support the fulfillment of important survival maintenance functions such as hunger, thirst, sociability, nurturance, and exploration. Evolutionary theories of human behavior have asserted that subjective experience of adaptation attributes, such as survival ability and reproductive fitness, are reflected biologically in the operations of the mesolimbic dopaminergic system (probably the endpoint of, or nested within, a cascade of other neurobiological systems [e.g., glutaminergic, opioid, serotonergic]).[15] As noted by Sussman and Pakdaman, "early theorists suggested that humans experience innate and secondarily acquired appetitive needs [which are] invoked by interoceptive (e.g., hunger pangs) and environmental (e.g., sight or smell of food) stimuli that guide behavior toward rewarding outcomes which satiate those needs."[16] Addiction occurs when there is "an illusory satiation of appetitive needs via a learned behavior," such as feeling the need for alcohol to survive.[17]

Categorizing Addictions

The two general categories of addiction, also known as addictive behaviors, include *substance addiction* and *behavioral (process) addiction*. Substance addiction pertains to repetitive intake of a drug (such as alcohol) or of food and refers to manipulation of neurotransmission through introduction of exogenous ligands (e.g., recreational drugs) that cross the blood-brain barrier. Endogenous ligand (neurotransmitter) function is altered by being acted on via the exogenous ligands. A substance addiction, therefore, is an addictive behavior but is not a "behavioral addiction." Behavioral addictions, on the other hand, have a relatively recent history, as they pertain to engaging repetitively in types of behaviors that do not involve direct intake of substances into the body.[18] Behavioral addiction refers to manipulation of endogenous ligand function through engagement in repetitive behavior. Endogenous ligand function becomes dependent, in time, on performance of those behaviors. The First International Conference on Behavioral Addictions in 2013 demonstrated a global research consensus on the existence of multiple types of addictions, including behaviors such as shopping, internet use, and sex.[19]

The word *addiction*, then, has come to define a relationship or reaction to the things we do or what we consume. Establishing a stable definition of this changeable term is crucial to making inferences about how addiction maps onto other concepts, such as impulsivity or compulsivity.[20] In general, addiction, unlike compulsion, "involves the attempt to achieve some appetitive effect and satiation through engagement in some behavior."[21] Differentiating "addiction" from other disorders such as "obsessive-compulsive disorder (OCD)" has proved challenging. It might be argued that the difference between an OCD and an addiction is that only negative reinforcement operates with OCD, whereas both positive and negative reinforcement operate with addictions.[22] Yet, while positive reinforcement may lead to addiction to such substances as cigarettes, the maintenance of that addiction may be primarily through negative reinforcement.[23] One reductio ad absurdum argument stemming from this positive-negative reinforcement issue would be that early on the behavior is an addiction but later it becomes an instance of OCD.[24] Such determinations have an impact on the development of policies and methods of prevention and control. Before May 2013, for example, gambling was considered an impulse control disorder (*DSM-IV*),[25] but later it was changed to an addiction (*DSM-V*), which meant that one could now receive third-party payments for treatment.

As forms of addiction continue to shift, and as some behaviors and substances have only very recently come to be categorized as addictions or addictive by researchers and practitioners, we must attend both to specific cases and to the bigger social and cultural picture to recognize patterns that persist regardless of substance or behavior. By breaking down seemingly capacious and wily phenomena into some of their basic parts, we can begin to provide a framework for thinking through the shifting attitudes, belief systems, and economic demands that contribute to the way medicine, science, law, and society approach the topic of addiction. The following overview provides a selective list of literary, historical, and familiar anecdotes about the substances and behaviors that have come to represent the story of addiction and thus contribute to its definition.

Substance Addictions: A Short History

The earliest and most common way to categorize various addictions has been around the substances one might take, such as those featured in this issue: opium, alcohol, and tobacco are among the most studied, as they have the longest literary, cultural, and treatment histories. What follows is a review of some of the attitudes and anecdotes that have put these various substances at the center of addiction's history.[26]

Alcohol

Alcoholism has been the subject of considerable research and attention over time and across a range of disciplines, and its history in the United States includes the founding of Alcoholics Anonymous in 1935, as well as the establishment of the National Institute on Alcohol Abuse and Alcoholism in 1974. While these modern-era organizations suggest that treating alcohol addiction is a relatively recent movement, concern over the misuse and dangers of alcohol have been addressed in historical and literary writings for thousands of years. Alcohol consumption is mentioned in recorded history beginning approximately twelve thousand years ago in China.[27] Problematic use of alcohol has likely occurred as long as alcohol has been imbibed. Writings from Herodotus (450 BC) to records from Pompeii (70 CE) and the proclamations of Domitian (80 CE) begin to indicate concern about widespread drunkenness in Rome. The passage of the "Gin Act" in England in 1751, to give another imperial example, reflects emerging policies that address the dangers of drinking in the modern era. Roy Porter notes, "The medical writers of Georgian England had no doubt that heavy alcohol consumption was often responsible for ill-health and disease, and not least was one of the triggers of madness (and for this reason much health advice literature was at pains to moderate consumption)."[28] As Phil Withington's essay in this issue demonstrates, the concept of the drunkard (one who likes to drink) was distinct from the "sin of drunkenness," which included both alcohol and tobacco.[29]

Tobacco

As Withington notes, "Tobacco was first popularized as an accompaniment and possible incitement to drinking." And while suspicion that tobacco causes various diseases dates to at least the seventeenth century, its material value overshadowed any concerns about disease. Apparently, during the American Revolution, in the 1770s, George Washington requested that people send tobacco to the battlefront if they couldn't send money.[30] By 1839 flue curing—a method for drying out tobacco leaves that enhanced smoothness of the inhalation, giving the tobacco smoke a light, sweet flavor and a high nicotine content—had increased the likelihood of compulsive use. Identification of nicotine as the chemical that induced compulsive use of tobacco occurred in the 1920s and 1930s.[31] The public consensus that nicotine was addictive, and the driving force behind regular tobacco use, occurred with publication of the surgeon general's report on nicotine addiction in 1988.[32]

Opiates

Literary representations of opium, particularly from the nineteenth century reflect its dangers and value(s), both economic and aesthetic, as Thomas De Quincey and Samuel Taylor Coleridge famously relied on and wrote about their use of opium. Coleridge's "Kubla Khan" was inspired by a laudanum-induced dream, and De Quincey's *Confessions of an English Opium-Eater* has come to stand in for the range of highs and lows that accompany opium use.[33] Social embarrassment while using opium (e.g., talking nonsense about politics, necessitating friends to apologize for the person with the acknowledgment that the individual was using opium) and a tendency to walk among the poor in London at night (potentially dangerous behavior) were documented as consequences of overuse. The personal and the political impact of opium noted by Breen and Zieger in this issue speak to its range and reach as addiction became a necessary aspect of nation building.

Recognition of the increasing prevalence of opium misuse as a form of addiction led to developments of patent medications to treat it. The German pharmaceutical company Bayer sold an over-the-counter morphine derivative under the trade name Heroin from 1898 to 1910, reflecting an increased popularity of opiate use as a medication, which was presumably more acceptable than uses outside the clinical domain. Recent lawsuits and settlements related to the opioid crisis contribute to the ongoing public struggle with the short-term effectiveness of opiate-based pain medications, on the one hand, and, on the other, the awareness of their addictive properties, which pharmaceutical companies capitalized on.[34]

Cocaine

Some of the replacement medications used to treat opiate addictions led to new problematic drug use. In 1880 Edward C. Huse wrote about the use of cocaine for the cure of an opium habit.[35] In "The Nightmare of Cocaine,"[36] a man from the United States wrote about the development of his addiction to cocaine while fighting in France in World War I. He reportedly substituted cocaine for alcohol use and believed that he fought much better. Subsequently, he used cocaine regularly and experienced a sustained period of his life that included rushing thoughts and haphazard traveling, lack of sleep, weight loss, tolerance and withdrawal symptoms and cravings, loss of spouse, and social isolation. William Halsted, later chair of the Johns Hopkins University Department of Surgery, began in 1884 a lifelong struggle with cocaine that left him remote and eccentric, with occasional absences from work, after being considered very outgoing earlier in his life.[37]

Both opium and cocaine were contained in numerous products back in 1900.[38] By 1900 some 250,000 Americans (of 75 million) were opiate addicts, and 200,000 were cocaine addicts. Controlling for overlap in drug use, about 1 in 200 Americans (0.5 percent) was an opium or cocaine addict.[39] In 1905 Samuel Hopkins Adams, a famous muckraker, exposed the patent medication industry's use of great amounts of opium and cocaine in their medicines.[40] In present times, 0.3 percent of Americans abuse these drug types, which are now illegal (not including modern pharmaceutical opiates), representing a relative decrease in percentage prevalence, though the population is much larger.[41]

Marijuana

Essays in this issue speak to the devotional use of cannabis as well as the larger political associations of cannabis with colonial rebellion, revealing the range of historical sources and anecdotes about the impact on individual consumption. To turn to other examples, in "The Tale of Two Hashish-Eaters,"[42] marijuana was referred to as a "hilarious herb" that was purchased frequently and without good sense, as one person spends his daily wage to purchase marijuana, while others engaged in socially embarrassing behaviors, such as dancing naked in public under its influence. In 1857 Ludlow explained that his preoccupation with marijuana use stilled his pursuit of all other types of excitement. With continuous intoxication, his attempts to quit led only to relapses, cravings, depression, abnormal dreaming (including dreaming that he was intoxicated), and the search for a physician's assistance.[43] Recent state legislation, legalizing marijuana, puts this drug in a class with alcohol: both are legal substances associated with leisure, relaxation, and religious ceremony, but they also remain potentially addictive.

Food

There is no ancient history regarding food addiction. Binging and purging behaviors were noted in ancient Rome, though this may have reflected not consistent patterns of dysfunctional behavior but popular behaviors adopted during ritualized banquets to continue to gorge on food. Thinking about food or eating as an "addiction" appears to be a recent notion, since roughly the 1950s.[44]

Behavioral Addictions: An Even Shorter History

Identifying specific substances continues to dominate the ways clinicians, researchers, and communities organize their thinking about and management of addiction. Concerns about "gateway drugs" or a "slippery slope" refer to the relationship among substances and their impact on society, families, and individuals. Behavioral addictions, also referred to as "process" addictions,[45] have been studied empirically since the 1980s.[46] When we turn to these behaviors (processes) our attempts to define addiction take on a new dimension and add another layer of complexity to these models. As Grant et al. note, "The essential feature of behavioral addictions, according to the *DSM-IV*, is the failure to resist an impulse, drive, or temptation to perform an act that is harmful to the person or to others."[47] The determining factor, then, of a behavioral addiction is its expression: "With an addictive behavior, over time, persons may become preoccupied with the behavior, exhibit a loss of control over the behavior, and suffer negative life consequences as a result."[48] Heidi Sinclair, Christine Lochner, and Dan J. Stein argue in "Behavioural Addiction: A Useful Construct?" that "while the construct of behavioural addiction may be useful in clinical practice and in research contexts, further work is needed to assess the extent of its diagnostic validity and clinical utility."[49]

Categorizing such addictions is relatively recent and includes a "a range of excessive behaviors, such as gambling, video game playing, eating disorders, sports and physical exercise, media use, sex addiction, pathological working, and compulsive criminal behavior."[50] But even this list is in the beginning stages and has not been recognized in the same way as substances. Gambling is now "included in DSM-5 under the rubric of substance-related and addictive disorders."[51] The International Classification of Diseases and Health Problems (ICD-11), which, like the *DSM*, is an influential way of categorizing disease, classifies gambling as an addiction as well as a gaming disorder; however, it considers sex addiction an impulse control disorder.

Determining whether a behavior reaches the level of addiction—is maladaptive—is complicated by historical associations with vice and sin rather than disease. These behaviors range from pleasurable, popular, possibly voluntary, and wicked.[52] Terms such as *lust*, *gluttony*, and *greed* appear both in the Bible and in Alcoholics Anonymous materials and map onto what we might think of as addictive behaviors involving sex, food, gambling, and shopping.[53] Unlike the Ten Commandments, the seven deadly sins are a list not from the Bible but from Pope Gregory I, who revised a previous list of sins to arrive at the seven: lust, gluttony, avarice, sloth, wrath, envy, and pride. These sins overlapped and were conceived in relationship to one another, so that one sin might lead to others.[54]

By the end of the nineteenth century, sins, evils, or, as Norman Morand Roumane and Russell H. Conwell termed them, "social abominations or the follies of modern society" (1897), included opium and alcohol use, as well as cursing and divorce, slum lords and sweatshops. With their list of abominations and warning to the public, Roumane and Conwell sought to "uplif[t] humanity so that we might have a greater degree of purity in our homes, in our society, and in our nation."[55] Among these "abominations," the editors include chapters on "gambling" and "fashion slaves" (shopaholics),[56] anticipating the modern methods of cataloging and pathologizing behaviors.

Gambling has been the most studied of the behavioral addictions, as luck-oriented rituals have been written about since at least 4000 BCE.[57] Matheson notes that "rampant gambling in Rome led Caesar Augustus (ca. 20 BCE) to limit the activity to only a week-long festival called 'Saturnalia' celebrated around the time of the winter solstice, while Emperor Commodus (192 CE) turned the royal palace into a casino and bankrupted the Roman Empire along the way."[58] References to the problems of gambling in "The Pardoner's Tale" from Chaucer's *Canterbury Tales* (ca. 1400 CE) and Dostoyevsky's "The Gambler" (1866) indicate early and lasting recognition that gambling was a problem and that, in the case of the individual gambler, the solution was to quit completely.

Some behaviors characterized as a loss of control were initially conceptualized as manias or morbid appetites.[59] Andre Matthey's writings about diseases of the spirit ("manias") in 1816 shaped subsequent views of behavioral addictions such as kleptomania.[60] Often associated with imbecility, hysteria, and even menopause, the kleptomaniac became "a cultural stereotype of a debilitated female."[61] Sex is another behavior that was considered a "mania"[62] and has become part of the discourse of addiction. While the problems or dangers associated with out-of-control sexual behavior have been noted for centuries (for example, the myth that excessive masturbation would interfere with producing children), it was not until the 1970s that sex was imagined as an addiction.[63] For some scholars, however, sex addiction is a social construct that seeks to "'repathologize forms of erotic behavior,'" which benefits self-help and medical industries.[64]

While theft and uncontrolled sex are behaviors with negative connotations and potentially dangerous consequences, *workaholism*, coined by Wayne Oates in *Confessions of a Workaholic* (1968),[65] turns addiction into something productive and even admirable. Oates was a professor of the psychology of religion and pastoral care who discussed that topic from the perspective of a practitioner, asserting that while his addiction was more acceptable than others, being a workaholic was not healthy. Later researchers sought to distinguish someone who is admirably committed to an activity from someone who suffers from that commitment. Spence and Robbins found that "in comparison to others, the workaholic is highly work involved, feels compelled or driven to work because of inner pressures, and is low in enjoyment of work."[66]

Some behavioral addictions have yet to be identified. Addiction to the internet could not happen until the invention of the internet. *Internet addiction* was coined as a hoax by Ivan Goldberg in 1995[67] but then was studied seriously by Kimberly Young and Mark Griffiths in 1998.[68] Failing to recognize the distinctions among various behaviors and substances may trivialize and diminish the concept of addiction,[69] just as conflating forms of addiction may misdirect focus to the individual rather than societal issues,[70] or lead to negative consequences that may be due both to societal and individual factors.[71] While the identification of behavioral addictions has led to serious medical and therapeutic interventions, the general concept of addiction has persisted in popular culture and can connote both serious concern and lighthearted hyperbole. It is important to hold on to the subtle differences, even as we strive for a common language and story.

The *DSM* Approaches to Addiction

As the essays in this issue suggest, the concept of addiction is productively porous but also frustratingly inconclusive. While some researchers and practitioners search for intrinsically logical causal models of addictions, most tend to use extensional criteria, that is, a list of multiple criteria that, if met, qualify someone as suffering from an addiction.[72] The *DSM* offers the best-known extensional definition of addiction,[73] and its role in medical education and clinical practice cannot be underestimated. As Horowitz notes in his preface to *DSM: A History of Psychiatry's Bible*, "Since publication of the manual's third edition in 1980, its diagnoses define what mental disorders are considered legitimate, how patients conceive of their problems, who receives government benefits, and which conditions psychotropic drugs target and insurance companies will pay to treat."[74]

The following review of the *DSM* reflects cultural and clinical debates over how researchers have tried to understand and address addiction over time and as a condition that is itself defined by time. As some aspects of the *DSM* change, the emphasis on temporality persists: when diagnosing addiction, the question of *what* (substance or behavior) is followed by *how long* and *how often*. The temporal register of addiction provides some unity, a foundation on which other parts of the definition are built.

DSM-I

Definitions of substance abuse or dependence have varied dramatically since the initial publication of the *DSM-I* in 1952.[75] In the *DSM-I* the category for "drug addiction" was vague in scope. "Alcoholism (addiction)" and "drug addiction" were categorized under the larger heading of "personality disorders" and the subheading of "sociopathic personality disturbance" and referred to a mental condition in which a person has a long-term pattern of manipulating, exploiting, or violating the rights of others, suggesting that these behavior abnormalities (i.e., intake of a substance) stem from certain personality features that persist over time.

DSM-II

The *DSM-II*, published in 1968, included a category of drug dependence composed of physiological (addiction) and psychic (state) components to make the definition less vague. Drug addiction or dependence referred to opium, synthetic analgesics, barbiturates, other hypnotics and sedatives, cocaine and other psychostimulants, cannabis, hallucinogens, and other drugs (e.g., volatile solvents). Tobacco and caffeine use did not explicitly appear in any category.

Notably, this second version of the *DSM* moved from the personality-based definition of alcoholism in the original *DSM* toward a more physiological one conceived independently of relation to other disorders in the *DSM-II*. In addition, four categories of alcoholism were defined (episodic excessive, habitual excessive, addiction, and other or unspecified), and physiological and psychological tracks were delineated. Physiological dependence on alcohol included withdrawal symptoms of gross tremor, hallucinosis (alcohol-related hallucinations or psychosis), seizures, delirium tremens, and tolerance. Several alcohol-related diseases (e.g., alcoholic hepatitis) were considered clinical features. A behavioral, psychological, and attitudinal track included drinking despite medical and social contraindications or loss of control.

DSM-III

First published in 1980 and revised in 1987, the *DSM-III* distinguishes between abuse and dependence. In the *DSM-III-R* psychoactive substance abuse requires a maladaptive pattern of use that is demonstrated by continued use despite persistent social, occupational, psychological, or physical problems caused or worsened by use, or by recurrent use in physically hazardous situations, for at least a one-month duration or presenting at least one symptom two or more times over the previous year. This section opens with the explanation that "this diagnostic class deals with behavioral changes associated with more or less regular use of substances that affect the central nervous system. These behavioral changes in almost all subcultures would be viewed as extremely undesirable."[76] The references to specific amounts of time mark "abuse" or "dependence." Further, at least three of the following nine criteria were necessary for a classification of psychoactive substance use dependence, and some of the symptoms of the disturbance must have persisted for at least one month or must have occurred repeatedly over a longer period:

1. Substance often taken in larger amounts or over longer periods than intended;
2. Persistent desire or one or more unsuccessful efforts to cut down or control substance use;
3. A great deal of time spent in activities necessary to get the substance (e.g., theft), taking the substance (e.g., chain smoking), or recovering from its effects;
4. Important social, occupational, or recreational activities given up or reduced because of substance abuse;
5. Continued substance use despite knowledge of having a persistent or recurrent social, psychological, or physical problem that is caused or exacerbated by use of the substance;
6. Marked tolerance—need for markedly increased amounts of the substance to achieve intoxication or desired effect (e.g., doubling quantity from early use), or markedly diminished effect with continued use of the same amount;
7. Characteristic withdrawal symptoms;
8. Substance often taken to relieve or avoid withdrawal symptoms; and
9. Frequent intoxication or withdrawal symptoms when expected to fulfill major role obligations or when use is physically hazardous.

With the publication of the *DSM-III*, drug dependence was no longer included under a more general category of personality disorders, reflecting its importance as a separate entity. Thirteen drug categories classified in the *DSM-III* were retained in the *DSM-IV* (i.e., alcohol, amphetamines, caffeine, cannabis, cocaine, hallucinogens, inhalants, nicotine, opioids, phencyclidine, sedatives/hypnotics/anxiolytics, polysubstance [three groups of substances of equal preference, not including caffeine or nicotine], and "other" or "unknown" [e.g., anabolic steroids, betel nut]).

DSM-IV

The *DSM-IV* appeared in 1994, with a text revision published in 2000. The editors acknowledge that "the term mental disorder [from the manual's title] unfortunately implies a distinction between 'mental' disorders and 'physical' disorders that is a reductionistic anachronism of mind/body dualism" (xxii). Such acknowledgment recognizes the challenges and limitations of such categorizations, of language, to capture individual cases.

"Substance use disorder" was defined as a maladaptive pattern of drug use leading to clinically significant impairment or distress, as manifested by one or more of four symptoms or criteria in a twelve-month period:

1.   Recurrent drug use may result in a *failure to fulfill major role obligations* at work, school, or home. Repeated absences, tardiness, poor performance, suspensions, or neglect of duties in major life domains suggests that use has crossed over into abuse.

2.   Recurrent drug use in situations in which it is *physically hazardous* is a sign of abuse. Operating machinery, driving a car, swimming, or walking in a dangerous area while under the influence indicates drug abuse.

3.   Recurrent drug-related *legal problems*, such as arrests for disorderly conduct or for driving under the influence, are indicative of abuse.

4.   Recurrent use despite having persistent or recurrent *social or interpersonal problems*, caused or exacerbated by the effects of the drug, is indicative of abuse. For example, getting into arguments or fights with others, passing out at others' houses, or otherwise acting in a socially disapproved way is indicative of abuse.

Substance use that leads to decrements in performance of major life roles, physically dangerous action, legal problems, or social problems indicated substance *abuse* disorder in the *DSM-IV* and *DSM-IV-TR*. Seven other criteria, if met, constitute "substance dependence." A diagnosis of substance *dependence*, a more severe disorder, was intended to subsume a diagnosis of substance abuse. The criteria for substance dependence provided by the *DSM-IV* and *DSM-IV-TR* included three or more of the following seven symptoms in the same twelve-month period:[77]

1.   *Tolerance is experienced.* There is either a need for markedly increased amounts of the drug to achieve the desired drug effect or a markedly diminished effect with continued use of the same amount of the drug.

2.   *Withdrawal is experienced.* Either a characteristic withdrawal syndrome occurs when one terminates using the drug or the same or a similar drug is taken to relieve or avoid the syndrome.

3.   The drug often is taken in *larger amounts or over a longer period* than was intended. For example, an alcohol-dependent man may intend to have only two drinks on a given evening but may end up having fifteen drinks.

4.   There is a *persistent desire or unsuccessful effort to cut down or control drug use*. For example, an alcohol-dependent man may decide to become a controlled drinker. He may intend to drink only two drinks every evening; however, he ends up having fifteen drinks on some evenings, two drinks on some evenings, and twenty drinks on other evenings.

5.   *A great deal of time is spent on activities necessary to obtain the drug, use the drug, or recover from its effects.* For example, a person may travel long distances or search all day to "score" a drug, may use the drug throughout the night, and then may miss work the next day to recover and rest. In this scenario, two days were spent for one "high."

6.   *Important social, occupational, or recreational activities are given up or reduced because of drug use.* For example, the drug abuser may be very

high, passed out, or hung over much of the time and thus may not visit family and friends like he or she did before becoming a drug abuser.

7. *Drug use continues despite knowledge of having a persistent or recurrent physical or psychological problem* that is likely to have been caused or worsened by the drug. For example, someone who becomes very paranoid after continued methamphetamine use and is hospitalized but continues to use it after release from the hospital exhibits this last symptom.

DSM-V

In May 2013 the current diagnostic criteria for "substance use disorder" were established.[78] The number of drug classes is reduced slightly: phencyclidine is considered a hallucinogen; amphetamines and cocaine are combined into one "stimulant" category; there is no separate polysubstance category. These criteria now apply to ten drug categories: (1) alcohol, (2) caffeine, (3) cannabis, (4) hallucinogens (which subsumes phencyclidine and "other hallucinogens"), (5) inhalants, (6) opioids, (7) sedative/hypnotic/anxiolytic substances, (8) stimulants (which includes amphetamine-type substances, cocaine, and other or unspecified stimulants), (9) tobacco, and (10) "other" or "unknown" substances (e.g., anabolic steroids, antihistamines, betel nut).

The criteria are mostly a recombination of the *DSM-IV* criteria. First, the abuse and dependence categories are combined into one "substance use disorder" diagnosis. Second, the legal consequences criterion was removed (due to considerations including relatively low prevalence of legal problems, or sensitivity of that criterion). Finally, a "craving" criterion (strong desire or urge to use the drug) was added to the diagnosis. Substance use disorder is diagnosed if the individual reports two or more of the following, involving recurrent use over the last twelve months:

1. Use more than intended (larger amounts or longer period)
2. Desire, but inability, to quit or cut down
3. Consumes life (great deal of time to obtain, use, or recover from effects)
4. Craving, an intense desire or urge to use [new criterion]
5. Failure to fulfill major role obligations at work, school, or home
6. Continued use despite related social problems
7. Other social, job, or recreational activities are neglected or given up
8. Hazardous use (physical danger)
9. Continued use despite related psychological or physical problems
10. Tolerance
11. Withdrawal

Criteria 1 through 4 are intended to reflect impaired control. Criteria 5 through 7 are intended to reflect social impairment. Criteria 8 and 9 are intended to reflect risky use. Finally, criteria 10 and 11 are intended to reflect pharmacologic effects. One may speculate whether using these criteria will end up increasing the prevalence of diagnoses such as alcoholism.[79]

The *DSM-V*, like previous *DSM* systems, does not have a specific food addiction category,[80] although the manual does mention that some individuals may report eating-related symptoms resembling those typically seen in persons with substance use disorders, such as craving and compulsive use. The manual also mentions that this might reflect involvement of the same neural systems (e.g., regulatory self-control and reward). However, the authors mention that not enough is known about shared and distinct factors to address potential overlap and instead provide a separate category for "Feeding and Eating Disorders."[81]

New to *DSM-V* is the non-substance-related disorder category, which currently includes only gambling disorder. This disorder involves four or more of the following, involving recurrent behaviors over the last twelve months:

1. More money gambled to get desired excitement (tolerance-like)
2. Restlessness or irritability when trying to quit or cut down (withdrawal-like)
3. Repeated unsuccessful efforts to control, cut back, or stop gambling
4. Preoccupation with gambling (reliving past experiences, planning next venture, thinking how to get more money to gamble)
5. Frequent gambling when feeling distressed (e.g., helpless, guilty, anxious, depressed)
6. "Chasing" losses (returning to gamble and get even)
7. Lies to conceal extent of involvement
8. Relationship, job, or educational opportunity jeopardized or lost because of gambling
9. Reliance on others to provide money to relieve related debt

The *DSM-V* refers to other "behavioral addictions" that are not included as formal disorders at this time (such as sex, exercise, or shopping addictions) because of a lack of peer-reviewed evidence to establish the diagnostic criteria and course. However, the authors of the *DSM* encourage more research on other potential behavioral addictions.

The evolution of the *DSM* criteria is a testament to the impact of historical context on the definition of addiction, and these changes demonstrate heterogeneity of definition over time, which may or may not reflect enhanced understanding. While there is the tendency to consider *DSM* criteria exchangeable, and while multiple criteria summed to some number is diagnostic, there are several possibilities regarding how such elements of an addictive behavior might be interrelated. First, each of the elements alone, or in combination with some or all of the others, may be a *necessary* condition of addiction. Second, each of the elements alone, or in combination with some or all of the others, may be a *sufficient* condition of addiction.

An alternative conceptualization when considering constituents of an addiction is that of "family resemblances." Family resemblances refers to things which could be thought to be connected by one essential common feature that may in fact be connected by a series of overlapping similarities, where no one feature is common to all.[82] Consider the physical or other features of a family, for example. We may say that all the family members appear similar (e.g., on any number of elements in the family set, such as weight, eye color, hair, even last name), although no two are identical in descriptors (elements) examined and two of them in the group (set) may have no feature in common. Likewise, two people may be labeled as "addicted" but have no elements in common. For example, one "addict" may experience only tolerance and withdrawal, whereas another may experience only social and role consequences. Or a gambling "addict" may exhibit lying and preoccupation, whereas another may exhibit mood-related gambling and withdrawal-like symptoms. If such a nonoverlap of criteria exists, we can expect to discover new phenomena of addiction that bear only a family resemblance to the ones we now recognize.[83]

Summary and Conclusions

Heterogeneity of phenomena, vagueness in conceptual boundaries, and use of numerous definitional elements may make consensus regarding a "correct" definition of addiction elusive.[84] Some authors argue that to consider a substance or behavior an addiction requires data regarding co-occurring disorders, clinical characteristics, genetic contributions, and central/peripheral neurobiological factors.[85] Of course, an exploration of these different sources of data may reveal different patterns of findings across "addicts" who reportedly suffer from the same addiction (the effects on mesolimbic dopamine, however, appear reasonably consistent).[86] More generally, it is difficult to identify a unifying framework when there is so much heterogeneity in extensional diagnostic features.

While a global perspective may add more confusion conceptually in terms of defining when a behavior is or is not an "addiction problem," it also reflects some of the need for humility and flexibility in labeling people. Internationally, there may be some variation on when a repetitive behavior is considered an addiction, or at least a problem. For example, there may be differential tolerance of public drunkenness or of drinking shots of hard liquor in restaurants. Physical hazards or legal enforcement may vary depending on the environment (rural versus urban settings). One may conjecture that a person is more likely to be charged with "driving under the influence" in locations in which public transportation is scarce and police enforcement stringent. Also, norms vary on what is addictive sexual, work, or eating behaviors. It is not uncommon for persons in some countries to choose to work over sixty hours per week, whereas such behavior might be considered workaholic in another country.[87] One possible common criterion is that to the degree that one's ability to fulfill context-based roles or duties (e.g., spouse, parent, coworker, or citizen) is compromised, one is deemed to suffer from addiction.[88]

Future approaches to addiction—theoretical models and empirical research—must consider the issues involved when relying on criteria-based definitions of addiction, fuzzy boundaries when comparing addictive behavior to compulsive and impulsive behavior, and global variations in the perceptions of what is or is not addictive behavior. In the meantime, this essay has gestured at some of the productive overlap of definitions, and at the large community of scholars from fields as diverse as literature, philosophy, history, sociology, medicine, and psychology that grapple with the challenge of defining this familiar and widespread phenomenon.

STEVE SUSSMAN is professor of population and public health sciences, psychology, and social work at the University of Southern California. He studies etiology, prevention, and cessation within the addictions arena, broadly defined, as well as translation research and program development. He is editor of *Evaluation and the Health Professions* (since 2010), and his most recent books are *Substance and Behavioral Addictions: Concepts, Causes, and Cures* (2017) and *The Cambridge Handbook of Substance and Behavioral Addictions* (editor; 2020).

ERIKA WRIGHT is lecturer in the English Department at the University of Southern California (USC) and assistant professor of clinical medical education at USC's Keck School of Medicine; she is also associate director of USC's Humanities, Ethics, Art, and the Law program and Narrative Medicine MS program. She is author of *Reading for Health: Medical Narratives and the Nineteenth-Century Novel* (2016).

Notes

1   The *DSM* is the most popular extensional diagnostic source for mental disorders. "Over the past seventy years, the *Diagnostic and Statistical Manual of Mental Disorders*, or *DSM*, has evolved from a virtually unknown and little-used pamphlet to an imposing and comprehensive compendium of mental disorder" (Horwitz, *DSM*).

2   O'Brien, "Addiction and Dependence in DSM-V," 866.

3   O'Brien, "Addiction and Dependence in DSM-V," 867.

4   Sussman and Sussman, "Considering the Definition of Addiction."

5   Sussman, "Commentary."

6   Kalivas and Volkow, "Neural Basis of Addiction"; Nathan, Conrad, and Skinstad, "History of the Concept of Addiction."

7   Lemon, *Addiction and Devotion*, xii.

8   Alexander and Schweighofer, "Defining 'Addiction.'"

9   Levine, "Discovery of Addiction."

10   Kor et al., "Should Hypersexual Disorder Be Classified as an Addiction?"; Koob and Le Moal, "What Is Addiction?"

11   Courtwright, *Age of Addiction*; Orford, *Excessive Appetites*.

12   Meyer, "The Disease Called Addiction."

13   Goodman, "Neurobiological Development of Addiction"; Koob and Le Moal, "What Is Addiction?"; Sussman and Sussman, "Considering the Definition of Addiction."

14   Leshner, "Addiction Is a Brain Disease, and It Matters," 46; Levy, "Addiction Is Not a Brain Disease (and It Matters)"; Sussman and Ames, *Drug Abuse*.

15   Blum et al., "Reward Deficiency Syndrome"; Kalivas and Volkow, "Neural Basis of Addiction."

16   Sussman and Pakdaman, "Appetitive Needs and Addiction."

17   Sussman, *Cambridge Handbook of Substance and Behavioral Addictions*.

18   Rosenberg and Feder, *Behavioral Addictions*; Sussman and Ames, *Drug Abuse*.

19   Seventh International Conference on Behavioral Addictions: Behavioral Addictions— From Past to Present, icba.mat.org.hu/2020 (accessed July 6, 2021); American Psychiatric Association, *DSM-V*; Demetrovics and Griffiths, "Behavioral Addictions"; Sussman and Ames, *Drug Abuse*; Sussman, Lisha, and Griffiths, "Prevalence of the Addictions."

20   Blum and Grant, "Considering the Overlap and Nonoverlap."

21   Sussman and Sussman, "Considering the Definition of Addiction," 4031.

22   Blum and Grant, "Considering the Overlap and Nonoverlap"; Kor et al., "Should Hypersexual Disorder Be Classified as an Addiction?"

23   Raines et al., "Initial Investigation"; Wise and Koob, "Circumspective."

24   Sussman, *Substance and Behavioral Addictions*.

25   Blum and Grant, "Considering the Overlap and Nonoverlap."

26   See Robinson and Adinoff, "Classification of Substance Use Disorders."

27   Nathan, Conrad, and Skinstad, "History of the Concept of Addiction"; Warner, "'Resolv'd to Drink No More'"; Trotter, *Essay*; Rush, *Inquiry*; Tracy, *Alcoholism in America*; Levine, "Discovery of Addiction."

28   Porter, "Drinking Man's Disease," 385. See also Warner, *Craze*.

29 See also Warner, "Before There Was 'Alcoholism.'"

30 US DHHS, *Health Consequences of Smoking.*

31 US DHHS, *Health Consequences of Smoking.*

32 US DHHS, *Health Consequences of Smoking.*

33 De Quincey, *Confessions*; Coleridge, *Selected Poems.* See also Zieger, *Inventing the Addict*; and Courtwright, *Forces of Habit.*

34 American Bar Association, "Opioid Lawsuits Generate Payouts, Controversy."

35 Jonnes, *Hep-Cats, Narcs, and Pipe Dreams.*

36 *North American Review*, "Nightmare of Cocaine."

37 Jonnes, *Hep-Cats, Narcs, and Pipe Dreams.*

38 For example, Bayer Heroin and Coca-Cola (Levinthal, *Drugs, Behavior, and Modern Society*).

39 Jonnes, *Hep-Cats, Narcs, and Pipe Dreams.*

40 Jonnes, *Hep-Cats, Narcs, and Pipe Dreams.*

41 Sussman, *Substance and Behavioral Addictions*; Sussman and Ames, *Drug Abuse.*

42 Schaffer Library of Drug Policy, "Tale of Two Hashish-Eaters."

43 Ludlow, *Hasheesh Eater.*

44 Courtwright, *Age of Addiction.*

45 Schaef, *When Society Becomes an Addict.*

46 E.g., Cook, "Self-Identified Addictions and Emotional Disturbances."

47 Grant et al., "Introduction to Behavioral Addictions."

48 Sussman, "Sussman on Matilda Hellman's 'Mind the Gap!'"

49 Sinclair, Lochner, and Stein, "Behavioural Addiction," 43.

50 Alavi et al., "Behavioral Addiction versus Substance Addiction." See also Farrugia and Fraser, "Prehending Addiction."

51 Sinclair, Lochner, and Stein, "Behavioural Addiction," 43.

52 Bernhard, "Voices of Vices"; Skolnick, "Social Transformation of Vice."

53 Alcoholics Anonymous, *Alcoholics Anonymous.*

54 See Treharne, "Gluttons for Punishment"; and Bloomfield, *Seven Deadly Sins.*

55 Roumane and Conwell, *Social Abominations*, iii.

56 Roumane and Conwell, *Social Abominations.*

57 Ferentzy and Turner, "Morals, Medicine, Metaphors."

58 Matheson, "Overview of the Economics of Sports Gambling."

59 Orford, *Excessive Appetites.*

60 Matthey, *New Research on Diseases of the Mind.*

61 Abelson, "Invention of Kleptomania," 124.

62 E.g., Orford, *Excessive Appetites*; Rosenberg and Feder, *Behavioral Addictions.*

63 Reay, Attwood, and Gooder, "Inventing Sex."

64 Quoted in Reay, Attwood, and Gooder, "Inventing Sex," 3.

65 Oates, *Confessions of a Workaholic.*

66 Spence and Robbins, "Workaholism," 162. See also Sussman, "Workaholism."

67 Beard and Wolf, "Modification."

68 Griffiths, "Internet Addiction"; Young, *Caught in the Net.*

69 Orford, *Excessive Appetites.*

70 Sinclair, Lochner, and Stein, "Behavioural Addiction."

71 E.g., Courtwright, *Age of Addiction.*

72 Sussman, *Substance and Behavioral Addictions*; Sussman and Sussman, "Considering the Definition of Addiction."

73 The International Classification of Disease is another extensional model used by clinicians.

74 Horwitz, *DSM.*

75 Freedman, Kaplan, and Sadock, *Modern Synopsis of Psychiatry.*

76 American Psychiatric Association, *DSM-III-TR*, 163.

77 American Psychiatric Association, *DSM-IV-TR.*

78 American Psychiatric Association, *DSM-V.*

79 Wakefield and Schmitz, "How Many People Have Alcohol Use Disorders?"

80 Pai, Vella, and Richardson, "Is Food Addiction a Valid Phenomenon through the Lens of the DSM-5?"

81 American Psychiatric Association, *DSM-V*, 329.

82 Sussman and Sussman, "Considering the Definition of Addiction"; Wittgenstein, *Philosophical Investigations.*

83 Sussman and Sussman, "Considering the Definition of Addiction."

84 Sussman, *Substance and Behavioral Addictions.*

85 Kor et al., "Should Hypersexual Disorder Be Classified as an Addiction?"

86 Sussman and Ames, *Drug Abuse.*

87 Sussman, *Substance and Behavioral Addictions.*

88 Quintero and Nichter, "Semantics of Addiction."

Works Cited

Abelson, Elaine. "The Invention of Kleptomania." *Signs* 15, no. 1 (1989): 123–43.

Alavi, Salman S., Masoud Ferdosi, Fereshte Jannatifard, Mehdi Eslami, Hamed Alaghemandan, and Mehrdad Setare. "Behavioral Addiction versus Substance Addiction: Correspondence of Psychiatric and Psychological Views." *International Journal of Preventive Medicine* 3, no. 4 (2012): 290–94.

Alcoholics Anonymous. *Alcoholics Anonymous.* New York: Alcoholics Anonymous World Services, 1976.

Alexander, Bruce K., and A. R. F. Schweighofer. "Defining 'Addiction.'" *Canadian Psychology* 29, no. 2 (1998): 151–62.

American Bar Association. "Opioid Lawsuits Generate Payouts, Controversy." September 2019. www.americanbar.org/news/abanews/aba-news-archives/2019/09/opioid-lawsuits-generate-payouts-controversy.

American Psychiatric Association. *Diagnostic and Statistical Manual of Mental Disorders (DSM-III-TR)*. Washington, DC: American Psychiatric Association, 1980.

American Psychiatric Association. *Diagnostic and Statistical Manual of Mental Disorders (DSM-IV-TR)*. Washington, DC: American Psychiatric Association, 2000.

American Psychiatric Association. *Diagnostic and Statistical Manual of Mental Disorders*. 5th ed. (*DSM-V*). Washington, DC: American Psychiatric Association, 2013.

Beard, Keith W., and Eve M. Wolf. "Modification in the Proposed Diagnostic Criteria for Internet Addiction." *CyberPsychology and Behavior* 4, no. 3 (2001): 377–83.

Bernhard, Bo J. "The Voices of Vices: Sociological Perspectives on the Pathological Gambling Entry in the Diagnostic and Statistical Manual of Mental Disorders." *American Behavioral Scientist* 51, no. 1 (2007): 8–32.

Blair, W. *An Opium-Eater in America*. July 1842. www.druglibrary.org/schaffer/heroin/history/blair.htm.

Bloomfield, Morton W. *The Seven Deadly Sins: An Introduction to the History of a Religious Concept, with Special Reference to Medieval English Literature*. East Lansing: Michigan State College Press, 1952.

Blum, Austin W., and Jon E. Grant. "Considering the Overlap and Nonoverlap of Compulsivity, Impulsivity, and Addiction." In *The Cambridge Handbook of Substance and Behavioral Addictions*, edited by Steve Sussman, 373–85. Cambridge: Cambridge University Press, 2020.

Blum, Kenneth, John G. Cull, Eric R. Braverman, and David E. Comings. "Reward Deficiency Syndrome." *American Scientist* 84, no. 2 (1996): 132–45.

Coleridge, Samuel Taylor. *Selected Poems*, edited by Richard Holmes. London: Penguin, 2000.

Cook, David R. "Self-Identified Addictions and Emotional Disturbances in a Sample of College Students." *Psychology of Addictive Behaviors* 1, no. 1 (1987): 55–61.

Courtwright, David T. *The Age of Addiction: How Bad Habits Became Big Business*. Cambridge, MA: Harvard University Press.

Courtwright, David T. *Forces of Habit: Drugs and the Making of the Modern World*. Cambridge, MA: Harvard University Press, 2001.

Demetrovics, Zsolt, and Mark D. Griffiths. "Behavioral Addictions: Past, Present, and Future." *Journal of Behavioral Addictions* 1, no. 1 (2012): 1–2.

De Quincey, Thomas. *Confessions of an English Opium Eater*. London, 1821.

Farrugia, Adrian, and Suzanne Fraser. "Prehending Addiction: Alcohol and Other Drug Professionals' Encounters with 'New' Addictions." *Qualitative Health Research* 27, no. 13 (2017): 2042–56.

Ferentzy, Peter, and Nigel E. Turner. "Morals, Medicine, Metaphors, and the History of the Disease Model of Problem Gambling." *Journal of Gambling Issues* 27 (2012): 1–27.

Freedman, Alfred M., Harold I. Kaplan, and Benjamin J. Sadock. *Modern Synopsis of Psychiatry*. Vol. 2. Baltimore: Williams and Wilkins, 1976.

Goodman, Aviel. "The Neurobiological Development of Addiction: An Overview." *Psychiatric Times* 26, no. 9 (2009): 1–14.

Grant, Jon E., Marc N. Potenza, Aviv Weinstein, and David A. Gorelick. "Introduction to Behavioral Addictions." *American Journal of Drug and Alcohol Abuse* 36, no. 5 (2010): 233–41.

Griffiths, Mark. "Internet Addiction: Does It Really Exist?" In *Psychology and the Internet: Intrapersonal, Interpersonal, and Transpersonal Implications*, edited by Jayne Gackenbach, 61–75. San Diego, CA: Academic, 1998.

Horwitz, Allan V. *DSM: A History of Psychiatry's Bible*. Baltimore: Johns Hopkins University Press, 2021.

Jonnes, Jill. *Hep-Cats, Narcs, and Pipe Dreams: A History of America's Romance with Illegal Drugs*. New York: Scribner, 1996.

Kalivas, Peter W., and Nora D. Volkow. "The Neural Basis of Addiction: A Pathology of Motivation and Choice." *American Journal of Psychiatry* 162, no. 8 (2005): 1403–13.

Koob, George, and Michel Le Moal. "What Is Addiction?" In *Neurobiology of Addiction*, edited by G. F. Koob and M. Le Moal, 1–19. London: Academic, 2006.

Kor, Ariel, Yehuda Fogel, Rory C. Reid, and Marc N. Potenza. "Should Hypersexual Disorder Be Classified as an Addiction?" *Sexual Addiction and Compulsivity* 20, nos. 1–2 (2013): 27–47.

Lemon, Rebecca. *Addiction and Devotion in Early Modern England*. Philadelphia: University of Pennsylvania Press, 2018.

Leshner, A. I. "Addiction Is a Brain Disease, and It Matters." *Science*, no. 278 (1997): 45–47.

Levine, Harry G. "The Discovery of Addiction: Changing Conceptions of Habitual Drunkenness in America." *Journal of Studies on Alcohol* 39, no. 1 (1978): 143–74.

Levinthal, Charles F. *Drugs, Behavior, and Modern Society*. 4th ed. Boston: Allyn and Bacon, 2005.

Levy, Neil. "Addiction Is Not a Brain Disease (and It Matters)." *Frontiers in Psychiatry* 4, article 24 (2013): 1–7.

Ludlow, Fitz Hugh. *The Hasheesh Eater: Being Passages from the Life of a Pythagorean.* New York, 1857.

Matheson, Victor. "An Overview of the Economics of Sports Gambling and an Introduction to the Symposium." *Eastern Economic Journal* 47 (2021): 1–8.

Matthey, André. *New Research on Diseases of the Mind.* Paris, 1816.

Meyer, Roger E. "The Disease Called Addiction: Emerging Evidence in a Two-Hundred-Year Debate." *Lancet* 347 (1996): 162–66.

Nathan, Peter E., Mandy Conrad, and Anne Helene Skinstad. "History of the Concept of Addiction." *Annual Review of Clinical Psychology* 12 (2016): 29–51.

North American Review. "The Nightmare of Cocaine by a Former 'Snow-Bird.'" No. 227 (1929): 418–22.

Oates, Wayne. *Confessions of a Workaholic: The Facts about Work Addiction.* New York: World, 1971.

O'Brien, Charles. "Addiction and Dependence in DSM-V." *Addiction* (Abingdon, UK) 106, no. 5 (2011): 866–67.

Orford, Jim. *Excessive Appetites: A Psychological View of Addictions.* 2nd ed. Chichester: Wiley, 2001.

Pai, Nagesh, Shae-Leigh Vella, and Katie Richardson. "Is Food Addiction a Valid Phenomenon through the Lens of the DSM-5?" *Australian and New Zealand Journal of Psychiatry* 48, no. 3 (2014): 216–18.

Porter, Roy. "The Drinking Man's Disease: The 'Pre-history' of Alcoholism in Georgian Britain." *British Journal of Addiction* 80, no. 4 (1985): 385–96.

Quintero, Gilbert, and Mark Nichter. "The Semantics of Addiction: Moving beyond Expert Models to Lay Understandings." *Journal of Psychoactive Drugs* 28, no. 3 (1996): 219–28.

Raines, Amanda M., Amanda S. Unruh, Mike J. Zvolensky, and Norman B. Schmidt. "An Initial Investigation of the Relationships between Hoarding and Smoking." *Psychiatry Research* 215, no. 3 (2014): 668–74.

Reay, Barry, Nina Attwood, and Claire Gooder. "Inventing Sex: The Short History of Sex Addiction." *Sexuality and Culture* 17, no. 1 (2013): 1–19.

Robinson, Sean M., and Bryon. Adinoff. "The Classification of Substance Use Disorders: Historical, Contextual, and Conceptual Considerations." *Behavioral Sciences* (Basel) 6, no. 3 (2016). doi.org/10.3390/bs6030018.

Rosenberg, Kenneth Paul, and Laura Curtiss Feder, eds. *Behavioral Addictions: Criteria, Evidence, and Treatment.* London: Academic, 2014.

Roumane, Norman Morand, and Russell H. Conwell. *Social Abominations or the Follies of Modern Society.* Whitefish, MT, 1897.

Rush, Benjamin. *An Inquiry into the Effects of Ardent Spirits upon the Human Body and Mind.* 8th ed. Boston, 1823.

Schaef, Ann Wilson. *When Society Becomes an Addict.* New York: HarperCollins, 1987.

Schaffer Library of Drug Policy. "The Tale of Two Hashish-Eaters (Traditional)." In *The Thousand and One Nights.* www.druglibrary.org/schaffer/hemp/arab1.htm (accessed December 15, 2020).

Sinclair, Heidi, Christine Lochner, and Dan J. Stein. "Behavioural Addiction: A Useful Construct?" *Current Behavioral Neuroscience Reports* 3, no. 1 (2016): 43–48.

Skolnick, Jerome H. "The Social Transformation of Vice." *Law and Contemporary Problems* 51, no. 1 (1988): 9–29.

Spence, Janet T., and Ann S. Robbins. "Workaholism: Definition, Measurement, and Preliminary Results." *Journal of Personality Assessment* 58, no. 1 (1992): 160–78.

Sussman, Steve, ed. *The Cambridge Handbook of Substance and Behavioral Addictions.* Cambridge: Cambridge University Press, 2020.

Sussman, Steve. "Commentary: Addiction, Stigma, and Neurodiversity." *Evaluation and the Health Professions* 44, no. 2 (2021): 186–91.

Sussman, Steve. "Steve Sussman on Matilda Hellman's 'Mind the Gap! Failure in Understanding Key Dimensions of an Addicted Drug User's Life' Addictive Effects." *Substance Use and Misuse* 47, nos. 13–14 (2012): 1661–65.

Sussman, Steve. *Substance and Behavioral Addictions: Concepts, Causes, and Cures.* Cambridge: Cambridge University Press, 2017.

Sussman, Steve. "Workaholism: A Review." *Journal of Addiction Research and Therapy,* suppl. 6, no. 1 (2012). doi.org/10.4172/2155-6105.S6-001.

Sussman, Steve, and Susan L. Ames. *Drug Abuse: Concepts, Prevention, and Cessation.* New York: Cambridge University Press, 2008.

Sussman, Steve, Nadra Lisha, and Mark Griffiths. "Prevalence of the Addictions: A Problem of the Majority or the Minority?" *Evaluation and the Health Professions* 34, no. 1 (2011): 3–56.

Sussman, Steve, and Sheila Pakdaman. "Appetitive Needs and Addiction." In *The Cambridge Handbook of Substance and Behavioral Addictions,* edited by Steven Sussman, 3–11. Cambridge: Cambridge University Press, 2020.

Sussman, Steve, and Alan N. Sussman. "Considering the Definition of Addiction." *International Journal of Environmental Research and Public Health* 8, no. 10 (2011): 4025–38.

Tracy, Sarah W. *Alcoholism in America: From Reconstruction to Prohibition.* Baltimore: Johns Hopkins University Press, 2005.

Treharne, Elaine. "Gluttons for Punishment: The Drunk and Disorderly in Early English Homilies." Twenty-Fourth Annual Brixworth Lecture, 2nd ser., no. 6. University of Leicester, 2007.

Trotter, Thomas. *An Essay, Medical, Philosophical, and Chemical, on Drunkenness, and Its Effects on the Human Body.* 4th ed. London, 1810.

US DHHS (Department of Health and Human Services). *The Health Consequences of Smoking—Nicotine Addiction: A Report of the Surgeon General.* Rockville, MD: US Government Printing Office, 1988.

Wakefield, Jerome C., and Mark F. Schmitz. "How Many People Have Alcohol Use Disorders? Using the Harmful Dysfunction Analysis to Reconcile Prevalence Estimates in Two Community Surveys." *Frontiers in Psychiatry* 5, no. 10 (2014): 1–22.

Warner, Jessica. "Before There Was 'Alcoholism': Lessons from the Medieval Experience with Alcohol." *Contemporary Drug Problems* 19, no. 3 (1992): 409–29.

Warner, Jessica. *Craze: Gin and Debauchery in an Age of Reason.* London: Profile, 2003.

Warner, Jessica. "'Resolv'd to Drink No More': Addiction as a Preindustrial Concept." *Journal of Studies on Alcohol* 55, no. 6 (1994): 685–91.

Wise, Roy A., and George F. Koob. "Circumspective: The Development and Maintenance of Drug Addiction." *Neuropsychopharmacology* 39 (2014): 254–62.

Wittgenstein, Ludwig. *Philosophical Investigations,* translated by G. E. M. Anscombe. Oxford: Blackwell, 1953.

Young, K. S. *Caught in the Net.* New York: Wiley and Sons, 1998.

Zieger, Susan. *Inventing the Addict: Drugs, Race, and Sexuality in Nineteenth-Century British and American Writing.* Amherst: University of Massachusetts Press, 2008.

Introduction

NAN GOODMAN

The coronavirus pandemic that began in late 2019 and that merged with other catastrophic global conditions to create a syndemic (see Cynthia J. Davis's note) has brought changes beyond our comprehension. Pandemic-inspired articles, novels, stories, poems, blogs, tweets, videos, songs, and artwork are being produced at a prodigious rate as we try to make sense of what we all have, to varying degrees, witnessed and experienced for the last two years and continue to confront with no clear end in sight. In this "Of Note" section we hear from two literary scholars, Davis and Stuti Goswami, who have been writing about the body, medicine, pain, and the deleterious effects of disease and other maladies for some time and who now offer their insights into how this pandemic resembles and differs from previous global health calamities. Their contributions revolve in turn around recently published work on the pandemic by other scholars, including Anjuli Fatima Raza Kolb's "Paravictorianism: Mary Shelley and Viral Sovereignty" (*Victorian Studies*, Spring 2020), Walter D. Mignolo's "The Logic of the In-Visible: Decolonial Reflections on the Change of Epoch" (*Theory, Culture, and Society*, December 2020), and a multiauthored symposium titled "Thinking through the Pandemic" (*Science Fiction Studies*, November 2020). Even as we marshal words to assess the damage the pandemic has done, however—the deaths it has caused and the racial and health care inequities it has perpetuated and aggravated—the theme of these essays and notes is the ineffability of their impact in the end. No matter how hard we try, it seems, this pandemic defies description. The question with which Davis opens her note echoes throughout. "Should we view the COVID-19 pandemic as an inflection point or as more of the same?" she asks. Acknowledging a similar uncertainty, Goswami observes: "The imprints left behind by the novel coronavirus in the lives of people are multidimensional and constantly evolving." But write we must, and so we offer these articles and notes as a way of bearing witness to the ineffability of our loss and of making good on our obligation to scrutinize it, for without that we will never find our way to the other side of this disaster. Committed to giving a forum to as many voices as we can on the subject, *ELN* will also follow this "Of Note" section with a special issue dedicated to the subject of the pandemic that is scheduled for publication in 2023, at which point, we hope, the world will look a little brighter.

ENGLISH LANGUAGE NOTES

60:1, April 2022 DOI 10.1215/00138282-9560298
© 2022 Regents of the University of Colorado

On Syndemics and Social Change

CYNTHIA J. DAVIS

Should we view the COVID-19 pandemic as an inflection point or as more of the same? Has the newly resurgent pandemic only deepened entrenched socioeconomic divisions or shone a light on them so glaring that structural change ensues? In what ways has the coronavirus sharpened established biomedical and geopolitical borders, even as, *qua* pandemic, it inevitably crossed them? And to what extent have the devastating effects of this first truly global pandemic been compounded by contemporaneous crises that made 2020 an annus horribilis for so many, although notably not all, of us? What we have all been living through (same storm, different boats) since late December 2019 deserves to be called a syndemic, a term originally introduced by the medical anthropologist Merrill Singer to designate two or more aggregated disease clusters in a given population but now used more loosely to describe any "fractured, stratified convergence of catastrophes."[1] Three 2020 journal publications—Anjuli Fatima Raza Kolb's "Paravictorianism: Mary Shelley and Viral Sovereignty," Walter D. Mignolo's "The Logic of the In-visible: Decolonial Reflections on the Change of Epoch," and a multiauthored *Science Fiction Studies* symposium titled "Thinking through the Pandemic"—explore the planetary ramifications of syndemics and the stories we tell about them.

These publications identify different sets of convergent crises. Kolb examines the conjunction between "the panicked and highly racialized discourse around disease and epidemic surveillance" and "the global security state that flourished in response to terrorism."[2] Mignolo explores the unprecedented global convergence of the COVID-19 pandemic and the related economic crisis, while the contributors to the symposium reliably reflect on the "tragic synchronicity" between the viral pandemic and the racial injustice protests following George Floyd's murder without losing sight of the intensifying climate crisis.[3] These variations notwithstanding, the authors all agree that the convergence they describe has worsened the already "unthinkable burdens that continue to fall disproportionately on those to whom colonial modernity, racial capitalism, and neoliberal globalism had already outsourced all the risks in the world."[4]

The three publications also differ in their conceptions of temporality. Both Kolb and Mignolo are concerned with what the latter calls the "unilinear timeline of Western modernity," retroactively constructed as an unbroken trajectory of civi-

ENGLISH LANGUAGE NOTES

60:1, April 2022 DOI 10.1215/00138282-9560309
© 2022 Regents of the University of Colorado

lized progress from ancient Greece to the modern world.[5] Yet Kolb traces a cyclical pattern in which the Greco-Persian Era, the Crusades, and the Romantic/Imperialist Era all connect to our present moment through their shared animation by a xenophobic "terror of Muslims, and the fear of a brown planet," embedded in "the discourse of a racialized world-ending pandemic."[6] Mignolo, for his part, interprets the unprecedented "extended and intense planetary 'now'" epitomized by the conjoined viral and financial crises not as a continuation but instead as a "change of epoch," a breaking point in the global process of Westernizing the planet.[7] Focused on "the present continuous and future imperfect," the symposium contributors on balance treat the current dystopian syndemic as a potentially galvanizing opportunity to "'emerge on the other side'" into a closer-to-utopian future informed by a "politics of hope."[8] Such narratives of progress, however, leave a lot to the imagination while potentially obscuring the fact that, as Mignolo reminds us, whatever happens next will not be the same everywhere and for everyone.[9]

Finally, the various essays offer different assessments of the possibilities for structural change opened up by syndemics. For Kolb, these possibilities are few, given the persistent dehumanizing and pathologizing of "sick and brown people" over time, where differences are matters more of degree than of kind.[10] Mignolo, by contrast, accentuates the prospect of radical change. The glossy Western narrative of modernization, "happiness, development and growth," he argues, can no longer effectively hide what has always been there: not only "the fear, isolation, despair, [and] broken relationships" among "the numerical majority of the planetary population" but also, and more positively, diverse knowledges, forms of ancestral wisdom, communal healing praxes, cooperative economies, and multiple local temporalities.[11] His investment in the restitution of these marginalized forms of knowing, being, and relating conveys his hope that the epochal change he discerns will be for the better, although he does acknowledge at one point, without further comment, that it could be for the worse.[12] The symposium contributors concede that the genre of science fiction serves as an imperfect "toolkit of diagnosis and prediction on a planetary scale," incapable of ever fully making sense of syndemics in their sheer scale, specificity, and unevenness.[13] Still, amid an "era of unfolding and overlapping material catastrophes,"[14] a number of them surmise that the powerful exercise of imagining better worlds might bring us closer to "seizing control from the closed futures of disaster capitalism" while rebuilding "the narrative of solidarities for possible futures."[15]

Yet as the current pandemic alone has shown, any such process of imaginative rebuilding assumes that members of the precariat would be inclined to demonstrate an ethos of solidarity, in the interest of healing of all sorts, that the more privileged among us have rarely if ever reciprocated. The enthusiasm with which so many Americans, among others, are embracing a "return-to-normal" narrative offers additional cause for wariness about the prospect of pandemic-induced social progress. The tendency among the global elite to prioritize some people's suffering, some people's lives, over others long predates and will likely outlast our current moment of crisis, as will the practice of the few taking advantage of "the unbearable situation of the many."[16] Creative fiction has immeasurable value, not least in its potential to do some of our most inventive dreaming for us. Still, as those of us who inhabit them know full well even if we don't always say so, cultural and imaginative realms will remain wobbly platforms for transformation unless buttressed by broader structural reforms that might someday relegate catastrophes, convergent, global, or otherwise, to our collective past.

CYNTHIA J. DAVIS is professor of English at the University of South Carolina, where she specializes in US literature and culture from the Civil War to World War II. Her essays have appeared in such journals as *American Literary History, American Literature,* and the *Arizona Quarterly.* Her latest book is *Pain and the Aesthetics of U.S. Literary Realism* (2021).

Notes

1   Anindita Banerjee and Sherryl Vint, in Banerjee and Vint, "Thinking through the Pandemic," 322.
2   Kolb, "Paravictorianism," 446.
3   Gerry Canavan, in Banerjee and Vint, "Thinking through the Pandemic," 333.
4   Banerjee and Vint, in Banerjee and Vint, "Thinking through the Pandemic," 323.
5   Mignolo, "Logic of the In-visible," 205.
6   Kolb, "Paravictorianism," 448.
7   Mignolo, "Logic of the In-visible," 206, 208.
8   Banerjee and Vint, in Banerjee and Vint, "Thinking through the Pandemic," 322.
9   Mignolo, "Logic of the In-visible," 216.
10 Kolb, "Paravictorianism," 457.
11 Mignolo, "Logic of the In-visible," 216, 208, 209.
12 Mignolo, "Logic of the In-visible," 209.
13 Banerjee and Vint, in Banerjee and Vint, "Thinking through the Pandemic," 322.
14 Canavan, in Banerjee and Vint, "Thinking through the Pandemic," 333.
15 Bodhisattva Chattopadhyay, in Banerjee and Vint, "Thinking through the Pandemic," 339.
16 Mignolo, "Logic of the In-visible," 207.

Works Cited

Banerjee, Anindita, and Sherryl Vint, eds. "Thinking through the Pandemic: A Symposium." *Science Fiction Studies* 47, no. 3 (2020): 321–76.

Kolb, Anjuli Fatima Raza. "Paravictorianism: Mary Shelley and Viral Sovereignty." *Victorian Studies* 62, no. 3 (2020): 446–59.

Mignolo, Walter D. "The Logic of the In-visible: Decolonial Reflections on the Change of Epoch." *Theory, Culture and Society* 37, nos. 7–8 (2020): 205–18.

Of Pandemic and Life's Propositions

STUTI GOSWAMI

The COVID-19 pandemic that has raged across the world since late 2019 is unprecedented on many grounds. Like previous pandemics, it has been widespread spatially and temporally. Like all pandemics in recorded history, it has also brought disease and death to millions. However, the nature of the virus and its adaptability to different environmental and climactic conditions have been unlike other pandemics in human history. With time, the virus has undergone mutation at multiple levels, and the extent of mutation is not fully known. This pandemic is no longer just a medical disease; it has evolved into a social malaise. Stigmas are associated with the disease as the pandemic has exposed the simmering fissures in human society and human relationships. As a consequence, the imprints left behind by the novel coronavirus in the lives of people are multidimensional and constantly evolving.

Three recent essays—"Paravictorianism: Mary Shelley and Viral Sovereignty," by Anjuli Fatima Raza Kolb; "The Logic of the In-visible: Decolonial Reflections on the Change of Epoch," by Walter D. Mignolo; and "Thinking through the Pandemic: A Symposium"—explore the multifarious and multidimensional nature of the COVID-19 pandemic across different planes of human existence. The pandemic has influenced a change in the perception of history and of the ways humans perceive themselves and their positionality in the world. For the first time, in uncountable years, humans, despite their "sophisticated biomedical infrastructures," have found themselves at the mercy of a disease whose cure is not fully ascertained.[1] "Thinking through the Pandemic" explores the near-surreal experience of this pandemic. It has fueled human imagination in ways nobody could have envisaged and has generated a new language register that will be a part of everyday human communication for years. The abundance of information on the pandemic has left people overwhelmed and in turn has influenced them psychologically and emotionally. All three essays touch on this psychosocial impact of the pandemic on human society.

Human happiness has also been altered. With the pandemic and subsequent lockdowns—total and partial—in different parts of the world for different stretches of time, digital dependence has increased across all age groups and on all fronts,

ENGLISH LANGUAGE NOTES

60:1, April 2022 DOI 10.1215/00138282-9560320
© 2022 Regents of the University of Colorado

from education to commerce to observation of customs and rituals. Both physical distancing and greater reliance on digital connection have left people more isolated. Working from home has blurred lines between personal and professional spaces, and the virtual has become the real as the term *normal* has acquired a whole new range of meaning. The culture of digital dependence due to the pandemic has also adversely affected individual self-worth and increased individuals' aggression and frustration.

Kolb's essay on the diplomatic tensions between Indonesia and the World Health Organization in 2006 over a naturally occurring viral flu that was linked to the war on terror explores how a pandemic can reaffirm racial stereotypes and facilitate religious or racial suppression. Kolb's essay examines the institutionalization of a viral pandemic in the context of nineteenth-century literary studies as the transitions of "a viral pandemic, climate change, racial capital, corporate kleptocracy, industrial agriculture, neoimperialism" are directed in favor of the privileged classes—racial, ethnic, socioeconomic.[2]

Kolb's observations bring us to the question of modernity, particularly of the West. Complicated by geopolitical tensions and turmoil in the global economy, the pandemic has exposed the inequalities that exist in the modern world. We are on the cusp of a "change of epoch," despite the apprehension and fear about the pandemic, Mignolo warns. In the new epoch familiar notions are increasingly defamiliarized, he explains. This includes Western notions of modernity and the temporal linearity of modernity. Mignolo raises the question not of how a war is waged against the disease but of how we can defend ourselves and "of the sickness of a civilization that cannot imagine any other way to deal with the nightmare."[3] For Mignolo, the COVID-19 pandemic raises questions that can be seen as marking the end of the epoch of Western hegemony and the colonizing of the mind. Agreeing with Mignolo, Kolb, and the symposium contributors, all we can say with certainty is that this pandemic has altered the perception and propositions of human life forever.

STUTI GOSWAMI is assistant professor in the Department of English at the Assam Royal Global University, Assam, India.

Notes

1   Anindita Banerjee and Sherryl Vint, in Banerjee and Vint, "Thinking through the Pandemic," 323.
2   Kolb, "Paravictorianism," 447.
3   Mignolo, "Logic of the In-visible," 206.

Works Cited

Banerjee, Anindita, and Sherryl Vint, eds. "Thinking through the Pandemic: A Symposium." *Science Fiction Studies* 47, no. 3 (2020): 321–76.

Kolb, Anjuli Fatima Raza. "Paravictorianism: Mary Shelley and Viral Sovereignty." *Victorian Studies* 62, no. 3 (2020): 446–59.
Mignolo, Walter D. "The Logic of the In-visible: Decolonial Reflections on the Change of Epoch." *Theory, Culture and Society* 37, nos. 7–8 (2020): 205–18.

Keep up to date on new scholarship

Issue alerts are a great way to stay current on all the cutting-edge scholarship from your favorite Duke University Press journals. This free service delivers tables of contents directly to your inbox, informing you of the latest groundbreaking work as soon as it is published.

To sign up for issue alerts:

1. Visit **dukeu.press/register** and register for an account. You do not need to provide a customer number.

2. After registering, visit **dukeu.press/alerts**.

3. Go to "Latest Issue Alerts" and click on "Add Alerts."

4. Select as many publications as you would like from the pop-up window and click "Add Alerts."

read.dukeupress.edu/journals

 UNIVERSITY PRESS